Contents

Contributors

Mike Berry is Professor of Urban Studies and Public Policy at RMIT University in Melbourne, Australia. He was Foundation Executive Director of the Australian Housing and Urban Research Institute and is a widely recognized expert in housing studies and policy. His research has informed recent housing policy developments in Australia and, with international colleagues, he has contributed to comparative analysis in the housing and broader urban fields over many years.

Cesar Costantino is a senior economist at Fannie Mae corporate strategy group. Costantino is a main contributor to the corporate economic, housing and mortgage market forecasts. Before joining Fannie Mae, Costantino worked for the World Bank's research department. Prior to that, he was a lead economist at the National Commission for the Defense of Competition, Argentina's federal antitrust agency.

Tony Dalton is Professor of Urban and Social Policy and a senior researcher with the RMIT University Australian Housing and Urban Research Institute Research Centre. His primary research interest is in the area of housing and social policy with a focus on the changing nature of housing markets and distributional outcomes in a period of social and economic restructuring.

Kees Dol is a housing market researcher at the OTB Research Institute for the Built Environment at Delft University of Technology, the Netherlands. His core interests are in the development of housing markets and housing demand. In the past ten years he has written various research reports for the Dutch Housing Ministry, local municipalities, housing associations and other NGOs, builders and developers. Recently, he has been commissioned by the Dutch Housing Ministry to investigate the impact of the financial crisis on a selection of Western European housing markets.

Doug Duncan is Fannie Mae's vice president and chief economist. Duncan spent more than 15 years at the Mortgage Bankers' Association. He began his tenure as senior economist, was promoted to senior economist and director of research, and later became senior vice president and chief economist. Before his time at the Mortgage Bankers' Association, Duncan was a LEGIS Fellow and staff member with the Committee on Banking,

Finance, and Urban Affairs for Congressman Bill McCollum in the US House of Representatives. He also worked on the Financial Institutions Project at the US Department of Agriculture. Duncan earned a doctorate in agricultural economics from Texas A&M University.

Ray Forrest is Chair Professor of Housing and Urban Studies at the City University of Hong Kong and Professor of Urban Studies at the University of Bristol, UK. He was Head of Bristol's School for Policy Studies (2001–04). From 2001 to 2005 he was Co-Director of the ESRC Centre for Neighbourhood Research and from 2004 to 2008 Associate/Acting Director of the Centre for East Asian Studies at Bristol. He is currently co-editor of *Housing Studies* and *Asian Public Policy*, and a member of the UK Academy of Social Sciences.

József Hegedüs is founding member of Metropolitan Research Institute, which was established in 1989 in Budapest, Hungary. He is an economist and sociologist (master in economics, PhD in sociology). He has been co-organizer of the East European Working Group of the European Network for Housing Research since 1989, and a member of Hungary's Housing Policy Council, a high-level advisory group in housing policy matters since 1996. He has been Affiliated Professor at Corvinus University from 2007. He has worked in several countries, including Bosnia-Herzegovina, Albania, Serbia, Georgia and Ethiopia as a short-term consultant. He has published several articles and book chapters related to the housing system in transition countries.

Yosuke Hirayama is Professor of Housing and Urban Studies at the Graduate School of Human Development and Environment, Kobe University, Japan, working extensively in the areas of housing and urban change, homeownership and social inequalities, as well as comparative housing policy. His work has appeared in numerous international and Japanese academic journals, and he is a co-editor of *Housing and Social Transition in Japan* (with Richard Ronald, Routledge, 2007). He has received academic prizes from the City Planning Institute of Japan, the Architectural Institute of Japan and Tokyo Institute of Municipal Research. He is also a founding member of the Asia-Pacific Network for Housing Research.

Soo-hyun Kim is currently an associate professor in the Graduate School of Urban and Real Estate at Sejong University in Seoul, Korea. He was previously Vice Minister of Environment in the Korean government. He also served as a secretary to the president for National Economy, Social Policy and Social Inclusion. He has studied squatter, poverty and public housing issues in Korea.

Anitra Nelson, Honorary Associate Professor of RMIT University (Australia) and attached to the RMIT-AHURI Research Centre, investigates housing affordability and environmental sustainability. She is an expert on Karl Marx's theory of money (*Marx's Concept of Money: The God of Commodities* (Routledge, 1999)), community-based sustainability (editor of *Steering Sustainability in an Urbanizing World: Policy, Practice and Performance* (Ashgate, 2007)) and has co-edited (with Frans Timmerman) a forthcoming book on non-market socialist solutions to contemporary environmental and financial crises (*Life Without Money: Building Fair and Sustainable Economies* (Pluto Press, 2011)).

Michelle Norris is a senior lecturer in the School of Applied Social Science, University College Dublin, Eire. Her research interests focus on housing policy and urban regeneration, particularly the management and financing of social housing, the regeneration of social housing estates and inner urban areas, and comparative analysis of housing provision in Europe. She is co-convenor of the European Network for Housing Research Working Group on Comparative Housing Policy and a member of the editoral board of the *International Journal of Housing Policy*.

Hoang Huu Phe, a trained architect, has studied at the Asian Institute of Technology and at the Bartlett School, University College London. He has written extensively on aspects of urban form, urban regeneration and housing policy in Vietnam. He is the director of the research and development division of Vinaconex, Vietnam's biggest state-owned construction firm.

Richard Ronald is Assistant Professor in Urban Studies at the University of Amsterdam and a Visiting Fellow at the OTB Research Institute at Delft University of Technology, the Netherlands. He has numerous publications on housing, urban and social change in Europe and Asia-Pacific. His most recent books include a monograph, *The Ideology of Home Ownership: the Role of Housing in Homeowner Societies,* and a number of co-edited works including *Housing and Social Transition in Japan* and *Home and Family in Japan*. Richard has been a recipient of the Japan Foundation Doctoral Research Fellowship and the Japan Society for the Promotion of Science Postdoctoral Fellowship. He is currently the review editor of the *International Journal of Housing Policy* and section editor of International *Encyclopaedia of Housing and Home* (Elsevier, forthcoming).

Chao Sun is Master of Real Estate Economics, Renmin University of China and researches real-estate finance and real-estate policy.

Jón Rúnar Sveinsson was born in Seyðisfjörður on the east coast of Iceland. He studied sociology at the University of Iceland, Lund University and Uppsala University. He has undertaken housing research in both Iceland and Sweden, pioneering research of the rental housing market in Iceland. He was among the founders of the Icelandic cooperative housing movement in the 1980s. He has worked on housing research at the State Housing Agency, the Housing Financing Fund, The Urban Studies Institute, Bifröst University and since 2005 has been an independent scholar at the Reykjavik Academy.

David Thorns is Professor of Sociology, distinguished sociologist and one of New Zealand's leading social scientists. His major research projects have addressed suburban and community research; the sociology of housing and residential mobility; social inequality and class formation, comparative urban research; restructuring and change within advanced capitalist societies; urban sustainability; comparative welfare state policy analysis and globalization and urban change. His work has been innovative and led to significant shifts in theoretical and research agendas.

Peter Williams is a consultant working in the areas of housing finance, markets and policy. He is Chairman of the UK government's National Housing and Planning Advice Unit (NHPAU). He is also Executive Chairman of the Intermediary Mortgage Lenders Association and a board member of the Kent Reliance Building Society, Consult CIH and Chairman of Thames Valley Housing Association. He is a visiting professor at the Centre for Housing Policy, University of York. He was previously Deputy Director General of the Council of Mortgage Lenders, Professor of Housing at the University of Wales, Cardiff, Deputy Director of the Chartered Institute of Housing and a board member of the Housing Corporation and Tai Cymru. He has authored and edited several books on housing and social change and is on the management board of the journal *Housing Studies*.

Nessa Winston is a lecturer in the School of Applied Social Science, University College Dublin. Her main research interests centre on sustainable housing policies and practices in urban and rural contexts. She is currently involved in an international project funded by the EU Seventh Framework Programme on the impacts of increasing inequalities. The focus of her research is on housing and inequality from a comparative perspective. She has received a number of research grants to examine housing, urban regeneration and sustainability, and continues to pursue her interest in the development of sustainable communities from a housing perspective.

Jianping Ye is Professor, Doctoral Adviser and head of Department of Land and Real Estate Management, Renmin University of China. He is also the managing director of China Land Science Society and China Land Appraisers Society. His main fields of research include land management, real estate operation and management, realty policy, realty investment analysis and price evaluation, urban operation and land development, and land coordination. His recent publications are *Real Estate Marketing* (Renmin University Press, 2000) and *Research on Land Property Right in China's Countryside*.

Ngai-Ming Yip is Associate Professor in the Department of Public and Social Administration, City University of Hong Kong. His research covers housing policy and management, spatial segregation and gated communities, urban policy and issues relating to neighbourhood and grass-roots governance.

Preface

This book originated in a two-day symposium held at the City University of Hong Kong in December 2009. Thirteen invited speakers presented specially prepared papers that were then discussed and debated among the small number of participants in a roundtable format. This arrangement, unlike the more conventional open-forum conference, allowed substantial time for an exchange of views and for an intensive but relaxed exploration of the different housing-market impacts of the financial crisis.

The primary objective of the symposium was to examine the ways in which the 2007 financial crisis had affected households. The housing market was at the centre stage of the crisis in terms of causes and consequences. Most of the research and commentary had, however, focused on the institutional casualties and the dramatic interventions by various governments to maintain a degree of stability in the current financial regime. There had been limited systematic exploration of the housing-market consequences for households, although it was evident that the impacts had been highly uneven both across and within different societies. The legacy of the recent past in terms of market entry points, employment and income status, borrowing capacity and debt exposure had produced a highly differentiated pattern of household vulnerabilities mediated by variations in institutional structures and policy histories. This differentiation could be observed at the international scale and within countries. In terms of housing-market consequences, therefore, a global financial crisis had not produced common outcomes. The symposium aimed to examine the particular factors at work in particular countries that had produced this unevenness.

The timing of the symposium was also important since sufficient time had to have elapsed for the household impacts to have become evident and for some solid empirical evidence to be available. It has to be said, however, that at the time of writing, events are still unfolding, the economic 'recovery' is fragile and the longer-term consequences for the financial system and for different groups of households remain uncertain. Moreover, the quality and availability of relevant evidence varies between countries. In some cases, detailed comparisons are possible between different groups in a population. In other cases, we have had to rely on more qualitative material or make broader geographic comparisons. Thus, while this collection fills a major gap in knowledge, it is inevitably work in progress.

The collection encompasses the experiences of the USA, the UK, Australia, New Zealand, Hungary, Vietnam, Japan, the Netherlands, South Korea, Iceland, Ireland, China and Hong Kong. This selection spans a wide range of housing systems and crisis impacts. There was an obvious desire to represent the major economies such as the USA, Japan and China, and some smaller countries that had been major casualties, notably Ireland and Iceland. Other countries such as the Netherlands and Australia were selected because they seemed to have escaped relatively unscathed–for the moment. We spent some time considering how best to group the chapters hoping that some clear themes would emerge from discussion at the symposium. In the end a quasi-geographical grouping seemed as good as any other. Some further comment on this is provided in the concluding discussion.

Finally, various acknowledgements and thanks are due. The Department of Public and Social Administration at the City University of Hong Kong provided the funding for the entire event. Particular thanks go to Davis Lau, who took charge of all the administrative arrangements, including organizing the venue and the website, and to Dr Ying Wu, who did an enormous amount of work in transforming all the chapters into the required format, pursuing straying contributors and ensuring that we almost met the deadline. Our thanks also to the staff at Edward Elgar for their patience, enthusiasm and impressive efficiency throughout.

1. Households, homeownership and neoliberalism

Ray Forrest

INTRODUCTION

As recently as the early 1980s, just as neoliberalism began to gather political and policy momentum, the discourse around homeownership was essentially rooted in a social project. The growth of homeownership was presented by politicians, and engaged by most analysts, as a core element in the spread of middle-class lifestyles from minorities to majorities. Whether it was the American Dream, the Australian Dream or the British version of a property-owning democracy, the ingredients were pretty much the same. Homeownership was associated with stability and security; it gave a 'stake in the system'; it represented an asset that could be handed down to children (Hamnett et al., 1991); it was associated with political conservatism and responsible communitarianism; it provided a general sense of well-being, of ontological security (Saunders, 1990; Forrest et al., 1990). It was implicitly imbued with the warm glow of family life. Of course, these and related associations with homeownership were subject to both theoretical debate and empirical challenge. Nevertheless, although homeownership was increasingly recognized as the primary source of household wealth for the majority of households (see, e.g. Forrest and Murie, 1995), it was the political, social and cultural features of the tenure that were most prominent in academic and political debate.

It was also acknowledged, however, that the image of homeownership that dominated derived from a time when, in many societies, it was the minority tenure of a relatively secure upper- and middle-class section of society whose housing experiences were typically rooted in a period of expanding employment opportunities, rising real incomes and high inflation. The more it encompassed a broader cross-section of populations in a changing economic climate, the more likely it was to draw in more households in vulnerable and marginal circumstances which might experience difficulties. Inevitably, therefore, the characteristics associated with homeownership would change with its changing social composition.

1

The English caricature of leafy, semi-detached suburbia was, of course, always an idealized misrepresentation of the general character of home-ownership. Nevertheless, until the very recent past, housing problems in the Anglo-American literature were mainly linked to rental tenures. Achieving homeownership was a 'step on the ladder': if not always a smooth upward trajectory to higher social status, certainly an assumed move away from housing difficulties and low social status. The risks for lower-income households and those in more vulnerable and insecure circumstances of moves into homeownership were recognized. Governments explored and pursued a variety of low-cost homeownership initiatives and forms of shared ownership. Exclusion from homeownership was seen as accentuating existing social divides through the accumulation of housing wealth that a postwar, baby-boom generation of homeowners had generally experienced. Those in rental tenures faced a new form of social stratification in which earned incomes combined with housing wealth to widen social inequalities, with implications for life chances across the generations. In 1987, Nigel Lawson, then UK Chancellor of the Exchequer (echoing similar views in other countries), had referred to the emergence of a new 'inheritance economy' and a vision of millions of pounds 'cascading down the generations', an idea taken up by numerous subsequent politicians. The academic literature was similarly preoccupied with equity gains and the distributional impact of rising real house prices and a developing policy focus on 'asset-based' welfare reflected the growing prominence of the residential sphere as a store of accumulating wealth.

Although these discussions were situated in references to the increasing commodification of housing (Harloe, 1981; Forrest and Williams, 1984), they were typically concerned with shifting tenurial patterns, the developing critique of the state in welfare provision, the nascent privatization policies of the early 1980s and the gathering momentum of neoliberalist influences. In particular, where countries had large social rental sectors, such as in the UK, this process of commodification progressed from sales to sitting tenants through to the eventual buying and selling of previously state-owned properties on the private market. These kinds of policies promoted in a number of counties provided a significant boost to home-ownership sectors at relatively low risk for the purchasers because of high discounts on market values. While securitization may have been an interest of some economists, the mainstream housing-policy literature at this time remained for the most part focused on a shift from direct to indirect housing subsidies and did not anticipate a more fully fledged version of commodification in which dwellings would be traded like other commodities. Dwellings were still 'bricks and mortar'; all that was solid had not yet 'melted into air'. As Hannsgen (2007) observes, however, by the early twenty-first century the relationship between homeowners, prospective homeowners and the institutions that lent them mortgages had changed substantially.

A once sleepy industry, directed towards a social purpose, had given way to an industry in which profit, as opposed to homeownership and security, became important. Savings and loans shifted their attention away from making profits by supporting homeownership and toward profit-making as such. (Ibid., p. 11)

THE GLOBAL FINANCIAL CRISIS OF 2007 – THE USUAL SUSPECTS?

The more extensive neoliberalization of homeownership sectors and its association with greater volatility, instability and periods of financial crisis has generated a growing literature. The relationship between households, housing and economic crises inevitably created more casualties in homeownership sectors as the tenure expanded. Asset deflation impacted more directly on household circumstances where homeownership was the dominant tenure. Nominal, as opposed to real, house-price falls could generate pervasive negative equity–a term almost unknown before the late 1980s. The bursting of the housing bubble in Japan in 1990, the more general impact of the Asian financial crisis in 1997 or apparently more localized recessions such as the steep house-price falls in the UK in the late 1980s contributed to a growing recognition of the importance of the relationship between residential sectors and macroeconomies (see, e.g., Deep and Domanski, 2002; Farlow, 2005). And rather than housing being a store of wealth to be simply passed down to the next generation, with deregulation it became a new source of liquid wealth to be mobilized for a variety of purposes. Indeed, various analyses indicated that domestic consumption in the USA and elsewhere had been maintained primarily through refinancing schemes and equity release (Brenner, 2004). Given the significance of US domestic consumption for international trade, it appeared that homeownership had shifted to a pivotal position in relation to the general health of the global economy. But this increasingly complex financial system, with residential mortgaging at the centre, began to unravel in 2007 and reached crisis point in late 2008, prompting what now seem rather premature proclamations of the end of neoliberal capitalism. Was this version of capitalism in terminal crisis? And as part of that regime, was the institutional form of homeownership that had developed in many countries also fatally compromised? Was a major rethink required about residential property ownership–its social meaning and financial structure?

Were dwellings about to become perceived as primarily homes again, use values rather than exchange values–something to live in rather than securities to be traded across the globe with the kinds of consequences that had unfortunately become so evident? Of course, we had been here before, albeit in the context of more localized crises. Was this crisis different? It certainly was for many homeowners around the world.

What was evidently different was the extent and depth of the institutional crisis, with prominent investment banks, commercial banks and other related institutions going to the wall. And when nationalization, a term supposedly banished from the neoliberal policy lexicon forever, re-emerged as a key strategy to prop up ailing institutions, it was clear that things were serious. In relation to the social project of homeownership, what was evident was that the neoliberal model of asset-based securitization had failed spectacularly to deliver.

As the crisis has unfolded, the weight of analysis has been on the causes of the crisis–who and what is to blame? Here there are conflicting accounts and analyses at varying levels of abstraction. Popular versions scapegoat greedy bankers making easy money from unsophisticated purchasers, bamboozled by innovative products, impenetrable jargon and comforted by the myth that property prices would keep rising. As Stiglitz (2009) argues, however, there may indeed be a number of guilty parties to the crime, but there is a need for a sober analysis of the causes if future crises are to be avoided. Also, he observes that

> The notion of causation is, however, complex. Presumably, it means something like, 'If only the guilty party had taken another course of action, the crisis would not have occurred.' But the consequences of one party changing its actions depend on the behaviour of others: presumably the actions of other parties too, may have changed. (Ibid., p. 229)

There are also analyses of the underlying causes of the crisis that operate at very different levels of scale and abstraction–at the systemic level of the capitalist world system; at the international level of a particular conjuncture of financial practices and regulatory structures; and at the national level in relation to specific institutional configurations and practices. If taken together, these help explain both the apparently increasingly crisis-prone nature of the global economic system and the differential impacts.

Given the primary focus of this book, the key issue is the extent to which homeowning households are going to remain exposed to the vicissitudes of an increasingly unstable financial system. From some analytical vantage points, this seems highly likely. Wade (2008), for example, has argued that the 'globalization model itself needs to be rethought' (p. 20) and Arrighi's (1994, 2010) authoritative analysis of the history of different capitalist regimes would point to the current phase of financialization as signalling the coming end of US hegemony, as it in did previous periods, in the context of a crisis of capitalist overaccumulation that has been gathering momentum for the last three decades. Drawing on Phillips (1993), Arrighi observes that periods of financialization, unlike those of industrialization, can only benefit small elites to the detriment of the vast majority of the population. From this perspective, then, homeownership was simply caught up in the latest relentless wave of financialization, following the dot.com and other previous bubbles. Structural fundamentals rather than the actions of particular institutions or actors are thus at the root of the problem.

None the less, as this book shows, specific institutional factors and government policies clearly make a difference, as does the nature and degree of financial integration of particular national finance systems. Whilst the underlying processes may be similar, vulnerabilities shift over time, evident in the geographies of the Asian financial crisis as opposed to the more recent upheavals. Debates at this level tend to focus on the extent to which the problems were associated with too much regulation or too little–or the nature of neoliberal reregulation. Friedman's (2009) extensive review, drawing on a collection of papers on the causes of the financial crisis, offers a detailed institutional analysis of the interaction of policies and practices in the USA. Friedman's finger points to the US government and the ratings agencies as being among the key culprits in what at times seems a rather tortuous defence of bankers. They were, it seems, not greedy but ignorant and misguided. They were ignorant of the unreliability of the ratings provided by Moody's and the other rating agencies, and ultimately victims of well-intentioned but ill-conceived government policies to promote higher levels of homeownership among lower-income households. 'The evidence, then suggests that bankers were not imprudent in the sense of ignoring risks that they knew about. Rather they were ignorant of the fact that triple-A rated securities might be much riskier than advertised' (Friedman, 2009, p. 148). Investment banks were apparently ignorant of the oligopoly status of the main rating agencies and their protection through an accumulation of legal and regulatory barriers to competition. Flawed models and inaccurate data lay behind ratings that, if they were wrong, had little effect on their business, protected as they were from market competitors.

Ultimately Friedman suggests that it was the lack of market competition rather than the operation of unregulated markets that lay behind the crisis, combined with the unintended consequences of regulatory interference. And, he asks, if bankers were simply greedy, why did so many lose substantially from investments they had made (or, of course, were given) in their own institutions? Whatever the merits of Friedman's undoubtedly detailed analysis, the overall picture is of a financial melange truly out of control–a system in which tranches of unaffordable mortgages taken out by poor householders became valuable commodities to be traded across the globe. As Ferguson (2009, pp. 9–10) more provocatively comments,

> These CDOs had been so sliced and diced that it was possible to claim that a tier of interest payments from the original borrowers was as dependable a stream of income as the interest on a ten-year US treasury bond and therefore worthy of a coveted triple-A rating. This took financial alchemy to a new level of sophistication, apparently turning lead into gold.

Whilst Stiglitz (2009) would list many of the same culprits, he stresses that references to the effects of the Community Reinvestment Bank Act, which required banks to direct more funding to lower-income communities for homeownership, and the operation of Fannie Mae and Freddie Mac as primary underlying causes of the crisis are unwarranted and 'clearly just an attempt to shift the blame'. He also suggests that simplistic economic theory was a key factor. 'It is America's fully private financial markets that invented all the bad practices that played a central role in this crisis.' He continues, 'the government didn't intend for people to buy homes beyond their ability to afford them. That would generate ephemeral gains, and contribute to impoverishment: The poor would lose their life savings as they lost their home' (ibid., p. 337).

THE USUAL VICTIMS?

This takes us to the primary concern of the book. Which households bore the brunt of the aftermath of the 2007 crisis? Stiglitz refers to 'the poor' and generally it is those households in the most precarious economic circumstances that suffer most when housing booms turn to busts. In the Asian financial crisis it was typically those on the economic margins, those in the least secure jobs, and often women, who bore the brunt of the downturn (see Ramesh, 2009). At a general, global level, the latest crisis is no different in the sense that it is those with very little to lose who probably lose most proportionately. The credit crunch has little direct impact on those who have no access to credit. In those countries that are marginal to the global financial system, where only a small minority own homes or have mortgages, it is the daily pressures of subsistence survival rather than the consequences of collapsing financial systems and sub-prime crises that are uppermost. None the less, they are far from immune from the contagion effects of a major cutback in global trade. The marginal become even more marginal in such circumstances. For instance, the collapse of export trade in China saw a massive shakeout of migrant workers, some ten million, according to some official estimates, as firms dependent on trade relations with the West collapsed into bankruptcy.

It is appropriate, therefore, to remind ourselves of the daily realities of slum living for a growing segment of the world's population (UNHSP, 2003) before adjusting our focus to the housing systems of more affluent countries. This is not to evoke a moral position but precisely because the neoliberal turn that reshaped the financial and mortgage systems of many of the advanced core capitalist economies has had an even more devastating effect on housing conditions in sub-Saharan Africa, in parts of Latin America and Asia. The same ideology and processes that drove financialization also shaped the structural adjustment programmes that prescribed privatization, cutbacks in social services and the opening of weak economies to free trade. The retreat of the state was highlighted in the UN Report (UNHSP, 2003) as a key factor behind the rapid and pervasive increase in slum settlements around the world. The housing crisis at an international level was already getting worse rather than better before the 2007 financial meltdown. Discussions about the speed and extent of a 'recovery' refer to a situation in which significant populations will be as marginal after, if not more so, as before the crisis. In relation to housing opportunities and conditions, sub-prime and sub-Saharan, signify the enormous social distance between precarious inclusion and comprehensive exclusion.

So, when housing markets go from boom to bust, the usual victims are those who were last to get in – those who buy at the peak of the house-price cycle with high loan-to-value ratios. The most vulnerable are typically younger households, on lower incomes, buying the most marginal properties and stretching themselves to the limit to get a foot on the last rung of the property ladder before it is raised beyond their reach. To paraphrase Bootle (1997), those are the households that are caught when 'the music stops'. The prize is suddenly transformed into a liability with no one to pass it to. Vulnerability is, however, a product of a combination of factors, and homeownership sectors contain households in highly varied circumstances in relation to personal circumstances, financial circumstances, the timing of market entry and debt exposure. This is easily forgotten. Prices may tumble but many longstanding homeowners own outright or have accumulated sufficient equity to weather a financial storm. In most cases, negative equity poses real and practical difficulties only if it combines with income loss, relationship breakdown or some other circumstance that forces a sale (Forrest et al., 1999). The solution for most is to simply sit tight, maintain mortgage payments and hope for better times–which in the past have usually come. And as housing-market instability has increased, and crises have become more numerous, there is always the usual refrain of lessons learnt and changing attitudes. The next cohort of prospective owners will have a different perspective on, and different expectations of, house purchase. Houses will be things to live in rather than commodities to buy and sell in order to ratchet up equity. Lenders will be more risk-averse in future house-price booms. Loan-to-income ratios will not be allowed to grow dangerously as affordability becomes more problematic. Borrowers will be more closely scrutinized in terms of their risk profile and given better financial advice.

But none of this happens–at least not so far. If there is a lesson learnt from previous busts, it is that lessons are usually quickly forgotten as market conditions change. The competitive pressures of deregulated mortgage markets are part of the explanation, producing, it seems, reck-lessness rather than greater market efficiency. There are also, however, more mundane, human factors at work. The uneven impacts of financial crises relate not only to cohorts within particular populations, but also to cohorts over time (Forrest, 2008). New cohorts of younger, first-time buyers looking to purchase properties in the hyper-inflating housing markets of the early to mid-2000s and others in marginal economic cir-cumstances but desperate to get on the housing ladder, had no experience or memory of the serious and often personally devastating impacts experi-enced by some homeowning households in previous periods. Homeowners and potential homeowners tend to see the future in terms of the present. For example, Case and Shiller (2003) have shown that, however irrational it seems, in periods of house-price inflation people tend to expect a contin-uing, and often substantial, annual upward trend. Moreover, the passing of time also affects institutions in the sense that ageing and staff turnover in lending organizations progressively erase memories of past and less benign market conditions.

This crisis has, however, been deeper and more pervasive, and rocked the structural foundations of the global economy. Moreover, the chapters that follow document that in some cases lessons were learnt, or are being learnt, in terms of more regulatory scrutiny of lending practices. The Asian financial crisis certainly gave a salutary lesson to many financial institutions in that region and occasioned, in some cases, new regulations on loan-to-value ratios and liquidity requirements (and see Ngai-Ming Yip, Chapter 13 in this volume).

The impacts on households of a housing-market crisis take, of course, many forms. Some are fairly immediate, direct and easily measured, such as home repossessions and increasing mortgage arrears. In this context, local institutional practices and welfare systems can make a significant difference in relation to the circumstances in which properties are repossessed and eviction orders issued. The wider economic impacts may, however, take longer to feed through, as is evidently the case at the present time. The repercussions on households internationally and intra-nationally will be strongly affected by the pattern of recovery in relation to world trade. A sluggish recovery or double-dip recession will prolong or exacerbate unemployment and underemployment. Households that may have cut back on expenditure in other areas in order to maintain mortgage payments could find their coping strategies unsustainable in the longer term if the general economic climate and their personal financial circumstances do not get any better, or, indeed, worsen. The standard statistical indicators of housing-market stress, such as arrears or possessions, reveal only the most overt casualties of a housing-market crisis and inevitably conceal a mass of households that may be hanging on precariously to homes, jobs and living standards.

An important element in the contemporary calculus regarding household vulnerability to economic downturns has been the substantial increase in secured and unsecured household debt. In 1996, across OECD countries, average household debt, with mortgages as the overwhelmingly dominant part, was close to average annual disposable income. By 2007 it was near 170 per cent (Andre, 2010). Rising real incomes for many, combined with low nominal interest rates, financial deregulation and, until the credit crunch, a widespread house-price boom, have all contributed to this trend. Money has appeared to be cheap–although low inflation has obscured its real cost–and in countries such as the UK and the USA it became progressively easier to extract housing equity for remortgaging, to pay off other debts or to maintain or enhance living standards. In the USA, equity extracted from homes to pay off non-mortgage debts amounted to an average of $60 billion a year between 1991 and 2005. And the total equity extracted doubled between 2001 and 2005, from $627 billion to $1428 billion. The overall total in that period of some $5 trillion is truly staggering, and is indicative of the growing significance of house-price inflation and equity growth to the US consumption patterns and to the wider global economy (Greenspan and Kennedy, 2008). Similar trends were observed in many of the core capitalist countries, albeit not on the same absolute scale as in the USA. Rising household debt in itself does not, however, necessarily indicate a higher level of risk or vulnerability, and many commentators took a rather sanguine view of the trends before the 2007 crash. Rising debt was generally regarded as a function of rising affluence and an inevitable consequence of higher levels of homeownership and property values. As Greenspan (2005) observed, short of a period of appreciable overall economic weakness, households, with the exception of some highly leveraged subprime borrowers, do not appear to be faced with significant financial strain. With interest rates low, debt service costs for households have been essentially stable for the past few years.

Unfortunately, it subsequently emerged that we were not that short of a period of overall economic weakness.

Households may accumulate higher levels of debt for a variety of reasons. There is a sharp difference between a higher-income household trading up to a higher-value property and increasing the overall size of their mortgage and borrowing by a household trying to cope with unsustainable and unsecured credit-card debt. Higher debts can be generated by constraint rather than by choice. Moreover, the rising costs of entry into homeownership have made more households dependent on two incomes. The loss of one income can trigger immediate difficulties. More generally, the psychology of high debt exposure is rapidly transformed when economic conditions shift from benign to hostile and when asset values are deflating rather than inflating.

There is a tendency, however, to assume that rising household indebtedness is mainly associated with the more recent neoliberal regime–and a deregulated, highly competitive lending environment has certainly encouraged and enabled more households to borrow more. However, Montgomerie (2009) provides a more nuanced view in her analysis of household indebtedness in postwar USA. She shows, *inter alia* that the growth of unsecured borrowing, the most expensive form of debt, preceded the credit boom, was well established by the early 1990s and was associated with sustaining daily consumption rather than with the purchase of assets. Specifically, Montgomerie argues that the more conventional framework of financial inclusion and exclusion does not take sufficient account of the financially debilitating experience of *inclusion* for many low-income households. From this perspective, the sub-prime phenomenon is merely a more recent example of a longstanding trend in which the development of financialization is fuelled by a revolving door of indebtedness targeting those most in need but with the least ability to repay–reminiscent of the old joke, 'now you can borrow enough to get completely out of debt'. More generally, Montgomerie argues that the rising indebtedness of middle-income US households is associated with the maintenance of a postwar lifestyle that became progressively unsustainable because of changes in the nature of labour markets, income trajectories and state support. 'Taking this evidence into consideration we must see that growing social anxiety, declining wage growth and dwindling state support contributed to households' need to borrow in an effort to maintain a standard of living established by a previous generation' (Montgomerie, 2009, p. 18).

INTERGENERATIONAL DYNAMICS

In assessing the household impacts of the global financial crisis, it is also necessary to take account of more complex intergenerational dynamics. In previous housing-market busts, the wider economic fallout was considerably more limited regionally, nationally and institutionally. Major banks did not fail, the evident collateral damage and international contamination was in the main restricted to particular countries or regions (the Asian financial crisis being the most extensive before the more recent crisis) and, as indicated earlier, as regards housing-market casualties it was generally younger, first-time buyers who bore the brunt. The household impacts of the global financial crisis have, however, been more pervasive and have affected those at different points in the life course.

The global house-price boom, the expanding number of ageing homeowners in many societies and the affordability problems faced by a younger generation of homeowners and aspiring homeowners have focused much academic and policy attention on the intergenerational impacts of housing-related inheritance and *inter vivo* (lifetime) transfers. As Williams (Chapter 3 in this volume) shows, parental assistance has become an increasing necessity for access to homeownership in many high-price housing markets. However, falling share values in some key corporations, falling property values and low or almost negative interest rates have affected significantly the financial circumstances of some older homeowners. Savings have shrunk and in some cases all but disappeared. Particularly in the financial sector, where many elderly households assumed that savings and dividends were safe, some share portfolios have become virtually worthless. And where governments have been forced to nationalize or part-nationalize ownership, shareholders typically face at least a dividend freeze for the foreseeable future. Whilst governments have been concerned to protect depositors rather than shareholders, it is not the case that these two groups are mutually exclusive or that shareholders are necessarily relatively better off. Many elderly homeowners have relied on modest dividends to boost retirement incomes. And many homeowners nearing retirement face uncertain pension payouts.

In the UK, for example, these difficulties have been compounded by a bulge of endowment mortgages reaching maturity. Endowment mortgages were particularly popular financial products in the 1980s when savings plans involving investment in shares or bonds, and often property portfolios, were sold as attractive ways to pay off mortgages combined with the prospect of a bonus payout above the outstanding mortgage debts on maturity. These products typically mature after 25 years–meaning that a wave of maturing policies coincided with the credit crunch. In December

2008 the BBC reported that some 50 000 endowment policies were now maturing every month (BBC News, 2008).

A cohort of older homeowners, therefore, which expected to be paying off mortgages and be left with a lump sum from their endowment policies, may find that they still owe money on their mortgages and will have to fund the difference from some other source.

The general point is that households over the life course are experiencing differentiated impacts of the current financial crisis. Whilst sections of a younger generation struggle to pay mortgages or get on the ladder at all, in many cases the financial circumstances of their parents, or grandparents, have also been transformed. These developments, which require more detailed empirical analysis, suggest the need for at least some revision of previous assumptions about intergenerational assistance in the housing sphere. The heady predictions of the past, with masses of housing-related wealth passing down the generations as the bulge of asset-rich baby-boomers retired–and ultimately, expired–may now have to be qualified in a situation where the value of these assets may have been significantly deflated. Some asset-rich, income-poor elderly households will have been transformed to being both asset and income poor. For some families the flow of assistance may go into reverse–with better-off younger generations assisting their parents. Whatever the individual circumstances of families, the aggregate effect is likely to be a reduction in the ability of many parents to help their offspring gain an independent position in the property market.

The broader social consequences of affordability difficulties on family formation have been evident for some time. The difficulties of raising a sufficient deposit for house purchase, combined with rising educational costs and greater concern about job security, have seen a reversal of trends evident over most of the postwar period in many countries for children to leave home at an earlier age (Forrest and Hirayama, 2009). Echoing commentaries on 'parasite singles' in Japan, a study by The Prudential in 2003 referred to the UK phenomenon of 'kippers' (kids in parents' pockets eroding retirement savings) (BBC World News, 2003). According to this study, there were almost 7 million over-18-year-olds living with parents, some well into their thirties. A more recent study has coined another term, 'Baby Boomerangers,' referring to the new trend of children returning to the parental home to avoid the credit crunch (Abbey Mortgages, 2009). The Director of Abbey Mortgages observed:

> Millions of Britons have realised that sometimes you have to take one step backwards in order to go two steps forward. So while returning home or delaying your plans to move out might feel like a sacrifice, it's actually a great opportunity to save enough money to put down a deposit on a property of your own.

This is especially important in the current market where the bigger the deposit, the better the mortgage rate you will be eligible for.

Whatever the robustness or generalizability of these findings, it is likely that a long period of growing affordability difficulties for younger generations, combined with a new set of difficulties in the current financial crisis, has involved a further process of 'refamilization' under increasingly stressful circumstances. The new ingredient in this equation is that, for many families, financial resources are now compromised and uncertain across the generations. Coping strategies may now involve a wider mobilization of resources with children, or grandchildren, no longer able to assume a parental asset base on which to draw.

FACTORS AFFECTING DEGREE OF VULNERABILITY OF HOUSEHOLDS TO A HOUSING-MARKET CRASH

For households, the financial crisis has therefore impacted differentially, and in new ways, across cohorts within countries, within cohorts within countries and internationally. The nature and scale of these impacts are still relatively under-researched and the medium- to longer-term effects are still unfolding. Indeed, the primary aim of the chapters in this book is to provide additional and new evidence across a range of countries that have been hit in varying degrees and in varying ways by the 2007 financial meltdown. As emphasized earlier, the bulk of commentary and analysis so far has focused on institutional damage, institutional recovery, the macroeconomy and issues of regulation, reregulation and deregulation. And considerable effort has focused on attributing blame and in uncovering the interconnections and dynamics between institutional actors, nationally and internationally, that contributed to the mess. However, to return to Stiglitz's analogy, it doesn't really matter who pulled the trigger if you are in the firing line. If you have lost your job and cannot pay escalating mortgage costs on a property with declining resale value, it is little comfort to know it is the ratings agencies rather than the bankers who should shoulder more of the burden of the blame. Nevertheless, various factors in varying combinations have acted to mitigate, delay or exacerbate the severity of the impact on households. Box 1.1 attempts to summarize some of these contingent factors. None in itself is sufficient to explain the differences. They cannot, for example, be attributed to the degree of global financial integration of particular national financial systems and their exposure to toxic investment. As some of the chapters that follow

---

BOX 1.1   KEY FACTORS AFFECTING IMPACTS ON HOUSEHOLDS

- **Level of home ownership** – extent to which sector includes low-income and vulnerable households
- **Size of social rental sector** – extent to which low-income households are in social renting, the safety-net effect
- **Size of the private rental sector** – e.g. capacity to absorb unsold dwellings, impact on rents
- **Structure of home ownership sector** – temporal patterns of growth, outright versus mortgaged owners, extent of discounted purchase through transfers from state sector
- **Steepness and speed of upward price trajectory and steepness and duration of decline**
- **Overall debt exposure** – extent of secured and unsecured household debt
- **Lending regime** – e.g. loan-to-value ratios, extent and nature of high-risk mortgages
- **Income effects** – severity and pattern of any rise in unemployment, wage cuts
- **Specific institutional factors towards housing distress** – e.g. policies towards repossessions and arrears, mortgage rescue schmes
- **Nature of government responses to crisis** – e.g. recovery packages, economic stimulation

---

demonstrate, an understanding of the impacts on households requires a historical perspective on the development of national housing systems and financial structures to appreciate the path-dependent nature of the differential impacts of the global crisis.

A key factor affecting the severity and extent of the financial meltdown and its interactions with housing systems was the proportion of households in the sector. It is self-evident that where homeownership is the overwhelmingly dominant tenure form, more households are likely to be directly affected by any concoction of falling asset values, more vulnerable employment and high-risk, unstable lending with the potential for rapidly rising costs. Where homeownership accommodates a large proportion of the population, it will inevitably include a highly differentiated group of owners in terms of their financial circumstances, job security and property type and condition (Forrest et al., 1990). The term 'homeownership' merely describes a mechanism for paying for housing and offers little analytical purchase beyond that. The particular profile of homeowners within and between societies needs further scrutiny. Thus, it is not possible to read off the impact of the global financial crisis on households simply from the proportionate size of the tenure.

Numerous other specific factors come into play, including the pattern of development of homeownership, specific national policies including social assistance policies, the relative proportions of outright and mortgaged owners, the relative proportions of debt and equity among mortgaged owners, the particular lending and regulatory regimes of its financial system as well as the more general economic context. For example, where there has been a rapid growth of homeownership among younger, newly formed households–where it is a relatively immature tenure–there are likely to be proportionately more households exposed when there is a steep fall in property values and a steep rise in mortgage costs. Equally, where significant numbers of households have been recruited into the tenure via privatization policies, in which purchase costs have been discounted from market value or where governments have operated some other forms of low-cost purchase, some low-income households may be cushioned to some degree.

Where social rental systems remain relatively large, this is likely to represent an important safety net for low-income groups. If unemployment rises steeply, they may lose their jobs but not their homes. In this context, neoliberal policies have increased the risk exposure of households in housing systems through a combination of aggressive downsizing of not-for-profit forms of housing provision and through the equally aggressive marketing of high-risk loans to entice ever-increasing numbers of households to buy at initially low cost.

The book aims to explore the different ways in which these and other factors have combined in specific national contexts to produce varied outcomes in terms of the severity and pervasiveness of household impacts. The selection of countries reflects a number of considerations. An underlying theme was differential integration. Was there a strong relationship between the degree of financial integration in the global system and the casualty count in homeownership? So, for example, were homeowning households in Vietnam and Iceland in strongly contrasting positions of exposure? Or, to put it more simplistically, were you less exposed if you put your money under the bed rather than in the bank, and borrowing for housing was through more informal means? The selection was also guided by more general knowledge about the effect of global geography of the crisis on housing markets. The USA and the UK were essential inclusions representing the epicentres of the crisis because of the apparent severity of their housing-market slumps. Japan was also an important case, given its longstanding economic problems and with a housing market that had remained depressed throughout the 1990s in contrast to housing markets elsewhere, most notably in the USA and the UK. In the Netherlands and Australia the impact had apparently been relatively mild, although these countries were fully integrated members of the global economy. There were evidently important mediating factors at work at national level.

The East Asian financial crisis of 1997 had a dramatic negative effect on the economies and housing markets of most countries in the region, yet, as was intimated earlier, the more severe 2007/8 crisis seemed to have had a more modest impact on the region–at least compared with much of Europe and the USA. With some exceptions, the negative effects in terms of house prices and housing-market activity were limited and short-lived. Following the crisis, the region had the lowest average unemployment rates and the level of non-performing loans was modest and much lower than the levels during the Asian financial crisis.

CONCLUDING OBSERVATIONS

At the time of writing the economic atmosphere and general discourse is one of a mild but fragile recovery. The economic crisis in Greece and the likely emergence of other European nations facing similar fiscal deficits is part of that evident fragility. Key economic indicators remain highly volatile and sensitive to 'bad' news. There is also the question of who, and what, will be included in any recovery, and what will be left in its wake. The transfer of private debt to the public purse as the price paid to rescue the financial system has added significantly to the fiscal pressures on many governments. We are entering a period of fiscal austerity with a rising tax burden for households and a significant shakeout of employment in the public sector. There are likely to be more job losses and more households facing declining incomes. Moreover, the period of low interest rates may be coming to an end, seeing more households facing higher mortgage costs in conditions of growing financial insecurity. For households, therefore, it will be a highly uneven recovery, with growing contrasts between the most resilient and least resilient. Some households have benefited from a period in which mortgage costs fell, property bargains were available to be snapped up and where the best mortgage deals were available to those with the lowest risk profiles. We are now very much in prime, rather than sub-prime, territory, with the exclusion of the riskiest households from lines of secured or unsecured credit. And for all the rhetoric of more robust regulatory frameworks for the financial sector, the most evident institutional consequence of the crisis is a banking sector in which many institutions have emerged with greater economic presence and power. As Watkins (2010) observes, 'the great winners of the 2008 crisis have been the banks. With the exception of Lehmann brothers, the Treasury–Wall Street nexus has looked after its own. After a period of frenzied mergers, the surviving banks are famously bigger than ever before and still more essential to the system' (p. 9).

It was the logic of neoliberalism that drove forward the onward sale of mortgage portfolios and the growth of precarious financial 'products' aimed at reducing entry costs to homeownership for younger and/or lower-income households. These routes to increased homeownership seem to have reached an unfortunate conclusion. If so, what will be the new route? Despite the recent market failures, any serious expansion of more direct forms of intervention by governments in the housing sector to provide low-cost access to homeownership will be strongly resisted.

The homeownership of the pre-neoliberal era, which was more restricted in access, was about solidity and security–part of the Fordist social contract of relatively stable employment and wages, stronger trades unions, an expanding welfare state and regulated financial institutions. The neoliberal social contract involved shrinking welfare, more flexible and less secure employment, and a greater individualization of risks and rewards. Rising property values, cheap debt and the greater ability through financial deregulation to cash in the equity of the house to maintain or enhance consumption were important elements in that social contract.

Whatever the shape of the new era for homeownership, or whether it will emerge as a new era in any meaningful sense, the most defining characteristic will be an end to the promise of middle-class homeownership for an ever-expanding proportion of populations. Any new era will involve a greater degree of exclusion, or voluntary non-involvement, from home purchase, sharper contrasts in the housing trajectories of generations, more hybrid ownership forms (shared equity, shared ownership), more differentiated lending sources and terms, and a further fragmentation of homeownership along a number of social, spatial and temporal dimensions. These issues are discussed further in the concluding chapter.

REFERENCES

Abbey Mortgages (2009), 'Britain's baby boomerangers,' Press Release, 9 February, available at https://www.abbey.com/csgs/Satellite?c=GSNoticia&cid =1210620447841&idInfArchive= accessed 14 May 2010.

Andre, C. (2010), 'A bird's eye view of OECD housing markets', Economics Department Working Papers No. 746.

Arrighi, Giovanni ([1994] 2010), *The Long Twentieth Century*, London and New York: Verso.

BBC News (2008), 'Grim future for endowments', available at http://news.bbc. co.uk/1/hi/programmes/working_lunch/7788016.stm., accessed 25 June 2009.

BBC World News (2003), 'The kippers who won't leave home', 17 November, available at http://news.bbc.co.uk/2/hi/business/3276039.stm, accessed 20 July 2009.

Bootle, Roger (1997), *The Death of Inflation: Surviving and Thriving in the Zero Era*, London: Nicholas Brealey.

Brenner, R. (2004), 'New boom or new bubble?', *New Left Review*, **25**, 2nd series, 57–103.

Case, K. and R. Shiller (2003), 'Home buyers, housing and the macro-economy', paper prepared for the Reserve Bank of Australia Conference on Asset Prices and Monetary Policy, Sydney, August.

Deep, A. and D. Domanski (2002), 'Housing markets and economic growth: lessons from the US refinancing boom', *BIS Quarterly Review*, September, 37–45.

Farlow, A. (2005), 'UK house prices, consumption and GDP in a global context', Department of Economics, Oxford University, available at http://www.econom-ics.ox.ac.uk/members/andrew.farlow/, accessed 26 September 2009.

Ferguson, Niall (2009), *The Ascent of Money*, London: Penguin.

Forrest, R. (2008), 'Globalisation and the housing asset rich: demographies, geographies and policy convoys', *Global Social Policy*, **8** (2), 167–87.

Forrest, R. and Y. Hirayama (2009), 'The uneven impact of neoliberalism on housing opportunities', *International Journal of Urban and Regional Research*, **33** (4), 998–1013.

Forrest, Ray and Alan Murie (eds) (1995), *Housing and Family Wealth – Comparative International Perspectives*, London and New York: Routledge.

Forrest, R. and P. Williams (1984), 'Commodification and housing: emerging issues and contradictions', *Environment and Planning A*, **16**, 1163–89.

Forrest, R., P. Kennet and P. Leather (1999), *Homeownership in Crisis? The Experience of Negative Equity in Britain*, Aldershot: Avebury.

Forrest, Ray, Alan Murie and Peter Williams (1990), *Homeownership: Fragmentation and Differentiation*, London: Unwin Hyman.

Friedman, J. (2009), 'A crisis of politics, not economics: complexity, ignorance, and policy failure', *Critical Review*, **21** (2), 127–83.

Greenspan, Alan (2005), 'Remarks by Chairman Alan Greenspan', Globalization at the Council on Foreign Relations, New York, 10 March.

Greenspan, A. and J. Kennedy (2008), 'Sources and use of equity extracted from homes', *Oxford Review of Economic Policy*, **24** (1), 120–44.

Hamnett, Chris, Chris Harmer and Peter Williams (1991), *As Safe As Houses: Housing Inheritance in Britain*, London: Paul Chapman.

Hannsgen, G. (2007), 'A random walk down Maple Lane? A critique of neoclassical consumption theory with reference to housing wealth', *Review of Political Economy*, **19** (1), 1–20.

Harloe, Michael (1981), 'The recommodification of housing', in Michael Harloe and Elisabeth Lebas (eds), *City, Class and Capital*, London: Arnold, pp. 17–50.

Montgomerie, J. (2009), 'The pursuit of (past) happiness? Middle-class indebtedness and American financialisation', *New Political Economy*, **14** (1), 1–24.

Phillips, Kevin (1993), *Boiling Point: Republicans, Democrats and the Decline of Middle-class Prosperity*, New York: Random House.

Prudential (2009), 'Britain's baby boomerangers', Press release, 9 February.

Ramesh, M. (2009), 'Economic crisis and its social impacts: lessons from the 1997 Asian financial crisis', *Global Social Policy*, **9** (supp.), 79–99.

Saunders, Peter (1990), *A Nation of Homeowners*, London: Unwin Hyman.

Stiglitz, J. (2009), 'The anatomy of a murder: who killed America's economy?', *Critical Review*, **21** (2), 329–39.

United Nations Human Settlements Programme (UNHSP) (2003), *The Challenge of Slums*, London: Earthscan Publications.

Wade, R. (2008), 'Financial regime change?', *New Left Review*, **53**, Second Series, 5–22.

Watkins, S. (2010), 'Shifting sands', *New Left Review*, **61**, 5–27.

2. Effects of the recent credit cycle on homeownership rates across households: what we know and what we expect

Doug Duncan and Cesar Costantino*

INTRODUCTION

After 1994, the homeownership rate in the USA departed from its historical secular pattern and increased from 64.0 percent in that year to a peak of 69.0 percent in 2004. Although it is currently trending down, the US homeownership rate is still above the levels recorded before 1998. This chapter summarizes its history and explains what factors are behind its recent behavior.

Once a new household is formed, the decision to own versus to rent would be determined only by the relative cost of each alternative if the housing units were the same in location and characteristics, and there were no frictions in the credit markets. However, housing units are different in location and characteristics almost by definition. Moreover, in many cities rental housing often is very different than the rest of the housing inventory, and these differences end up affecting tenure choice. Finally, credit markets are not frictionless, thus households most often need to pass a number of screening tests, for example meeting credit-risk score requirements, and be ready to hold an equity position in the investment if they want to become homeowners. All these factors contribute to the tenure decision of a household.

The aggregate homeownership rate is just the average across all households. If households were homogeneous, we would be able to infer directly the aggregate homeownership rate from any household's tenure decision.[1] Since they are not, the US homeownership rate is affected by the composition of the household population, which can be sliced and diced along many relevant dimensions affecting preferences and their budget constraint, for example age, ethnicity, marital status, family composition, income and wealth. Trends in the composition of the household population can affect the aggregate homeownership rate even when within each sub-group the rate remains unchanged.

Our research suggests that the recent behavior in this variable is explained by the current credit cycle, that is the easing and subsequent tightening in credit conditions in the residential mortgage market,[2] and by the change in the demographic profile of the household population. We present evidence and also discuss findings by other researchers showing that the change in credit availability and cost affected households differently as a function of age, ethnicity and income.

Looking beyond the current credit cycle, two factors will support the long-term outlook for the homeownership rate: demographics and household attitudes. The rising share of age cohorts that typically own homes will contribute positively and help stabilize homeownership rates in the coming decade. In addition, we provide fresh evidence that the most important considerations in the decision to become a homeowner are not driven purely by financial factors–like price and interest rates–and that most households still have a positive attitude towards owning a home. With some caveats, also discussed in the chapter, these two factors will put a floor to the downward adjustment in the US homeownership rate in the medium term.

The next section presents a summary of the literature. Then we discuss the US historical experience, especially during the most recent economic cycle. After reviewing the determinants of household tenure choice, this section explores how the decline in homeownership from its record high in 2004 has affected the household population. The final section offers an expectation of how the homeownership rate in the USA will adjust in the medium term, reflecting our view of the equilibrium rate.

LITERATURE REVIEW

There is a wealth of research providing insight into factors influencing homeownership participation. The next paragraphs are not meant to provide an exhaustive discussion of the existing literature, but only to present the research findings that can shed light on the recent household tenure choices.

Obviously, a household's budget constraint is one of the main factors affecting tenure choice. Linneman and Wachter (1989) provide evidence that homeownership rates are lower for households with lower current income and assets due to their inability to meet underwriting requirements. Using Panel Study of Income Dynamics (PSID) data, Boehm and Schlottmann (2004) find that in addition to achieving homeownership at a slower rate, those in the low-income and minority demographic groups are more likely to exit homeownership than are moderate- and high-income whites. Turner and Smith (2009) use the same data and come to similar conclusions. Controlling for household composition, housing finance, employment and wealth, low-income homeowners and minority home-owners are still more likely to exit homeownership than higher income and non-minority homeowners.

The relative cost between owning and renting is a function of, among other things, mortgage interest rates. However, Painter and Redfearn (2002) assessed the effects of mortgage interest rates on homeownership rates over time and across regions and found that, after controlling for socioeconomic variables such as income, age of households, housing prices and population, the effect of mortgage rates was not statistically significant.

In a series of papers, Garriga et al. (2006) and Chambers et al. (2007, 2008, 2009a, 2009b) also study the relationship between the homeown-ership rate, mortgage-market conditions, and household decisions on homeownership within the context of the recent housing boom. In their 2006 paper, they evaluate changes in demographics, mortgage rates and housing policy, as well as financial innovations in the mortgage market. Their findings suggest that mortgage innovation led to disproportion-ate growth in homeownership among minorities and people 35 years of age and under. In a subsequent paper (2009a), they compare the relative effect of financial innovation, demographic changes, low interest rates, and favorable housing policy on the homeownership rate. Their primary finding is that innovation in the mortgage market played a much more significant role in the dramatic spike in homeownership rates in the USA from 1994 to 2004 than the other common explanations. More specific-ally, they find that the homeownership rates of younger demographics and minorities were disproportionally boosted by new mortgage products.

HOMEOWNERSHIP IN AMERICA

Historical Trends in Homeownership

American culture currently places a high value on homeownership. A new nationwide housing survey conducted on behalf of Fannie Mae between December 2009 and January 2010 polled homeowners and renters on their attitudes toward homeownership, among other things. The survey findings provide fresh evidence that a majority of Americans (65 percent) still prefer owning a home. However, this survey also finds that safety and quality of schools are cited as top reasons to own (Figure 2.1). This introduces some caveats regarding the future of preferences toward homeownership.

Which of the following factors would be most important to you in deciding to buy a house?
Multiple responses permitted

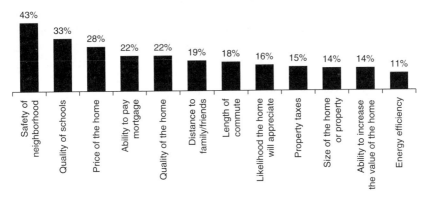

Note: The graph indicates that there is a strong emotional component to owning, based on a sense of security for your family – significantly stronger than any of the more economic considerations.

Source: 2009 Fannie Mae National Housing Survey.

Figure 2.1   Safety, education most important considerations in home purchase

Note that the two most important factors cited are not related to the housing-unit characteristics, affordability or even geographic location, but to the degree of access to safety and education. This suggests that households believe that rental housing, more often than not, does not deliver proper access to these goods. Thus a change in government policy towards allocating more resources to districts where rental housing is prevalent or subsidizing rental housing in districts with good safety and education could reduce the appeal of owning a home. In addition, we need to consider the possibility that many of the single-family housing units exit the for-sale segment and re-enter the market as rental units. In some locations, this also could lead to a new equilibrium where the appeal of homeownership becomes diminished after households realize that there is a new pool of rental units with access to safety and education levels that previously were only accessible through the for-sale housing market.

The difficulty in predicting the future path of homeownership is compounded by the fact that tenure choice might change household behavior, which in turn can affect safety, schools and home quality, and also by the fact that the benefits/costs of those behaviors often spill over to the neighborhood. For example, Coulson and Li (2010) find positive externalities arising from homeownership and include a discussion of the empirical literature on the benefits/costs of homeownership. Also, consistent with the theory of externalities, Engelhardt et al. (2010) find that the effect of homeownership on expenditure on interior repairs is positive and statistically significant while the effect on expenditure on exterior repairs is not significant. Complex interactions between household behaviors and tenure decision, alongside exogenous factors like credit availability and affordability, have determined the homeownership rate in the past and will do so in the future.

It is not clear that the current attitude towards homeownership was so prevalent in the distant past. Less than half of American households owned their homes at the start of the twentieth century. Homeownership remained fairly stable until the Great Depression, after which many homeowners lost their homes as a result of soaring personal bankruptcies, mortgage foreclosures and unemployment. Many more were unable to restructure or refinance their existing balloon mortgages or get access to credit to buy a home due to the severe credit contraction. In the following two decades, the homeownership rate climbed substantially, reaching more than 60 percent by 1960 (Figure 2.2), as a result of innovations in the mortgage finance markets.

Among others, Chambers et al. (2009a) attribute the increase from 48 percent after the Second World War to 64 percent during the mid-1960s to innovations in the mortgage-finance industry pushed by the Federal Housing Administration (FHA). They argue that the introduction of the fixed-rate 30-year mortgage, which since then has constituted the backbone of the mortgage-finance market, might explain 10 percentage points of the increment in the homeownership rate.

The homeownership rate remained within a tight interval during the 1965–97 period. From the late 1960s up to the 1980 recession, the rate increased steadily from 63 percent to 65.5 percent. The two severe recessions in the early 1980s caused the homeownership rate to deteriorate significantly. It was not until 1997 that the rate regained the levels seen before the 1980s recessions.

By the end of 2004, 69.2 percent of Americans owned their homes – a record high – thanks in part to loosened underwriting practices that eased down-payment constraints and innovative mortgage products that lowered initial monthly mortgage payments and the cost of credit for any given household risk profile. Young and middle-income households saw the largest increases in homeownership rates.

Figure 2.3 shows that, no matter what the previous history was, after 1997 all regions of the USA experienced a similar upward trend until the bursting of the real-estate bubble.

In the West, there is a slight downward trend until 1997, while in the

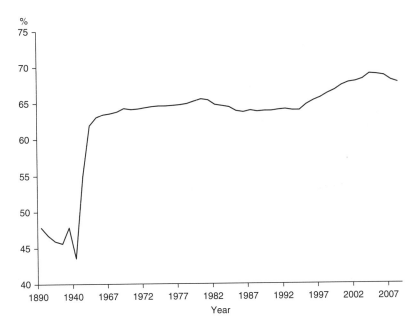

Source: Census Bureau.

Figure 2.2   US homeownership rate: 1890–2008

Northeast region the trend appears to be increasing almost linearly until the bursting of the real-estate bubble.

At the state level, the 'rust belt' and the 'bubble' states have very similar behaviors within each group. Pennsylvania and Michigan have been experiencing a decreasing trend since the late 1990s, while Ohio has not experienced a monotonic decreasing trend but its homeownership rate today is lower than in the late 1990s, which suggests that the current trend is the result of the real-estate bust and deteriorating fundamentals. In most of the 'bubble' states the picture is different, with a post-bubble decreasing trend but levels that are still above those registered in the late 1990s, Nevada being the exception to the rule.

Recent Changes in Homeownership and the Displaced Households

Since the end of 2004, the homeownership rate has trended down. Initially, the decline was modest. As early as 2005 the delinquency rate for subprime loans started to trend up sharply, even though the economy continued to grow. As the housing market started to decline and the economy

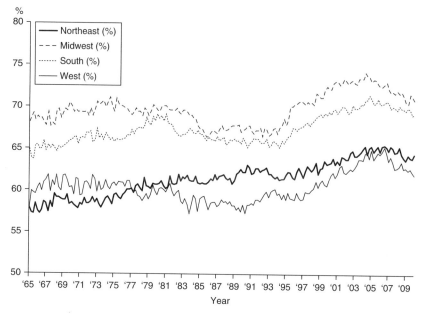

Source: Census Bureau.

Figure 2.3   Regional homeownership rate

slipped into recession, the homeownership rate suffered more pronounced drops.

Since the fourth quarter of 2006, when the homeownership rate started to decline rapidly, and up to the second quarter of 2009 the total number of occupied households has increased by 1.35 million units. This increase reflected a surge of 1.89 million renter households and a drop of 536 000 owner-occupied households.

Figure 2.4 shows that the number of renter households increased significantly in 2007 and 2008 as the recession deepened, while the number of owner households declined during the period. This recent development reversed the long-term trend between 1994 and 2004, when the number of owner households surged while the number of renter households fell. During the recent economic downturn, renting has become an attractive alternative as a growing number of consumers have delayed homeownership pending the recovery of the housing market and due to the increase in underwriting requirements. According to a study by the Joint Center for Housing Studies of Harvard University (2006), the number of renters was projected to increase by 1.8 million during the 2005–15 period, given

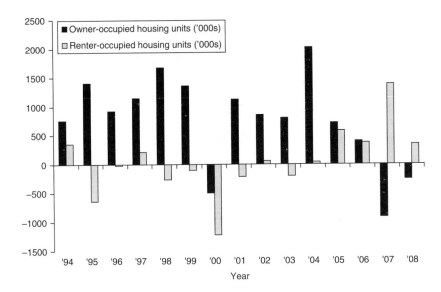

Source: Census Bureau.

Figure 2.4   Annual change in owner and renter households

expected population trends. In fact, renter households surged by 2.7 million just between 2005 and 2008. According to the Census Bureau, between 2004 and 2009 the increment in the rentership rate increased monotonically as the cohort became younger – which by definition mirrors the decrease in the homeownership rate across those households.

One of the impacts of the recent housing downturn has been a dramatic rise in the foreclosure rate since the end of 2006. Those who have lost their homes through foreclosure often become renters, although many have moved in with friends or relatives and some became temporarily homeless. In a survey by the National Coalition for the Homeless (2009), respondents were asked to estimate the percentage of their clients who had become homeless due to foreclosure, whether after eviction from homes they had been renting or owned. The median response was 10 percent, with the mean response being 19 percent. Survey respondents also were asked to identify the top three living situations for those who lost their homes due to foreclosure (Figure 2.5).

If the foreclosure inventory continues to rise, the growth in renter households could soon return to levels not seen since the early 1990s and increase even among households that traditionally leaned heavily toward ownership. Since professionally managed rental apartment housing starts

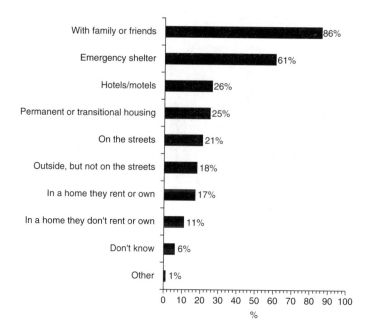

Note: Percentages add up to more than 100% as respondents were asked to choose the three most common situations.

Source: National Coalition for the Homeless (2009).

Figure 2.5   Where do displaced homeowners turn?

continue to be depressed, in the short run the supply of rental homes will likely come from the foreclosure pipeline. As suggested by Nechayev (2009), the housing market will go through a process of mix-and-match between newly minted prospective renters and newly minted rental single-family units. Households that had to leave their homes due to foreclosure will probably need to relocate if the labor-market conditions are weak in their current location. For example, rust belt states such as Michigan have shown negative net migration for some time, but now the emigrants will leave the state with almost no equity and a bad credit score, which will likely constrain them to become renters in non-professionally managed rental units.

Household Characteristics and the Homeownership Rate

The decision to own or rent depends on household preferences and budget constraint, which change with a variety of demographic factors including

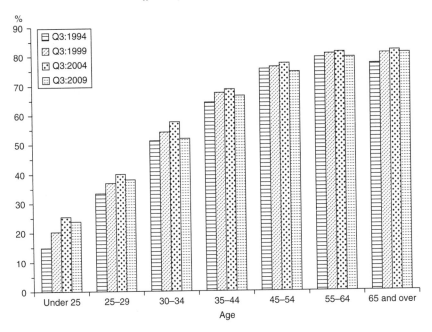

Source: Census Bureau.

Figure 2.6   Homeownership by age, selected years

age and household type and composition, as well as economic factors such as mortgage-credit conditions and home prices.

Homeownership rates vary considerably across family structure, age, racial, ethnic and income groups. Only about 25 percent of households under 25 are owners, along with about one-third of those aged 25 to 29. The rate increases to more than 60 percent for those aged 35 and above. The rate continues to rise with age, reaching a maximum of around 83 percent when households reach 70–74 years old. After that age, the rate starts to trend down. This suggests that the aging of the baby-boomers during the next decade will be positive for homeownership.

Between 1994 and 2004, homeownership rates increased for every age group. That improvement has reversed in the wake of the economic downturn (Figure 2.6). Note that the under-35 subset of the population was the main beneficiary of mortgage innovation and consequently it was especially hard hit when credit conditions worsened.

Between 1994 and 2004, homeownership rates increased for each race and ethnic group. However, black and Hispanic households' increment,

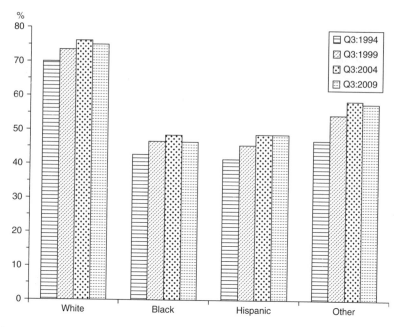

Source: Census Bureau.

Figure 2.7   Homeownership by race or ethnicity, selected years

13 percent and 18 percent respectively, was proportionately larger than the non-Hispanic white households, 9 percent, between the third quarter of 1994 and the third quarter of 2004.

Even with these gains, the homeownership rate among minority households still lagged significantly below that of non-Hispanic white households (Figure 2.7).

The non-Hispanic white homeownership rate was 75.0 percent in the third quarter of 2009, compared with 46.4 percent and 48.7 percent for blacks and Hispanics, respectively. The black homeownership rate declined by 2.0 percentage points from the third quarter of 2004 to the third quarter of 2009, compared with a 1.1 percentage point drop for non-Hispanic white and no change for Hispanic homeownership rates.

Finally, income is an important driver of homeownership. The homeownership rate is less than 50 percent for households in the lowest income bracket, compared with more than 90 percent for those in the highest income bracket. According to Chambers et al. (2009a), homeownership rates by income have increased for each income cohort during the boom phase of the current real estate. However, the increase was proportionally larger for the middle-income groups, which are also the groups where the mass of households is larger.

The income and wealth gap between owners and renters widened during the period of surging homeownership. According to the American Housing Survey (AHS), median renter real income dropped 6 percent to $26 000 between 1995 and 2005, compared with an increase of 8 percent to $55 000 for homeowner income during the same period. This is not surprising, as one would expect that the probability of becoming an owner rises with renter's income. According to Harvard University's Joint Center for Housing Studies' tabulation of the AHS (2006), in 2005, about 41 percent of renters were in the lowest income quartile ($21 000 or less), compared with only 17 percent of homeowners. Finally, the Survey of Consumer Finances (SCF) also shows a widening inequality in the net worth of homeowners and renters during the period of rapid increase in the homeownership rate. Between 1995 and 2004, the median net worth of homeowners increased by 44 percent, while the median net worth of renters fell by 33 percent. This probably happened because rapid home-price appreciation contributed to the disparity and again because renters with the highest wealth were the most likely to turn into homeowners.

Figure 2.8 shows historical leveraging of homeowner households. The current bust phase of the credit cycle has both reduced equity and raised leverage for them. As a consequence, we expect the owner/renter gap in wealth to narrow somewhat in the future.

One of the main issues is whether the recent experience will adversely affect homeowners' and renters' consumption/saving behavior. Between 1995 and 2001, the share of homeowners who reported that they saved steadily increased, but since 2001 the share has been declining partly due to the rapid home-price appreciation during the housing boom, which allowed homeowners to consume more as their household wealth increased. That trend has likely reversed already, given the massive destruction in housing wealth of homeowners during the recession.

Another salient characteristic of homeowners is that they also are historically far less mobile than renters (Figure 2.9). The downward trend in annual migration for homeowners will likely continue as the share of mortgages with negative equity rises, making it more difficult for them to move even when there are job opportunities elsewhere.

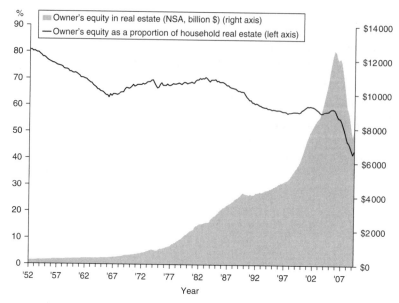

Source: Federal Reserve Board.

Figure 2.8   Increasing leverage; decreasing equity

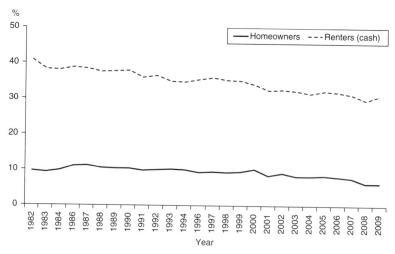

Source: Ruggles et al. (2010).

*Figure 2.9   Renter versus homeowner mobility (annual migration rate by
homeownership status)*

Table 2.1   Homeownership rate summary statistics

	1965–97		1965–2008	
	Average	Std dev.	Average	Std dev.
Homeownership rate: USA	64.39	0.63	65.2	1.69
Civilian unemployment rate: 16 yr +	6.15	1.56	5.86	1.48
Real GDP (Bil.chained 2005$) % change, year to year	3.31	2.22	3.18	2.04
Disposable personal income (Bil. chained 2000$) % change, year to year	3.40	1.67	3.32	1.64

Sources: Bureau of the Census, Bureau of Labor Statistics, Bureau of Economic Analysis.

OUR EXPECTATIONS

The new instruments that allowed households to access mortgage financing played a significant role in the dramatic increase in the homeownership rate between 1994 and 2004. This section assesses to what degree this factor influenced household-tenure choice.

The homeownership rate remained within a tight interval during 1965–97. Table 2.1 shows summary statistics for the homeownership rate and a host of factors that are usually mentioned in the literature as potential explanatory variables. It is noteworthy that when we add the period 1998–2008 to the sample, the change in the variability of the explanatory variables is much lower than that of the homeownership rate. We take this as a strong hint that we should focus on what was different this time around, that is, increased credit availability and cheap risk pricing.

In this section we propose a simple model that explains the recent behavior of the homeownership rate as a function of the volume of sub-prime and FHA originations and changes in the age distribution of the household population. The volume of sub-prime and FHA lending most likely captures the increased credit availability and cheap risk pricing that fueled the increase in the homeownership rate and continues to support it above historical levels. We find that the volume of sub-prime and FHA originations explains most of the recent increases in age-adjusted homeownership rates.

In order to control for the change in household age distribution, we calculate the homeownership rate as the average of the age-specific homeownership rates weighted by 1999 Q1 age-cohort population shares. We regress this variable on the volume of sub-prime and FHA originations.

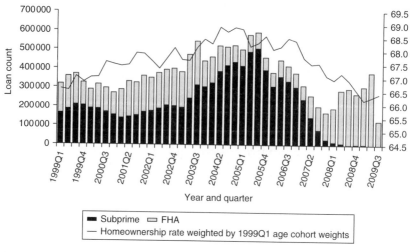

Sources: Fannie Mae, True Standings Servicing.

Figure 2.10   *Sub-prime and FHA loan populations (homeownership rate and loan originations)*

We had access to data on the number of loans originated by quarter and by different loan types in the USA from the beginning of 1999 to the third quarter of 2009 from True Standings Servicing. These data cover loan-level data on more than 80 percent of the nation's active first mortgages (more than 39 million loans) including all of the Fannie Mae and Freddie Mac portfolios. Figure 2.10 shows the sub-prime and FHA loan populations.

We show in the appendix that a very simple autoregressive distributed lag model was able to account for 84 percent of the variability in the homeownership rate and that the volume of sub-prime plus FHA loans is statistically significant.[3] Figure 2.11 shows the actual and fitted values from our model.

As a result, as Figure 2.12 shows, we can use our empirical model plus different assumptions on the availability of cheap credit to infer equilibrium homeownership rates that mimic the recent historical experience.

Figure 2.12 clearly shows that the homeownership rate long-run value could be sustained at the recent peak levels provided credit availability and risk pricing return to levels seen during 2003–05, either through increased private investor risk appetite or government action. Note that for the solid-lines forecast, we are implicitly keeping the age distribution constant at the 2009Q3 level.

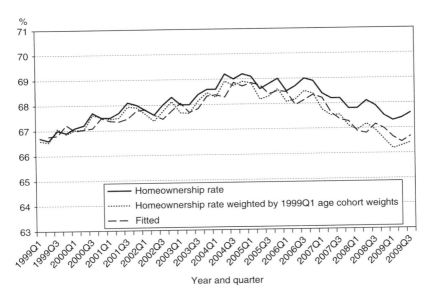

Sources: Census Bureau, Fannie Mae.

Figure 2.11 *The homeownership rate, accounting for demographic trends (homeownership rate, homeownership rate net of demographic changes and fitted values)*

CONCLUSIONS

For a variety of reasons, US households place a high value on homeownership. However, historically young and minority households have found it difficult to access credit markets due to their inability to meet downpayment and underwriting requirements. All that changed during the boom phase of the current credit cycle and as a result these households experienced a very significant increase. The unwinding of the credit boom has led to a decline in the homeownership rate that, we think, is not over yet.

We expect a long-run lower rate of homeownership than the peak, probably around 66 percent. The credit-expansion variable was a powerful explanatory variable and its role is consistent with the role of leverage in the financial markets crisis. In the future, new households will find it more difficult to obtain credit to purchase a home and existing ones that had to return their homes to their creditors will find even more barriers to ownership.

Finally, the current housing crisis might affect preferences toward

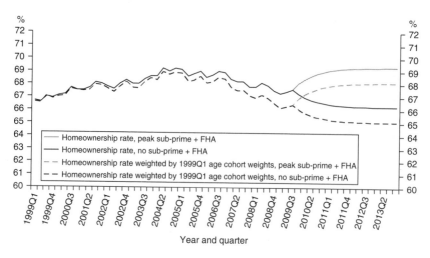

Note: Solid-line forecasts maintain the age distribution constant at the 2009Q3 level.

Source: Fannie Mae.

Figure 2.12   *Homeownership rate forecast scenarios (homeownership rate scenarios: sub-prime + FHA originations at 2003–2005 levels versus no sub-prime + FHA originations)*

homeownership. There is evidence that households currently do not value ownership because of the expected benefits from being the residual claimants on this asset. Survey findings seem to suggest that owning a home is not important *per se*, but the access to certain goods that traditionally have come attached to for-sale properties is, and this might change as for-sale properties migrate to the rental market and former property owners become renters.

NOTES

*   We would like to thank Manhong Feng, Stephen Gilbert, Yang Hu, Brian Hughes-Cromwick, Richard Koss, Ryan Kurth and Orawin Velz for their contributions and research assistance. This chapter presents opinions, analyses, estimates, forecasts and other views of Fannie Mae's Economics & Mortgage Market Analysis (EMMA) group, and should not be construed as indicating Fannie Mae's business prospects or expected results, which are based on a number of assumptions, and are subject to change without notice. Although the EMMA group bases its opinions, analyses, estimates, forecasts, and other views on information it considers reliable, it does not guarantee that the information provided in these materials is accurate, current or suitable for any particular purpose. Changes in the assumptions or the information underlying these views could produce

materially different results. The analyses, opinions, estimates, forecasts, and other views published by the EMMA group represent the views of that group as of the date indicated and do not necessarily represent the views of Fannie Mae or its management.

1. In this case the homeownership rate would be 1 or 0 at any point in time.
2. In a paper that explains the recent increase in mortgage defaults, Mian and Sufi (2009) find that during the 2001–5 period mortgage credit increased due to a shift of the supply curve driven by financial intermediation.
3. The appendix also shows a model including prime loans that count as another explanatory variable. Prime loan volume proved not to be statistically significant in explaining the dependent variables' behavior while sub-prime + FHA volume remained significant.

REFERENCES

Boehm, Thomas P. and Alan M. Schlottmann (2004), 'The dynamics of race, income, and homeownership', *Journal of Urban Economics*, **55** (1), 113–30.

Chambers, Matthew S., Carlos Garriga and Don E. Schlagenhauf (2007), 'Mortgage contracts and housing tenure decisions', Federal Reserve Bank of St Louis Working Paper No. 2007-040A.

Chambers, Matthew S., Carlos Garriga and Don E. Schlagenhauf (2008), 'Mortgage innovation, mortgage choice, and housing decisions', *Federal Reserve Bank of St Louis Review*, **90** (6), 585–608.

Chambers, Matthew S., Carlos Garriga and Don E. Schlagenhauf (2009a), 'Accounting for changes in the homeownership rate', *International Economic Review*, **50** (3), 677–726.

Chambers, Matthew S., Carlos Garriga and Don E. Schlagenhauf (2009b), 'The loan structure and housing tenure decisions in an equilibrium model of mortgage choice, Federal Reserve Bank of St Louis Working Paper No. 2008-024A.

Coulson, Edward and Herman Li (2010), 'Measuring the external benefits of homeownership', Working Paper, Department of Economics, Penn State University.

Engelhardt, Gary V., Michael D. Eriksen, William G. Gale and Gregory B. Mills (2010), 'What are the social benefits of homeownership? Experimental evidence for low-income households', *Journal of Urban Economics*, **67** (3), 249–58.

Fannie Mae (2009), Fannie Mae National Housing Survey, available at http://www.fanniemae.com/about/housing-survey.html.

Garriga, C., W.T. Gavin and D. Schlagenhauf (2006), 'Recent trends in homeownership', *Federal Reserve Bank of St Louis Review*, September/October, **88** (5), 397–411.

Joint Center for Housing Studies of Harvard University (2006), *America's Rental Housing: The Key to a Balance National Policy*, Cambridge, MA.

Joint Center for Housing Studies of Harvard University (2009), *The State of the Nation's Housing*, Cambridge, MA.

Linneman, Peter and Susan Wachter (1989), 'The impacts of borrowing constraints on homeownership', *Real Estate Economics*, **17** (4), 389–402.

Mian, Atif R. and Amir Sufi (2009). 'The consequences of mortgage credit expansion: evidence from the U.S. mortgage default crisis', *Quarterly Journal of Economics*, **124** (4), 1449–96.

National Coalition for the Homeless (2009), *Foreclosure to Homelessness 2009: The Forgotten Victims of the Subprime Crisis*, Washington, DC.

Nechayev, Gleb (2009), 'Where have all the renters gone?', *About Real Estate*, **10** (19).

Painter, Gary and Christian L. Redfearn (2002), 'The role of interest rates in influencing long-run homeownership rates', *Journal of Real Estate Finance and Economics*, **25** (2/3), 243–67.

Ruggles, Steven, J. Trent Alexander, Katie Genadek, Ronald Goeken, Matthew B. Schroeder and Matthew Sobek (2010), 'Integrated public use microdata series: Version 5.0 [Machine-readable database]', Minneapolis: University of Minnesota.

Turner, Tracy M. and Marc T. Smith (2009), 'Exits from homeownership: the effects of race, ethnicity, and income', *Journal of Regional Science*, **49** (1), 1–32.

APPENDIX: REGRESSION RESULTS

Dependent variable	Homeownership rate weighted by 1999Q1 age cohort weights
Number of observations read	43
Number of observations used	42
Number of observations with missing values	1

Analysis of variance

Source	DF	Sum squares	Mean square	*F*-value	Pr > *F*
Model	2	18.9014	9.4507	105.5	<0.0001
Error	39	3.4936	0.0896		
Corrected total	41	22.3951			

Root MSE	0.2993	R^2	0.844
Dependent mean	67.6550	Adj. R^2	0.836
Coeff. var.	0.4424		

Parameter estimates

Variable	DF	Estimate	Std error	*t*-value	Pr > |*t*|
Intercept	1	17.3354	5.7609	3.0100	0.0046
Lagged dependent	1	0.73362	0.0875	8.3900	<0.0001
Lagged sub-prime + FHA (000s)	1	0.00184	0.0006	2.9200	0.0057

Dependent variable	Homeownership rate weighted by 1999Q1 age cohort weights
Number of observations read	43
Number of observations used	42
Number of observations with missing values	1

Analysis of variance

Source	DF	Sum squares	Mean square	*F*-value	Pr > *F*
Model	3	18.9499	6.3167	69.67	<0.0001
Error	38	3.4451	0.0907		
Corrected total	41	22.3951			

Root MSE	0.3011	R^2	0.846	
Dependent mean	67.6550	Adj. R^2	0.834	
Coeff. var.	0.4451			

Parameter estimates

Variable	DF	Estimate	Std error	*t*-value	Pr > |*t*|
Intercept	1	17.03215	5.8103	2.93	0.0057
Lagged dependent	1	0.73777	0.0882	8.37	<.0001
Lagged sub-prime + FHA (000s)	1	0.00168	6.65E-04	2.53	0.0156
Lagged prime (000s)	1	4.11E-05	5.62E-05	0.73	0.4689

3. The credit crunch in the UK: understanding the impact on housing markets, policies and households

Peter Williams

INTRODUCTION

In many minds the UK has been at the heart of the global financial crisis (GFC), alongside the USA. This connection is at two levels. First, it is viewed as a country with high house prices, over-extended consumer credit, a highly developed mortgage market with a diversity of products and a high level of homeownership (though it peaked at 71 per cent in the early 2000s and is now down to 68 per cent, putting the UK in the middle of the distribution of developed countries by level of homeownership). Second, the UK has a globally very active financial services industry with 'cutting-edge' financial innovation. Indeed, the UK government worked hard to establish the UK as the world leader in financial services, and many segments of that industry, such as hedge funds, are headquartered in the UK. In European terms and before the GFC, the UK was the largest securitization market in terms of issuance and the largest mortgage market at over £1 trillion outstanding loan debt and a deeply competitive mortgage market. In that sense it was both connected and vulnerable.

The wider context of the GFC will be familiar to many, although there are divergent views of both causes and effects. In the simplest of terms, huge current-account surpluses were being generated in China and elsewhere as a consequence of 'the long boom' in the USA and other countries, which in turn were building large current-account deficits. Interest rates were driven to historically low levels and this fuelled a rapid growth in credit and a search for higher yields. Real estate and mortgages were two attractive markets, with the upshot that funds were readily available at historically attractive rates for them. As property prices increased, in consequence, more funds were attracted to them and borrowing on the back of real-estate assets became very easy. With intense competition to lend, there was a 'degradation' in credit standards that itself continued to fuel 'illusory' increases in property prices (Turner, 2009).

This in turn contributed to a growth in both the volume of securitized credit instruments and their complexity – the so-called structured credit products and credit derivatives. The finance market believed that it could offer investors combinations of risk, return and liquidity that were more attractive (and quicker to bring to market) than the direct purchase of actual assets. The view was taken that this reduced risk by allowing it to be spread beyond banks themselves to a wide range of investors in a range of countries and by avoiding the regulatory capital requirements that flowed from holding risk on balance sheet. But, in reality, much of this securitized credit was bought not by investors but by other banks, feeding a huge growth in the debt of financial companies. There was a significant growth in the leverage of assets when related off-balance-sheet vehicles were included. Long-term assets were being funded through shorter-term borrowing backed by insurance, interbank lending and central bank facilities. But, once confidence in the system began to fall, there was insufficient liquidity to cover the lines of borrowing that then needed to be unwound. The system proved to be very exposed to a self-reinforcing cycle of deleverage, falling asset prices and collapsing liquidity (Lanchester, 2010).

The GFC, or the credit crunch as it is known in the UK, has played out in different ways in different countries. But two key points must be borne in mind. First there is 'cross-contamination'. Although there were big differences between countries, what happened in one country affected another. For example, because US investors were major purchasers of UK securitized credit, the collapse of confidence in securitized credit generally had an immediate impact upon liquidity in the UK. Similarly, UK investors were major depositors in Icelandic banks (and Irish banks), and when the Icelandic system got into difficulties this had immediate knock-on effects in the UK (for example, three building societies lost their independence as a consequence of losses emanating from depositing funds in Iceland). Ireland's move to offer a high level of protection to depositors triggered a problem of its own as each country moved to prevent major bank runs. Countries that thought themselves immune from the GFC have found that over time they had exposures to degraded assets or that they were simply no longer able to access credit as before. Second, beyond the GFC there have been subsequent waves of reaction evident, not least in Europe, where we have seen a sovereign debt crisis built around the interventions made to stem the collapse of the financial system, and this is now leading to widespread public expenditure cuts that in turn may precipitate further decline and disruption. We need to view the GFC in its broad context.

More specifically, house-price 'bubbles' were not restricted to the USA and the UK; Australia, France, Ireland, Sweden and Spain were also having a boom and still being overvalued (*Economist*, 2010).

And in a salutary comment in a recent report the McKinsey Global Institute (2009, p.11) estimated that

> global residential real estate values fell by $3.4 trillion in 2008 and nearly $2 trillion more in the first quarter of 2009. Together with equity losses, this has erased $28.8 trillion of household and investor wealth as of the middle of 2009. Replacing this wealth will require a long period of higher saving. To put this in perspective, the world's households saved about 5 per cent of their disposable income in 2008, or $1.6 trillion: they would have to save that amount for 18 consecutive years to amass $28.8 trillion.

THE UNITED KINGDOM

The UK experience of the GFC has been profound and longlasting, with deep effects on society, economy and the polity. The UK was the last G20 country still in recession, albeit it has now (2010) edged its way out. UK government interventions and support to banks that were at the centre of the country's downturn have cost around £1 trillion. Factory closures, bank bailouts, losses of jobs and productive capacity have followed, along with much-diminished housing and mortgage markets, which, as in the USA and a number of other countries, were at the heart of the downturn, and it is to these we now turn.

UK Housing and Mortgage Markets

As already suggested, the UK experienced rapid growth in credit in a number of sectors before the GFC, including residential and commercial real estate, underpinned by a rapid expansion in securitization, much of it backed by overseas investors (Crosby, 2008). Securitization was used by a variety of UK lenders – some of the largest banks and a range of specialist lenders plus a small number of building societies. Northern Rock, a demutualized building society, had grown rapidly in the decade on the back of a highly developed securitization programme. When the securitization market froze, although the 'Rock' had matched its long-term lending with long-term securitization, it found itself with limited financing opportunities. Retail investors learned of its difficulties and sought to withdraw their deposits, with the result that the 'Rock' was unable to meet its obligations and had to be nationalized.

The 'Rock' was one of a number of banks that had grown rapidly on the back of a sustained housing and real-estate boom –Alliance and Leicester, Bradford and Bingley and HBOS had also followed this path and ultimately paid the price. Indeed, all the building societies that had demutualized in the 1980s and 1990s succumbed during the credit crunch – the mortgage bank business model they had developed proved to be very exposed. It had lasted less than 20 years.

By the mid-2000s it was clear that the ever-inflating UK housing and mortgage market was not sustainable – affordability pressures were becoming intense, the number of mortgaged homeowners was actually dropping, and first-time buyers were being squeezed from the market. The hope was that the market would slowly deflate, reflecting this continued squeeze (there is a debate in the UK as elsewhere as to whether there was a housing bubble or not – it can be argued either way – but see Wilcox and Williams, 2010 for a statement of the negative view). In essence, when one considers low interest rates and rising wages as captured in mortgage costs to income ratios, affordability was at acceptable levels. However, when measured by other ratios such as loan to income and house price to income ratios, it was very poor. Low interest rates were part of the structural adjustment to low inflation.

In 2007 total gross mortgage lending was £362.6 billion and the UK market passed the £1 trillion of outstanding mortgage debt. By 2009 gross lending had shrunk to £143.5 billion – a clear indication of the rapid deceleration that took place in the UK. In summary and through the credit crunch we have seen:

- house prices fall by 15 per cent to 20 per cent, but with strong regional and local variations;
- transactions fall by 50 per cent;
- lenders withdrawing >90 per cent loan-to-value loans and replacing them with <75 per cent loan-to-value loans;
- a number of lenders withdrawing from the equity release market;
- housing output down from 200 000 in 2007 to 90 000 in 2009;
- mortgage arrears and possessions rising – the number of borrowers more than 12 months in arrears rose from 15 300 in 2007 to 65 300 in 2009 while possessions rose from 25 900 in 2007 to 46 000 in 2009;
- negative equity rising from 1 per cent of homes in September 2007 to between 7 per cent and 11 per cent in spring 2009 (Hellebrandt et al., 2009);
- shrinkage in the volume of mortgage lending, the number of products available and pricing/terms;
- a contraction and then recovery of the private finance market for social housing;

- the withdrawal of many lenders from the low-cost homeownership market.

However, none of this has been as dramatic as some might have expected. Early assumptions were that prices might fall by 40 per cent and arrears and possessions rise to record levels (for example, the record was 75 500 possessions in 1991). However, such has been the scale of government and Bank of England intervention that those levels have not been reached. Reducing the bank base rate to 0.5 per cent has probably been the key measure – this has helped numerous households sustain their mortgage payments despite reduced incomes. Indeed, for some borrowers the credit crunch has meant they are hugely better off, with their required mortgage payment being much lower than they could ever have anticipated (Hellebrandt et al., 2009). This in itself has been a significant stimulus measure, encouraging households to spend as well as to pay down mortgage debt. At the same time, this measure, by reducing rates, has also meant a number of lenders no longer have profitable mortgage books and this, in combination with the need to offer high rates to retail depositors, has left most UK lenders with a major funding problem. Low rates have solved one problem but created another, and this now feeds into the even bigger dilemma about how to restore mortgage funding levels to ensure a viable and functioning housing market (CML, 2010).

The contraction of credit reflects the difficulties of individual banks and the lack of liquidity, and their reappraised risk appetite has also meant that alongside the changes in the housing market have come deep-seated shifts in the structure and shape of credit. This will have long-lasting effects, with substantial consequences for households. One feature of the credit boom was the expansion of lending to 'non-prime' households. With the huge appetite for mortgage securities and the ready availability of mortgage finance, lenders were able to develop a significant market in providing credit to households that were viewed as having impaired credit – missed payments, minor court judgments, even bankruptcy. Up until the 1990s many of these households could not have entered or stayed in the homeownership market. By the mid-2000s up to around 10 per cent of mortgage lending was to households with impaired credit. Although this is often seen as a 'bad' thing, it not only meant that these households were able to sustain their homeownership, albeit at a higher cost, but it reduced the default rate in the prime homeownership market. It is estimated that around 100 000 households a year moved from prime to non-prime. Without this new market there would have been significant collateral damage.

Unfortunately the whole arena of non-prime lending has become tainted on the back of the credit crunch and the severely sub-prime segment of the market. Given these are higher-risk households, a higher default rate would be expected. It is also the case that because the loans are higher risk, the charges are higher and thus households with weaker credit histories are paying more and in that sense are more exposed. A Fitch report on UK non-conforming residential mortgage-backed securities (Fitch, 2009) showed that 19 per cent of loans were three or more months in arrears, the same as in 2009 Q2, although there are significant variations around this reflecting specific tranches of loans both by lender and date of issue.

As already noted, the UK mortgage market has contracted in terms of volumes and the risks lenders are prepared to take. Although there are modest signs that this new conservatism is easing, a recent unpublished review of the results of the top eight lenders (Jenks and Williams, 2009) showed there had been a strong shift towards low-risk lending and that there was little appetite to increase overall lending volumes in the UK. Most obviously this is affecting first-time buyers and those with weak credit histories. However, in addition, many other borrowers are finding it difficult to remortgage away from their existing provider – there simply is no supply of alternative mortgages. Many existing purchasers are thus 'trapped on' the standard variable rate provided by their lender when their fixed rate or discounted deal came to an end. This group is vulnerable to any rate increase that might flow through if and when base rates are increased.

In 2010 there were only eight to ten active lenders in the UK mortgage market, down from over 100 at the height of the boom and before the crunch. Most of the 50 or so building societies are not lending or lending only small volumes, reflecting their difficulties in raising retail deposits against the competition from the biggest banks and at the same time being able to offer mortgages that are profitable. The specialist lenders who emerged in the 1990s as a strong competitive force in the UK mortgage market in terms of innovations in products and processes, and who took market share from the big players, are currently inactive. This is because most rely heavily on the securitization market for funding and this has been closed to them since 2007.

Although several new entrants are seeking to enter the UK mortgage market, including Metro Bank from the USA, and some UK entrants along with UK retail firms such as Tesco and Virgin, it is unlikely that this new 'competition' will result in more than an extra £5 billion of lending capacity in the next year or so. The UK markets and borrowers are thus left with a considerable dilemma as to where to go.

The credit crunch has forced a retreat from lending of all types, and shareholders and regulators are now demanding that lenders approach the market with a new conservatism. There is competition of sorts for lending 75 per cent loan-to-value mortgages to people with strong credit histories. There is little competition to lend at 90 per cent loan-to-value and none at 95 per cent. It is currently unclear if and when 95 per cent loan-to-value lending – historically where first-time buyers have been on the loan-to-value curve – will restart. We also have a deeply uncompetitive market with an effective oligopoly operated by the big eight lenders. In many respects they are reluctant winners because all are trying to restructure balance sheets and in some cases reduce lending. Being asked to lend more in an oligopolistic market has some clear downsides – concentration of risk, close involvement with government and the risk of being forced to take on weaker assets in a period when house prices are uncertain.

Government Intervention

The UK government has taken a very proactive stance in relation to the credit crunch. This flows from its understanding of the centrality of housing markets in the economy in terms of consumer confidence, access to housing wealth, impacts on consumption and production, housing's role in business-start ups and the speed with which housing spending feeds through into the economy (DTZ Consulting & Research, 2006). The UK is not unique in the role housing plays, but the UK government is strongly aware of the consequences of supporting/not supporting the housing market and not least the wider electoral impacts.

The range of government and Bank of England (BoE) intervention into housing and mortgage-market-related areas during the credit crunch has been considerable (see CML, 2010 for a detailed list). It has ranged from adjustments to stamp duty, support for mortgage interest payments (SMI) and mortgage rescue schemes through to credit and asset-backed guarantees, a special liquidity scheme to help generate cash for banks and an extended programme of 'quantitative easing' through which the Bank buys in assets from firms in exchange for cash (around £200 billion has been spent on this to date) although the BoE Monetary Policy Committee has recently agreed to put the scheme on hold.

Given the scale and breadth of intervention, it is hard to tell whether there is real market recovery or simply a temporary recovery underpinned by government. What we have now is a hugely complex patchwork of interventions with different termination dates and with complex unwinding to follow. Indeed, using the Bank of England special liquidity scheme as an example, banks will only be able to repay the debt when the market is restored to full activity/profitability. As matters stand at present, the planned cycle of debt repayment cannot be undertaken because the market recovery remains so muted. If government forces the pace, it runs the risk of undermining the recovery. If it waits, it could be a long time because the recovery process will be quite slow. The mortgage market might not be operating at a normal level of funding – say between £200 billion and £250 billion for up to five years. This points up the real tensions in the recovery process. In a major policy paper the UK Council of Mortgage Lenders (2010, pp. 4–5) suggested:

> UK policy measures have focused on bank capital and liquidity, and on tightening mortgage market regulation. Policy has been informed by a narrative that sees securitisation, wholesale funded lenders, and non-conforming mortgage credit as problematic because of the events in the US. Yet in the UK, residential mortgage backed securities (RMBS) and wholesale funded lenders have both performed comparatively well, despite an absence of government support. If this policy stance remains unchanged, the result will be a long term reduction in choice for consumers in the mortgage market.
>
> If there was one outstanding cause of the crisis in UK banking, it was not insufficient capital or poor quality mortgage lending in the UK, but the vulnerability of our banks' funding structure. Yet policymakers have focused on bank capital and liquidity, and even on fixing a mortgage market that was not the cause of the crisis. At the same time, policymakers have not yet identified or developed a sustainable funding model for the UK mortgage market going forward.
>
> The focus of government support on retail deposits, and senior unsecured bonds from banks and larger building societies, and the failure to provide meaningful support to the RMBS and covered bond markets, is seriously distorting the competitive landscape. It is creating a moral hazard where depositors and senior unsecured bondholders may feel they have no need to understand the risks they are running, because they will be supported by government.
>
> Ironically, given the lack of government support for RMBS and covered bonds, these funding instruments have demonstrated their effectiveness during the financial crisis. They allow non-AAA rated institutions to issue the AAA rated securities that the Bank of England (BoE) demands as collateral for deposit takers seeking to access the SLS. It is difficult to reconcile the BoE's negative attitude to RMBS with its demand for AAA securities, given that banks can only satisfy this requirement by creating retained RMBS or covered bonds.

The government has made much of its intervention in the housing market, and particularly around mortgage arrears and repossessions, because it recognized that in previous downturns repossessed housing stock had helped force down prices and undermined confidence and market recovery. When it announced its homeowner mortgage support scheme (HMS) in early 2009 it assumed that up to 10 000 households might be assisted. Basically HMS is a modest equivalent of the USA's loan modification programme. Lenders are being asked to allow borrowers in arrears to continue in arrears for up to two years, with the lender suspending possession action on the assumption that many households will be able to recover the situation and repay outstanding arrears and return to normal payments. If at the end of two years the lender still has to take possession, the government offers to meet 70 per cent of the cost of any losses. In practice the numbers passing through this and the mortgage rescue scheme (through which owners sell their homes to social landlords and become tenants) has been in the hundreds, but this is mainly a product of lenders moving to work with borrowers in difficulty and reaching agreements outside the HMS system (now numbered in their thousands). Government has also tightened the court order process, so lenders have to prove what steps they have taken to avoid possession and lenders have themselves taken a proactive stance helping thousands of borrowers in a range of ways.

Alongside the range of 'prevention' measures, the government also brought forward its housing spending plans through the Homes and Communities Agency (HCA) pumping several billions into building programmes with the aim of supporting a faltering development programme. The credit crunch had impacted very hard on house builders – with falling house and land prices their stock market value plummeted and their borrowings were very exposed (HBOS and RBS were the main lenders to the industry, and both were in great difficulty). If this was not bad enough, UK housing output is very low in relation to demand and long-term housing requirements. At peak, 200 000 homes were built/brought back into use in 2007. The actual requirement was for between 240 000 and 350 000 homes. With output now back below 100 000 there is a considerable backlog building up that threatens to ensure that the UK faces long-term affordability problems with all the pressures that this will put on wages, on household formation and on flexibility and mobility.

The HCA has sought to help builders keep their capacity and build on existing sites so that they can return to the market over the medium/long term. This has worked to a degree, with over £5 billion being spent in a two-year period. The problem now is that, having brought forward finance and with a public-sector deficit of around £200 billion built up across government, the future is about less public expenditure rather than more. Unless the market can support itself in 2010/11, there is likely to be very little public expenditure available to underpin it. A new search to find private finance to underpin government policy has begun (HCA, forthcoming).

The HCA has invested in land acquisition, site development, new social housing and in low-cost homeownership. It has put over £300 million into HomeBuy Direct, a joint scheme with housebuilders through which households get a 25 per cent equity loan shared between government and builder. The HCA has also been trying to kickstart faltering development most notably in what are called housing market renewal areas. These are areas in the North and Midlands of England, where the housing market was deemed to have failed in the 1990s. Abandonment, low levels of mortgaged transactions and high numbers of cash sales, rapid population turnover and a shift from ownership to private renting characterized these areas. A major programme of investment was put in place with the aim of rebuilding the housing market in each area. This involved selective demo-lition and the development of new homes. With the onset of the credit crunch this process largely ground to a halt. These were marginal areas during the housing boom and unsurprisingly they have been clear candi-dates for retrenchment given the downturn. Again, investment has been brought forward but it is in the context of a shrunken mortgage market and where conservative lending inevitably means that such areas are low priorities. Their recovery will be slow. Some local authorities in these areas are planning to introduce their own loan schemes to make up for restricted mortgage lending, although few schemes have been launched to date; and the policy emphasis is shifting from market renewal to economic regenera-tion and growth. This is fully discussed in the recent Northern Way report (Parkinson et al., 2010).

This discussion of market renewal brings to the fore the question of the geography of the credit crunch. It is clear that in the downturn and in the recovery there will be a geography of advantage and disadvantage that is based around the longstanding North/South divide in the UK. In a world where credit is rationed and where risk is given a higher priority, it is hard to see how government will respond except through much-strengthened regional economic policy through which disadvantaged areas are rendered more attractive.

The final area to discuss in relation to government intervention is regu-lation of financial markets. The credit crunch has triggered a widespread reappraisal of the effectiveness of regulation of lenders, products and processes both in the UK but also at the wider EU and global level. The UK had argued it had the best and strongest regulation of financial serv-ices through the Financial Services Authority (FSA). The UK mortgage market had been state-regulated since October 2004. However, the crunch had revealed that:

- the so-called tripartite regulatory regime for banks, which was conducted via the FSA, the BoE and HM Treasury, had not been

effective, as is evidenced by the failure of Northern Rock and
Bradford and Bingley and their subsequent nationalization and
the part-nationalization of the Royal Bank of Scotland and Lloyds
Banking Group;

- the new Basel II had been found wanting: it allowed banks to operate
  with much-reduced capital and the regulations had a pronounced
  procyclical effect – in other words they encouraged behaviour that
  amplified the cycle both on the way up and on the way down;
- the emergence of the 'too-big-to-fail' syndrome where governments
  were obligated to bail out large banks even though it was the banks
  themselves who made the mistakes;
- the securitization market had allowed risk transfer to take place
  with a lack of understanding of the underlying assets and the risks
  that were being passed. The market had not properly priced these. It
  raised important questions about the 'originate and distribute' business model through which lenders could fully pass on the mortgage
  risks they had taken on;
- the so-called non-banking or shadow banking system had emerged
  strongly in the 1990s and 2000s. In certain respects it was outside of
  the regulatory requirements faced by deposit-taking banks (though
  in practice the differences between the two sectors in terms of
  'capital requirements' were not as great as some argue because of the
  requirements imposed by bond holders);
- although first mortgages for owner-occupiers were regulated under
  the Financial Services and Markets Act, second mortgages were
  under consumer credit regulation and buy-to-let mortgages were not
  regulated at all. This added to the confusion and led to a degree of
  regulatory arbitrage;
- the regulatory regime put in place for mortgages in 2004 was judged
  to have failed. The FSA in its recent discussion paper (FSA, 2009)
  commented 'our existing regulatory framework has proved to be
  ineffective in constraining particularly risky lending and unaffordable borrowing'.

There is now an intense battle being fought out on the global stage
(and down to the national stage) as to how better to regulate banks. This
encompasses everything from the role of central banks and ratings agencies to the nature of mortgage products and sales processes. Focusing
narrowly on the UK mortgage market, the FSA's paper raises questions
about product bans, much tighter affordability and credit assessment,
stronger policing of the broker sector and its remuneration. Although it
is supposedly a consultation, the FSA has been strongly emphasizing its

wish to create a stronger and more intrusive regulatory regime. It recognizes that this will have external effects but gives little attention to what those might be. What this reveals is that the potential regulatory 'backlash' in the UK is being constructed with limited regard for the impacts it might have on the operational characteristics of the mortgage market and the wider housing market. If the credit crunch has resulted in a new conservatism, the regulatory response may well enforce that.

IMPACT OF THE CREDIT CRUNCH UPON HOUSEHOLDS

Although the empirical evidence on the impact of the credit crunch is still being assembled, we do know that, given the known distribution of income and wealth, the mortgage market in the Midlands and North of England plus Scotland and Wales is weaker (Northern Ireland is probably an exception here). More sub-prime lending was made in these areas (GE Money, 2008) and thus any contracted mortgage market will probably have a disproportionate effect on those areas. In essence, these areas benefited from the upswing in credit availability because lenders were looking to lend. As the market contracts, so the supply to these areas will fall disproportionately. This is an issue that has not yet been confronted. Indeed, with the effective closure of the non-prime market, there are perhaps up to 600 000 borrowers with nowhere else to go (if their credit history does not improve). The issue is not one just of new entrants but also the existing stock of borrowers. Little attention has been paid to this group, who may be one of the main victims of the credit crunch.

We also know that in the credit crunch specific groups have suffered particularly, again in mortgage terms. The number of first-time buyers has been falling for a sustained period as affordability pressures grew. The credit crunch then tightened the terms under which lenders were willing and able to advance mortgages to such buyers. The upshot of this is that some 80 per cent of first-time buyers were parentally supported (CML, 2009a). Of the 20 per cent who were not assisted, the average age has moved to 37, reflecting the real difficulty many have in accessing the market. Indeed, it is estimated that there are up to one million would-be owners who have not been able to enter the market (CML, 2009b). In addition, mortgage arrears and possessions have increased, though not (as shown earlier) to the level some had expected, partly reflecting government action. However, that support is short term, and with wage pressures alongside possible tax and interest rate rises, it has been argued the UK faces a second mortgage crisis (Aron and Muellbauer, 2010).

As this might suggest, homeownership in the UK is both shrinking and changing. It is becoming once again a more exclusive 'club' with all the implications that has for class, the distribution of wealth and social mobility. This can be evidenced via the Labour Force Survey (Williams, 2010) where the level of mortgaged homeownership among middle to lower socio-economic groups can be shown to be falling. While in the past different age cohorts in contrasting market situations have managed to secure similar rates of ownership over time (NHPAU, 2010), this pattern is going to be harder to achieve with a constrained credit supply.

The consequences of a restructured housing and mortgage market on the wider distribution of income and wealth are potentially huge. The Labour government has been pursuing an asset-based wealth strategy for some years, and particularly since 2005 (Toussaint and Elsinga, 2009). Increased homeownership was at the centre of this, with government espousing an ambition to take ownership up from 71 per cent of households to 75 per cent (as a target, the aspiration was and remains at 80 per cent – see Williams, 2007). Currently it has fallen to 68 per cent and it could go lower to 65 per cent. Given that this will be selective in both class and geographical terms, it poses very significant policy dilemmas.

With a squeeze on public expenditure about to begin, one question is: where will households excluded from homeownership go? Some will not form and many will simply live with parents longer or share with friends. This will have implications for household formation rates, fertility rates and much more. We might also expect to see increases in other measures such as occupancy rates (no bad thing?), homelessness and sharing. Logically, some households will go into renting. As indicated, the social rented stock will expand only slowly and thus much of the demand might be felt in the private rented sector (HM Treasury, 2010).

It is already evident that private renting has been growing and that many households that would have been mortgaged homeowners have now become renters. However, that sector has also grown on the back of easy credit to landlords. In the future there will be less money available, rates will be higher and regulations will be tighter. None of this suggests that it will be easy to expand this sector to meet pressures from homeownership. It suggests that the UK will face some acute housing pressures that will be borne selectively by certain types of households.

Alongside homeowners there has been a general tightening of credit as is evidenced in a recent Bank of England survey (Hellebrandt et al., 2009). This is affecting lower-income households who have relied on easy credit-card borrowing to meet daily bills and mortgages (*Roof*, 2010). Without such access we can expect more pressure on government support plus an increase in poverty. What the survey showed was that although some households are clearly worse off, some have benefited hugely from the fall in interest rates. But that reduction might be reversed over the next two years and the pressures of tighter and more expensive credit will become more evident.

Willetts (2010) has recently highlighted the privileged status of the 'baby-boomers' defined by him as those born between 1945 and 1965, arguing that this group are 'dumping too many problems on the younger generation'. Certainly many of the housing-related problems identified in the downturn were being borne by younger and poorer households and in the future the same will also be true. It is not a comfortable scenario.

CONCLUSIONS

The evidence points towards increasing pressures on some but not all households and a growing segmentation in the marketplace between those with good and poor credit standing. This has implications for future social polarization. In that sense the crunch takes the UK back to the past. With a huge public deficit and inevitable tax and rate rises alongside expenditure cuts, it is evident that neither the public nor politicians are clear how this might work out but it is a task the new Coalition government must undertake.

This chapter has very deliberately taken a macro view, situating the experience of households within the reworking of the wider housing and mortgage markets and beyond that to the UK economy. As this chapter has shown, the UK market has experienced falling prices and increased arrears and possessions along with stalled development and reduced supply, leading almost inexorably to long-term unmet demand, increased volatility and potential affordability pressures in the future. It is hard at this stage to gauge how quickly the UK might work itself out of some of these problems. The regulatory regime is still unfolding, as is the government and central bank strategy for unwinding their support to firms and markets, and all of this is caught up in both budget and electoral cycles.

Within the mortgage market, competition has been reduced and reworked. We have seen a number of lenders go out of business or merge, with the consequence that competition has been reduced along with the diversity of products. The regulatory reforms likely to be announced over the next 18 months from time of writing – October 2010 – by the Financial Services Authority will probably add to the problems identified by forcing a more conservative market despite the wider implications of this. Here we can see the real tension between the economics and politics of the response to the credit crunch, with the latter still dominating. As this might suggest, it has triggered a renewed focus on the debates regarding the state and the market. It has given renewed confidence to and support for state intervention and control, and has weakened those who argue for market forces. This in turn has re-emphasized national controls and national markets.

The credit crunch has changed the UK and it will go on changing it. It can be argued that the UK was vulnerable, reflecting its reliance on home-ownership, its highly developed mortgage market and its small private rented sector. It has been argued that it is only a matter of time before everything returns to normal. This might be a comforting thought and there will be normality in time, but it will be a new normality. It will be a more selective and expensive world, probably with even sharper divides and inequalities. Government will probably work to soften the edges and enhance flexibility in a range of markets, but the new harsher realities will still shine through. This suggests that socially, geographically and generationally the divides will be stronger. How that will reshape politics over time, only time will tell.

REFERENCES

Aron, Janine and John Muellbauer (2010), 'The second UK mortgage crisis: modeling and forecasting mortgage arrears and possessions', Spatial Economics Research Centre (SERC), London School of Economics, Discussion Papers with no. 0052.

CML (2009a), 'First-time buyers – are they really getting older?', *CML News and Views*, **15**, August, CML, London.

CML (2009b), 'How quickly will first-time buyers return to the market?', *CML News and Views*, **21**, October, CML, London.

CML (2010), *The Outlook for Mortgage Funding Markets in the UK in 2010 to 2015*, CML, London.

Crosby, J. (2008), *Mortgage Finance: Final Report and Recommendations*, London: HM Treasury.

DTZ Consulting & Research (2006), *Housing, Economic Development and Productivity: Literature Review*, for the Department of Trade and Industry, Reading: DTZ.

Economist, The (2010), 'Froth and stagnation', *The Economist*, 10 July, p. 75.

Fitch (2009), *UK Non-Conforming RMBS*, Performance Review Q309, Fitch Ratings, London.

FSA (2009) 'Mortgage market review', Discussion Paper 09/3, FSA, London.

GE Money (2008), *The Sub Prime Mortgage Market*, London: GE.

Hellebrandt, Tomas, S. Kawar and W. Waldron (2009), 'The financial position of British households; evidence from the 2009 NMG survey', *Bank of England Quarterly Bulletin*, **2**, 110–21.

HM Treasury (2010), *Investment in the Private Rented Sector*, a consultation, HM Treasury, London.

Homes and Communities Agency (forthcoming), *Housing Finance Group Report*, HCA, London.

Jenks, P. and P. Williams, (2009), 'Prospects for the UK mortgage market', unpublished report for Department of Communities and Local Government, London.

Lanchester, J. (2010), *Whoops! Why Everyone Owes Everyone and No One Can Pay*, London: Penguin.

McKinsey Global Institute (2009), *Global Capital Markets: Entering a New Era*, London: McKinsey and Company.

National Housing and Planning Advice Unit (2010), *How do Housing Price Booms and Busts Affect Home Ownership for Different Birth Cohorts?* Fareham, Hants: NHPAU.

Parkinson, Michael et al. (2010), *The Credit Crunch, Recession and Regeneration in the North, What's Working*, Northern Way, Newcastle upon Tyne.

Roof (2010) 'Backs to the wall', *Roof Magazine*, Shelter, London.

Toussaint, J. and M. Elsinga (2009), 'Exploring "housing asset-based welfare". Can the UK be held up as an example for Europe?', *Housing Studies*, **24** (5), 669–92.

Turner, Adair (2009), *The Turner Review: A Regulatory Response to the Global Banking Crisis*, London: FSA.

Turner, A. (2010), 'What do banks do, what should they do and what public policies are needed to ensure best results for the real economy?', speech at the Cass Business School, London, 17 March, available on the FSA website.

Wilcox, Steve and Peter Williams (2010), 'The emerging New Order?' *Contemporary Issues*, **4**, UK Housing Review, CIH and BSA, CIH, Coventry.

Willetts, David (2010), *The Pinch: How Baby Boomers Took their Children's Future – and Why They Should Give it Back*, London: Atlantic books.

Williams, Peter (2007), 'Home-ownership at the crossroads?', *Housing Finance*, May, CML, London.

Williams, Peter (2010), *Home Equity: Accumulation and Decumulation*, London: Resolution Foundation.

4. Housing in Iceland in the aftermath of the global financial crisis

Jón Rúnar Sveinsson

INTRODUCTION

In 1944, Iceland became an independent republic, thereby putting an end to a union of more than five and half centuries with the Kingdom of Denmark. After the Second World War, the new republic entered upon a path of rising economic prosperity, which, despite regular downturns,[1] has nevertheless on the whole been spiralling upwards for nearly 70 years.

The steepest rise of Iceland's economic fortunes occurred just after 2000, lasting until about 2007. But during the first week of October 2008, the economy turned dramatically downwards, when the Icelandic banking system collapsed during the onset of the global financial crisis.

These events severely affected the Icelandic economy. After an average growth rate (measured as GDP) of 4.0 from 1945 to 2008,[2] a sharp downturn of 10.6 per cent was forecast for 2009, together with a rise in unemployment from 1 per cent in 2007 to 9–10 per cent in 2009 and 2010 (Fjármálaráðuneytið, 2009a, p. 3). Iceland's currency, the króna, lost half of its value against the euro from 1 December 2007 to 1 December 2008.[3] This proved devastating for homeowners who had their mortgages wholly or partially in foreign currencies.

Iceland is among those Western countries that have been hit hardest at the onset of the global financial and economic crisis; it was possibly *the* hardest hit. The Icelandic banks were among the first in the world to fail at the beginning of October 2008, opening up for Iceland a perilous path of perhaps the most severe economic difficulties ever to hit a prospering Western democracy.

The collapse of the Icelandic banks and the economic crisis have had grave consequences for the country's economic and societal fabric. The economic sovereignty of the nation is seriously threatened and the ensuing political turbulence has sent shock waves through the country's political system, leading to the fall of the sitting government, early elections won by the two leftmost parties, the Social Democrats and the Left Greens, and thereafter the formation of Iceland's first entirely leftist coalition government.

THE GATHERING STORM

In April 1991, Davíð Oddsson, the leader of the Independence Party, became prime minister of Iceland, a post he was to keep for the next 13 years. His career, ending with the governorship of Iceland's Central Bank during the financial collapse, neatly coincides and interweaves with the rise and fall of Iceland's 'boom-time' economics.

From the beginning of the Icelandic economic surge in the second part of the 1990s until about 2002, the growth of the Icelandic economy could mainly be characterized as healthy and production-based. Iceland's joining of the European Economic Area[4] in 1994 was also an important factor in propelling Iceland's economic boom of the late 1990s (Jónsson, 2009, pp. 130–31). Oddsson's government had in the early 1990s entered on a path of extensive privatization of state-owned enterprises. From a neo-liberal standpoint, the government's privatization programme was considered a resounding success, putting Iceland at fifth position on the 'Index of Economic Freedom' in 2006 (The Heritage Foundation, 2006).

The culmination of the Oddsson government's 10–15-year-long privatization drive was to be the privatization of the two state-owned banks, Landsbanki and Kaupthing, in 2002 and 2003, respectively.[5] In accordance with the EEA agreement of 1994, the Icelandic banks were allowed to operate in the entire EEA, that is the EU countries, plus Iceland, Norway and the microstate of Liechtenstein. After the privatizations, the three Icelandic banks became progressively bigger actors on the European investment banking scene, coinciding with a simultaneous expansion of a number of Icelandic companies – the most auspicious one being Baugur Group, buying itself on a large scale into retail shopping in the UK and in Denmark. Soon the activities of the expansive Icelanders were noticed as far afield as Bulgaria, where they bought the national telephone company, and in Iceland itself, where the astonished locals of Reykjavik could follow the early-morning lift-offs and late-night landings of the handful of private jets of the new Icelandic multi-millionaires at the city's small airport.

The Icelandic banks grew at a phenomenal rate during the first years of their international expansion. In only a few years, Iceland had become the world's greatest banking nation in the sense that the size of the banks' total financial undertakings grew to become ten times greater than Iceland's GDP (A. Jónsson, 2009, p. 108; OECD, 2009). The growth of the Icelandic banks turned out, however, to be based on huge amounts of borrowing on the international financial market. The flow of money into Iceland's domestic economy kept growing, making the Icelandic króna much stronger than was realistic (Landsbankinn, 2009a).

In early 2006 the first warning signs came from abroad in the form of highly sceptical articles about Iceland's phenomenal '*Wirtschaftswunder*' in the foreign press. In February 2007 the credit ratings of the Icelandic state were downgraded and from March to May 2007 the króna fell by 20 per cent against the euro. But the signs that something might actually be more than a little wrong with Icelandic banking and the Icelandic economy faded away, for the time being. By the middle of 2007, the króna had regained much of its former strength, and 2007 in many ways turned out to be the zenith of the spectacular Icarian flight of the Icelandic economy.

With hindsight it is clear that the international foraging of the Icelandic banks and their great expansion would never have been sustainable. During most of 2008, up to the actual October collapse, the banks, aided by leading Icelandic politicians, tried in vain to keep themselves afloat during mounting signs of impending doom.

With the fall of the American Lehman Brothers investment bank on 15 September 2008 and the domino effects throughout the international financing that ensued, there probably was no way that the Icelandic banking system could have been salvaged. On 6 October, the prime minister of Iceland, Geir H. Haarde, gave an address to the nation on national television, warning of the danger of a national bankruptcy, ominously ending his speech with the words: 'God bless Iceland' (Jónsson, Á., 2009, p. 170, Arnarson, 2009, p. 18, OECD, 2009).

Two days later all three big Icelandic banks had collapsed and the UK government had applied provisions of the UK anti-terrorism legislation to freeze the assets of one of the banks, Landsbanki (Jónsson, Á., 2009, pp. 184–5). The Icelandic people were at first stunned by these momentous events. But within a few weeks a protest movement, demanding new elections and the government's resignation, started to gain momentum.

HOMEOWNERSHIP IN ICELAND

Icelandic housing policy has so far been directed towards homeownership, indicated by 85–90 per cent of all families in Iceland owning their dwelling. As early as 1960, the rate of homeownership in Iceland was 70 per cent, having risen from 56 per cent in 1940. By 1990, this figure was 89 per cent (Hagstofa Íslands, 1997, p. 374). The homeownership rate rose significantly during the 1940s as a result of the economic boom brought on by the allied occupation of the country during the Second World War. The figure from 1990 is based on the results of a large survey, as no later figures are available. The rate of homeownership in all probability remained at the 90 per cent level until the fatal year of 2008 brought the future of homeownership in Iceland into serious jeopardy, in which it remains at the time of writing.

The exceptional and long-time domination of homeownership as the preferential housing tenure in Iceland has its roots in a number of social and economic factors. The lack of large towns and big cities in Iceland is, of course, an important and to some extent self-evident factor.[6] Like the English-speaking inhabitants of overseas nations in North America and Oceania, Icelanders are also originally a nation of settlers from Europe (i.e. Norway and the British Isles), and this has been suggested as an explanation of Iceland's divergence from the other Nordic countries, a divergence that manifests itself in a long-running political dominance of centre-right parties, an overall less developed welfare society and a housing system strongly dominated by homeownership (Tomasson; 1980, Ólafsson, 2003; Sveinsson, 2006).

Iceland accordingly ranks among those advanced Western countries where homeownership has gained the greatest preponderance. When homeownership extends to as much as 90 per cent of a country's population, it is possible to talk of a *de facto* monotenurial housing system. This implies that ownership as such has spread nearly equally to all income groups and social classes, even though class differences are easily visible in the prevailing standard and quality of the housing owned by families with different social backgrounds. Renting has on the other hand been getting more and more marginalized in Icelandic society, seen as at most a temporary housing solution for young people before they enter owner occupation or a stigmatized tenure for the worst-off groups in Icelandic society.

But perhaps the most important reasons for the strength of homeownership are to be found in the emphasis official housing policy has put on homeownership as one of its main objectives.

The State Housing Agency, a state-run mortgage lending institution, founded in the mid-1950s, was from its inception primarily geared towards assisting individual families to acquire a house or a flat of their own. It had a forerunner in earlier state-run lending schemes to assist self-builders to complete their house building, and for many decades to come, self-building remained an important factor in the 'housing culture' of the Icelanders and does so, to some extent, up to the present (Sveinsson, 2000, pp. 91–6, 106–9).

The strong emphasis on owning rather than renting in Iceland can also be clearly seen in the fact that social housing was until recently mostly owned by the occupants of such dwellings. This could be called 'social owner occupation' and it originated as far back as the 1930s, with what were called 'Workers' dwellings'.

The labour unions were heavily involved in the building and the distribution of such flats (by means-tested criteria) and the number being constructed each year was often an important part of the collective bargaining process between the national employers' association and the trade unions' federation. In 1965, the construction of 1000 owner-occupied flats for trade union members was an important part of a general labour-market settlement. And in 1986 the labour unions agreed to channel funds from the union-run pensions funds to finance the State Housing Agency's general lending schemes towards the buying or building of owner-occupied dwellings (Sveinsson, 1993, 2000, pp. 116–20). At its peak, social owner occupation amounted to about 7 per cent of the Icelandic housing stock.[7]

On the other hand, socially rented flats have until the last few years remained a marginal tenure, nearly exclusively serving the needs of municipal welfare bureaux to house their clients. The construction of new social owner-occupier flats came to an end in 1999 and the systematic build-up of a stock of social rental flats is now seen as an important housing-policy priority. They have now reached approximately the same number as the social owner-occupier flats did in their heyday in the 1980s and the 1990s, albeit not representing the same proportion of the housing stock, which has grown considerably in the meantime (Sveinsson, 2010).

THE ICELANDIC HOUSING BOOM

As can be expected in a country of homeowners, the residential housing market in Iceland has become increasingly important in the overall economic framework. The market is most mature in the capital region, as the regional markets outside the capital area are small in size.

The Icelandic housing market did not experience a big downturn in the years around 1990, as happened for example in the UK and in the other Nordic countries. During most of the 1990s, housing prices remained relatively stable, albeit with a slight tendency to a decrease. Figure 4.1 shows the development of annual average housing prices in the Reykjavik area from 1994 to 2009.

As shown in Figure 4.1, housing prices in the Reykjavik area had started to rise slowly by 1998. By 2000, prices had risen by 31 per cent compared

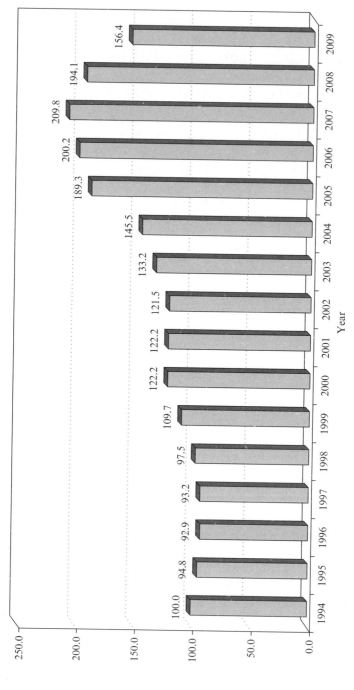

Sources: Fasteignaskrá Íslands (2010), Hagstofa Íslands (2010a).

Figure 4.1 Index of housing prices in the Reykjavik area (real terms), 1994–2009

with 1997. This was connected with increased economic growth in Iceland after 1995 and increased state lending after the former State Housing Agency in 1999 was turned into the Housing Financing Fund (HFF).

During the next two years, 2001 and 2002, housing prices again stagnated, only to start a new rise in 2003 and 2004 and to take a giant leap of 30 per cent in one year, from 2004 to 2005. In the Reykjavik area, housing prices reached their apex in 2007, 126 per cent higher in real terms than in 1996. By the end of 2007, prices started to fall and the average for 2009 was 25.5 per cent lower than 2007's average.

The reason for the big jump in housing prices in 2005 was above all the entry of the newly privatized banks on to the Icelandic housing mortgage market in August 2004. The state-owned HFF was at that time about to increase its maximum housing loans to 90 per cent of purchase prices or building costs.

The HFF had not yet implemented its 90 per cent loans, which meant that the banks managed to out-compete it, by being first to offer the new 90 per cent product on the mortgage market. Needless to say, the banks also competed among themselves in offering the highest lending and the lowest interest rates and the same maturity of 40 years as the HFF. Moreover, the HFF only lent 90 per cent of the value of a standard medium-sized house or flat, leaving the 'high end' of the housing market wide open to the banks. For a while, at least one of the banks would even lend 100 per cent of the purchase price of a property.

The HFF soon lost thousands of its clients, who grabbed the opportunity to refinance their housing loans at the HFF with new loans with better lending terms from the banks. The banks thus effectively took over the high end of the market for housing mortgages, while the HFF became more 'socially' oriented than before, granting loans to families with medium or low incomes and to families living in small towns and rural areas outside the Reykjavik area.

The influx of new lending capital at very favourable terms from the banks into the housing market obviously created a strong increase in homebuyers' purchasing power. This resulted in rising demand for housing and a steep rise in house prices, as described above.

Construction activity increased (see Figure 4.2) steadily from the year 2000, culminating in nearly 4500 building starts in 2007. Investment in residential construction increased by nearly 150 per cent from 1999 to 2007 (Fjármálaráðuneytið, 2009b, p. 19). In 2008, building activity remained high, but in 2009 the number of completed dwellings, compared with 2008, plummeted by 70 per cent and the building starts by 94 per cent. Thus the house-building industry has effectively collapsed and very few dwellings will probably be built in Iceland for at least some years to come.

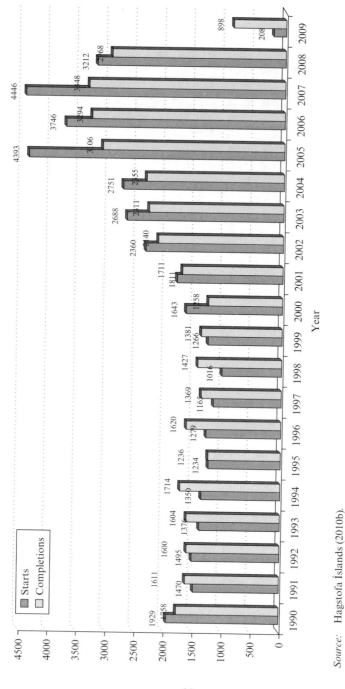

Source: Hagstofa Íslands (2010b).

Figure 4.2 Dwelling construction in Iceland, 1990–2009: building starts and completions, number of dwellings

THE COLLAPSE OF THE HOUSING MARKET

The property boom continued in the Reykjavík area until late 2007. By autumn 2008, just before the collapse of the banks and the onset of the economic crisis, housing prices had fallen by 15.8 per cent in real terms. After that, prices continued to decline and, by December 2009, housing prices in the Reykjavik area had fallen in real terms by 34.3 per cent since October 2007 (Fasteignaskrá Íslands, 2010).

A continued fall in prices is expected to take place over the next two years or so and by 2011 housing prices in the Reykjavik area might be down to a similar level as before the great surge of the market started in late 2004 (Seðlabanki Íslands, 2009).

The building boom of the last years before the banking crisis resulted in a considerable overproduction of new dwellings. This can be seen in many places in the Reykjavik area, where newly built houses and new flats stand empty in large numbers. Nationally, there may be around 3000 empty newly built dwellings, or what amounts to the dwelling construction capacity of about one year (Landsbankinn, 2009b, p. 7).

Housing construction investment is expected to have fallen by 45 per cent during 2009. A large part of that will go to the completion of projects that had started before the onset of the credit crunch. Also, the only functioning housing financing institution left in the country after the fall of the private banks is the HFF (Fjármálaráðuneytið, 2009b, p. 19, Landsbankinn, 2009b).

THE DIFFICULTIES OF HOMEOWNERS

After the onset of the economic crisis in the autumn of 2008, it became clear that homeowners in Iceland, especially younger families, would be hit hard by the consequences. Iceland has in fact had quite a long history of economic problems and housing-debt difficulties for at least a certain proportion of homeowners. During the early 1980s, Icelandic homeownership experienced a housing crisis, caused by the extreme inflation ravaging the economy at that time, peaking at 83 per cent in 1983 (Sveinsson, 2000, ch. 4). An important factor in the 1980s crisis was the indexation of all housing loans that had been introduced in 1979. When inflation rose to its all-time high in 1983, the consequences were quite serious for those young families who were at that time buying or building their first housing. This resulted in large protest meetings and the formation of a homeowners' grass-roots group.[8]

The governments of that time answered with a string of measures. The

State Housing Agency began an increasingly comprehensive debt relief programme, in 1985, and a big increase in the state-sponsored housing loans of the Agency was implemented.

Over time the proportion of families with serious debt problems decreased. However, the debt-relief activity by the State Housing Agency continued, as at any given time a certain number of families would for various reasons get into difficulties with their housing mortgages. One should bear in mind that because Iceland is a country with a very high rate of homeownership, the tenure includes a considerable proportion of low-income families. Thus the risk for debt problems can logically be predicted to be much bigger in an economic system where homeownership stretches over more or less the entire income spectrum of the society than in a society where homeownership has only 'trickled down' to the better-off part of the working class.

In 1996, the Ministry of Social Affairs (the government ministry that deals with housing issues in Iceland) initiated a pilot project by starting The Domestic Debt Advisory Service (Fjármálastofa heimilanna). It provides consultancy, at no cost, to people with serious debt-payment problems who have exhausted their financial resources. The Service assists people in getting an overview of their situation and helps them to make payment plans, choose remedies and acts as liaison in agreements with creditors, if required.[9]

THE MAIN EFFECTS OF THE BANKING CRISIS

The effects of the international financial crisis, mediated in Iceland through the devastating collapse of the three largest banks, can be broken down as follows:

The effects of the indexation of the housing loans   All long-term housing loans in Iceland are connected to the consumer price index. Always unpopular with the general population, the indexation of housing loans did not have a very great effect during the 1990s, when inflation in Iceland was quite low (that is, between only 2 and 4 per cent) and because of the steady increase in general purchasing power. But when the Icelandic króna began to plummet in the early months of 2008, prices of all imported goods began to rise. As the fall of the króna has continued, the consumer price index has risen by about 30 per cent since the beginning of 2008. This affects all housing loans directly, increasing their nominal value by the same 30 per cent.

Loans in foreign currencies   One of the new 'products' the banks started to market after their privatization was housing mortgages in foreign currencies. These loans had lower interest rates than domestic loans and were, of course, not indexed. For a time these loans, therefore, seemed like a great bargain for the general Icelandic public. The Icelandic króna was generally seen to be too highly valued and its extremely high exchange rate in 2004–06 was expected to slacken. A fall of perhaps 20 per cent of its value was expected to be in the pipeline. However, people, were ready to accept this, because the foreign loans would still be much cheaper than the domestic, indexed loans. Thus, when the euro rose not by 20–30 per cent but by more than 100 per cent, catastrophe was knocking at the door of all Icelandic homeowners who had taken out their housing mortgages in foreign currencies. The nominal value of these loans rose not just by 25 per cent, as the domestic index loans did, but on average by about 100 per cent.[10]

Fall of housing prices – loss of equity As described earlier, the fall in housing prices in the Reykjavik area now stands at nearly 35 per cent. This price fall is expected to continue throughout 2010 and to reach a low price plateau by 2011. At the same time, the nominal debt of all mortgage holders has been rising dramatically, as described above. For recent home-buyers this means inevitably that their housing equity has turned negative and seems likely to remain so for a number of years. Homeowners who bought their properties 15 to 25 years ago will, however, not find themselves in negative equity, but are likely to have lost a considerable part of the equity accumulated since the golden days of 2007, when housing prices were at their absolute zenith.

The rise of unemployment In the spring of 2009, unemployment in Iceland had risen to about 9 per cent. Those families that have already been hit by the catastrophic increase in their housing debt and where one or even both parents in a household have lost their job will probably have little chance of keeping their property.

The fall in the purchasing power of wages In the economic environment described above, it is no surprise that the purchasing power of wages has fallen. Although wages did not fall between 2008 and 2009, they have not kept pace with the wave of inflation that swept the Icelandic economy in 2008 and 2009.

A possible wave of emigration of young families During earlier recessions, most notably in the late 1960s, Iceland experienced short waves of net emigration. That this should happen now on a greater scale is one of the worst fears in Iceland. End-of-year figures for 2009 do show a decrease in the population from 2008, from 319 400 to 317 600 (Hagstofa Íslands, 2010c). A decrease of Iceland's population has not happened since 1889, when Icelandic emigration to North America was at its highest. Demographic forecasts now predict that Iceland's population of about 319000 will decrease to about 317000 in 2011 and thereafter begin to increase again (Hagstofa Íslands, 2010c). The emigrants are also likely to be predominantly young people, often young families, and educated. Moreover, people studying abroad – which is very common among Icelanders – are less likely to return to Iceland at a time of economic crisis. On the positive side, the possibility of seeking work abroad will to some extent make the problem of unemployment easier to bear.

THE INCREASED DEBTS OF HOMEOWNERS

At the end of 2007, there were very nearly 100000 homeowner households in Iceland – 27000 owned their property outright and 17500 owed more than 80 per cent of the property's valued market price[11] (Fjármálaráðuneytið, 2009b, p. 21). The total assets of these 100000 homeowners amounted to some 1570 billion Icelandic krónur.

Table 4.1 (based on statistics from tax returns) shows the equity status of Icelandic homeowners at the end of 2007 and the forecast for the end of 2009.

The total loss of housing equity (see the last column of Table 4.1) between 2007 and 2009 is 596 billion krónur, or 38.0 per cent. Thus the percentage of households in negative equity has increased from 7.5 per cent in 2007 to 28.4 per cent in 2009. In 2007, 35.1 per cent of all Icelandic homeowning households had housing equity of between 50 and 99 per cent. At the end of 2009, that figure will be down to 21.2 per cent.

Table 4.1   Equity position of homeowning households in Iceland, billions of Icelandic krónur

Equity position (%)	End of 2007			End of 2009 (forecast)			Loss of equity
	Households		Total equity	Households		Total equity	
	No.	%		No.	%		
100	27000	27.0	600	27000	26.9	540	−60
50–99	35121	35.1	809	21297	21.2	471	−338
20–49	20321	20.3	163	14618	14.6	126	−37
0–19	10057	10.1	21	8828	8.8	20	−1
Less than 0	7493	7.5	−23	28488	28.4	−183	−160
Total	99992	100.0	1570	100231	100.0	974	−596

Source: Fjármálaráðuneytið (2009b, p. 21).

The figure for the number of households that own their housing property debt-free is 27000. This group of homeowners consists mainly of people over 60. The age groups hardest hit by the loss of housing equity are those that are relative newcomers to homeownership, that is, people in the 30–45 age bracket.

REACTIONS TO THE ICELANDIC HOUSING CRISIS

After the Icelandic banks' collapse in October 2008, public discourse has been almost completely dominated by its effects on the whole of society and has involved intense soul-searching as to why this could have happened.

The plight of the Icelandic homeowners has also been very central in the debate. The government and the housing authorities have been severely criticized for their alleged ineffectiveness in dealing with the crisis, and a comprehensive package of measures to alleviate the difficult situation of the hardest-hit homeowners is being demanded. An example is the demand to write off 20 per cent of all housing debts with the banks and the HFF. This demand has been widely seen as just and logical, in the light of far-reaching debt write-offs of companies and businesses throughout the financial system in the turmoil that has followed in the wake of the banking collapse.

As in the 1980s, a homeowner pressure group has sprung into being, Hagsmunasamtök heimilanna (The Homeowners' Association). The Association has been very active in the housing debate and in the first half of October 2009, it organized a two-week 'mortgage strike', recommending that homeowners postpone their mortgage payments for two weeks.

Despite criticism of the housing authorities for doing very little, the HFF has been offering some solutions. Thus a partial payment plan can be arranged for borrowers who wish to catch up on past due mortgage payments. Also, refinancing defaulted payments is an option for borrowers who are behind on mortgage payments and unable to catch up. Extending the maturity of an existing mortgage for up to 70 years is a possibility, that is, the mortgage will mature in 70 years from the date of its issuance. Payment suspension for a period of 1–3 years is still another option (Íbúðalánasjóður, 2009).

Payment deferment is also a possibility: if payments according to a special 'payment deferment index' are lower than payments according to the consumer price index, the difference will be deferred until the payment deferment index rises above the consumer index. The deferred sum will thereafter be transferred to an adjustment account, which will be added to the principal of the loan (Íbúðalánasjóður, 2009).

The three big banks, now all owned by the Icelandic state,[12] offer similar options to their clients with difficult housing loans.

At the end of October 2009, the Icelandic Parliament passed new legislation on comprehensive measures to aid homeowners who were going through financial difficulties because of unbearable or very heavy debt load on their housing. The new law implies a general clause whereby all housing-loans indexation is put back to the beginning of 2008. After that, the loans are indexed according to the above-mentioned payment-deferment index. The deferred sum is then added to the principal of the loan and paid after the loan matures (for example 40 years). The deferred payments, however, can only go on for three years, the remainder of the loan, if there is any, will be written off (Félags- og tryggingamálaráðuneytið, 2009).

CONCLUDING REMARKS

Housing finance and housing markets were at centre stage in triggering the 2008 international financial crisis. Housing has also been central to the crisis management of 2009 in a number of countries around the globe and will be equally important in the reconstruction of the financial, economic and social fabrics in the post-crisis period into which the world is now moving.

The importance of housing for Iceland and the Icelanders after the bank collapse is also paramount. For one thing, the outcome of the present housing crisis for the young families who have only recently entered owner occupation will in many cases determine if they choose to emigrate to some of the neighbouring countries or decide to weather the storm and stay in Iceland. This age group, most often young parents in their thirties, is also important for the hoped-for resurgence of the Icelandic job market. People in this age bracket were heavily represented in the collapsed financial sector, where future job prospects may be problematic.

The overall management of the Icelandic crisis and the initiation of a healthy phase of economic reconstruction have so far been plagued by considerable difficulties. The biggest problem has been the Icesave dispute[13] with the UK and the Netherlands. This has not yet been resolved, despite renewed attempts by both the government and the parliament of Iceland and also by the entire population in a national referendum on 7 March 2010 (after the president's veto of the government's second attempt at a solution). The final settlement of the accounts over Icesave seems to be a prerequisite for the continued cooperation of Iceland with the IMF (International Monitory Fund), seen as vital for future management of Iceland's huge national debt.

In many countries, governments are being taught some hard lessons about the pitfalls of neo-liberal economics. One of these countries has been Iceland. What started out as very insecure loans in the housing sector in the USA, have contributed to the near breakdown of the booming homeowner housing market in Iceland.

What will probably happen is that the Icelandic state, or the now state-owned banks, will have to take over some thousands of houses and flats owned by those hardest hit by the economic crisis. People will not be thrown out on the street, but allowed to stay in their houses as tenants. Iceland thus seems inexorably to be going in the direction of a lower rate of homeownership in the near future. This is similar to what occurred in Iceland's Nordic neighbour Finland, after the economic downturn there in the early 1990s, following the break-up of the Soviet Union. At that time, the ownership rate in Finland fell by some 5 per cent. This is also very likely to happen in Iceland, and as in Finland, homeownership might take quite some time to recover.

Whether the entire Icelandic mindset associated with the national ethos surrounding homeownership will also change fundamentally is a wide open question.

NOTES

1. In fact deeper than experienced by most other OECD countries, see Jónsson, G. (2009).
2. Iceland's GDP average annual growth rates for 1945–2005 were as follows: 1945–55: 4.3 per cent; 1955–65: 5.0 per cent; 1965–75: 4.3 per cent; 1975–85: 4.3 per cent; 1985–95: 1.7 per cent; 1995–2005: 4.6 per cent (Hagstofa Íslands, 2009).
3. According to the Central Bank of Iceland (http://www.sedlabanki.is/?PageID=183), the euro was worth 89.76 Icelandic krónur on 1 December 2007 and 186.48 krónur on 1 December 2008. This amounts to a loss of value of 51.9 per cent.
4. The European Economic Area (EEA) was established on 1 January 1994 according to the agreement of three member states of the European Free Trade Association (EFTA), Norway, Iceland and Liechtenstein, and all the member states of the EU. The agreement makes it possible for these EFTA countries to take part in the European single market while still remaining outside the EU.
5. Landsbanki was the oldest Icelandic bank, established in 1886. Kaupthing had its origins in Búnaðarbankinn (The Agricultural Bank) founded in 1929. The third large bank, Íslandsbanki (renamed Glitnir in 2006), was already privately owned, orginating in 1990 in a merger of four smaller banks.
6. Iceland's urban structure is characterized by a strong monocentricity, as close to two-thirds of the population live in the Greater Reykjavik area. If the southwest region within a 60-kilometre radius centred on Reykjavik's city centre is considered, the percentage of the population living in that area is now between 75 and 80 per cent. Outside the southwest, only one town, Akureyri in the north, has more than 5000 inhabitants and just seven towns outside the southwest have from 2000 to 5000 inhabitants. Iceland's rural population, however, amounts to only 5.5 per cent of all Icelanders (Hagstofa Íslands, 2010c; Sveinsson, 2004).
7. The Icelandic social owner occupation is best described as a hybrid tenure, as the flats could not be resold on the open market, but went back to the local authority, to be sold

again to a new applicant according to the ascribed means-tested critera. In 2002, the restrictions on the resale of these flats were lifted and they became de facto unrestricted owner-occupier flats (Sveinsson, 2010).

8. On 24 August 1983, 2000 young homeowners took part in a protest meeting at a restaurant called Sigtún. The 'Sigtún group', as the grass-roots movement that ensued was called, managed to a certain extent to become a negotiating partner with the government and the housing authorities during the next 2–3 years (Sveinsson, 2000, ch. 4).

9. Today, the the Domestic Debt Advisory Service's operations are based on an agreement between, among others, the Ministry of Social Affairs, the Housing Finance Fund, the City of Reykjavik, the biggest banks, the Union of Local Authorities in Iceland, the National Church of Iceland, the National Association of Pension Funds, and the Icelandic Confederation of Labour.

10. In the years after 2003, it also became quite common in Iceland for people to buy new cars, often expensive city jeeps, with loans in foreign currency. After the fall of the króna, it is not unusual for the nominal value of a car loan in Icelandic currency to be twice as high as the selling price of the car that was aquired. This can, obviously, be very serious if the same family also happens to be in a difficult position with its housing loans.

11. According to the valutation of the Icelandic Property Registry (Fasteignaská Íslands).

12. Three new state-owned banks have been founded on the ruins of the three collapsed, private banks.

13. The Icesave dispute is a diplomatic dispute that began in 2008 between Iceland on one hand and the UK and the Netherlands on the other. The dispute centres on Iceland's repaying the UK and the Netherlands the reimbursement to UK and Dutch retail creditors in one of the Icelandic banks, Landsbanki, which was placed into receivership by the Icelandic Financial Supervisory when the Landsbanki collapsed in October 2008.

REFERENCES

Arnarson, Ólafur (2009), *Sofandi að feigðarósi* [Floating asleep into deadly waters], Reykjavik: JPV Forlag.

Fasteignaskrá Íslands [Icelandic Property Registry] (2010), 'The monthly development of housing prices in the Reykjavík area January 1994 to December 2009', www3.fmr.is/Markadurinn/Visitala-ibudaverds, accessed 15 March 2010.

Félags- og tryggingarmálaráðuneytið [Ministry of Social Affairs and Social Security] (2009), 'Ný lög girða fyrir óréttmætar afskriftir skulda' [New laws to stop unjust writing-off of debts], news release on 25 October, www.felagsmalara-duneyti.is/frettir/frettatilkynningar/nr/4545, accessed 28 October 2009.

Fjármálaráðuneytið [Ministry of Finance] (2009a), *Þjóðarbúskapurinn – Vorskýrsla 2009* [The Icelandic Economy – Spring Report 2009], Reykjavik: Fjármálaráðuneytið.

Fjármálaráðuneytið (2009b), *Þjóðarbúskapurinn – Haustskýrsla 2009* [The Icelandic Economy – Autumn Report 2009], Reykjavik: Fjármálaráðuneytið.

Hagstofa Íslands [Statistics Iceland] (1997), *Hagskinna – Sögulegar hagtölur um Ísland* [Icelandic Historical Statistics], Reykjavik: Hagstofa Íslands.

Hagstofa Íslands (2009) National accounts statistics 'paper title', www.statice.is/Statistics/National-accounts-and-public-fin/National-accounts-overview, accessed 14 October 2009.

Hagstofa Íslands (2010a), 'Consumer price index January 1994 to December 2009', www.statice.is/?PageID=1248&src=/temp_en/Dialog/varval.asp?ma=VIS01000%26ti=Changes+in+the+consumer+price+index+from+1988%26path=../Database/

visitolur/neysluverd/%26lang=1%26units=Indices%20and%20annualized%20 rates, accessed 15 March 2010.

Hagstofa Íslands (2010b), 'Statistics on residential construction', www.statice. is/?PageID=1229&src=/temp_en/Dialog/varval.asp?ma=IDN03001%26ti= Residential+buildings++in+Iceland+1970%2D2009+%26path=../Database/ idnadur/byggingar/%26lang=1%26units=Number/cubic%20meters, accessed 15 March 2010.

Hagstofa Íslands (2010c), 'Population statistics', www.statice.is/Statistics/ Population, accessed 15 March 2010.

Heritage Foundation, The (2006), World Heritage Foundation Website, on the 2006 Index of Economic Freedom, www.heritage.org/Research/Reports/2006/01/ Economic-Freedom-Advances-2006, accessed 17 September 2009.

Íbúðalánasjóður [The Housing Financing Fund] (2009), 'On measures for families with financial difficulties', www.ils.is/index.aspx?GroupId=630, accessed 22 October 2009.

Jónsson, Ásgeir (2009) *Why Iceland? How One of the World's Smallest Countries Became the Meltdown's Biggest Casualty*, New York: McGraw-Hill.

Jónsson, Guðmundur (2009), 'Efnahagskreppur á Íslandi 1870–2000' [Iceland's economic crises, 1870–2000], *Saga*, **XLVII** (1), 45–74. (Reykjavík.)

Landsbankinn [The National Bank of Iceland] (2009a), 'Statistics on the Icelandic króna's exchange rates', www.sedlabanki.is/?PageID=286, accessed 15 September 2009.

Landsbankinn (2009b), 'Hvenær aukast framkvæmdir á nýjum íbúðum á höfuðborgarsvæðinu?' [When will housing construction increase again in the Reykjavik Area?], www.landsbanki.is/Uploads/Maillist/Docs/fasteignamarka-durinn_okt09.pdf, accessed 24 October 2009.

OECD (2009), *OECD Economic Surveys – Iceland*, Paris: OECD.

Ólafsson, Stefán (2003), 'Contemporary Icelanders – Scandinavian or American?', *Scandinavian Review*, **91** (1), 6–14.

Seðlabanki Íslands [Central Bank of Iceland] (2009), Ársskýrsla 2008 [Annual Report 2009], Reykjavík.

Sveinsson, Jón Rúnar (1993), 'Social owner-occupation: the Icelandic workers' dwellings', paper presented at the ENHR Conference on Housing Policy in Europe in the 1990s, Budapest, 7–10 September 1993.

Sveinsson, Jón Rúnar (2000), *Society, Urbanity and Housing in Iceland*, Meyers: Gävle.

Sveinsson, Jón Rúnar (2004), 'The formation of urban homeownership in Iceland', paper presented at the ENHR Conference in Cambridge, 2–6 July 2004. See website: http://www.borg.hi.is/The%20Formation%20of%20Urban%20 Housing%20Policy%20in%20Iceland.pdf.

Sveinsson, Jón Rúnar (2006), 'Island – självägande och fackligt inflytande' [Ownership and union influence], in Bo Bengtsson (ed.), *Varför så olika? – Nordisk bostadspolitik i jämförande historiskt ljus* [Why So Different? Nordic Housing Policy from a Comparative Perspective], Malmö: Égalité, pp. 279–323.

Sveinsson, Jón Rúnar (2010), *Lokun félagslega húsnæðiskerfisins – Hvað kom í staðinn?* [The Closing of the Social Housing System – What Replaced It?], Reykjavik (forthcoming).

Tomasson, Richard F. (1980), *Iceland – the First New Society*, Reykjavik: Iceland Review.

5. Housing wealth, debt and stress before, during and after the Celtic Tiger

Michelle Norris and Nessa Winston

INTRODUCTION

Compared to many other Western European countries, the Republic of Ireland is distinguished by historically high rates of homeownership. In 1971, 60.7 per cent of Irish households were homeowners compared to 50 and 35 per cent of their counterparts in Britain and Sweden respectively (Kemeny, 1981). In addition to socio-economic factors such as the predominately rural and dispersed population distribution, these levels of homeownership rates were driven by extensive government support. Direct government supports for first-time homebuyers covered approximately 15 per cent of the costs of an average suburban home in the late 1970s and, during this decade, government provided half of all mortgage loans, as the commercial mortgage market was underdeveloped (O'Connell, 2005; Fahey et al., 2004). Furthermore, since the 1930s social housing tenants have enjoyed the 'right to buy' their dwellings, at a substantial discount from the market value and, uniquely in Western Europe, no ongoing taxes are levied on owner-occupied homes (O'Connell and Fahey, 1999). These supports appear particularly generous in view of the underperformance of the Irish economy, which, apart from a brief period in the 1960s/early 1970s, declined or stagnated for much of the twentieth century. As a result, population growth followed a similar pattern, as, despite a high birth rate, emigration was also high, particularly in the 1950s and 1980s (Kennedy et al, 1998).

From the mid-1990s, following the advent of the 'Celtic Tiger' economic boom, this situation changed radically (see Honohan and Walsh, 2002 for a fuller review). GDP per capita increased from 10 per cent below the European Union average in 1995, to 35 per cent above that for the EU15 in 2007 (Central Statistics Office, various years). Together with sharp falls in taxation and interest rates, rising employment and the liberalization of the mortgage credit market, this contributed to equally dramatic demographic and housing-market change. The population rose by 17 per cent and the number of households expanded by 14 per cent between 1996 and 2006 (Central Statistics Office, 2007a). Despite very high rates of new house building in recent years, annual house price growth jumped from 7.7 per cent per annum between 1990 and 1993 to 22 per cent per annum between 1996 and 2002 (Norris and Shiels, 2007). By the late 1990s the proportion of mortgages provided by government had fallen to 0.1 per cent, and average interest rates on new mortgages fell from 7.10 per cent in 1994 to 3.4 per cent in 2004 following Ireland's entry into European Monetary Union and entry of UK banks into the Irish mortgage-lending market in the post-2000 period (Norris et al, 2007; European Mortgage Federation, various years).

Since mid-2007, however, the Irish economy, government finances and housing market have declined both suddenly and sharply. GDP per capita grew by 5.3 per cent in 2007, but declined by 4.2 per cent in 2008 and by 8.4 per cent in the first half of 2009 (Central Statistics Office, various years). The unemployment rate rose from 4.6 per cent in 2007 to 12.5 per cent in November 2009, and the public balance of payments, which had been positive for most of the 1997–2007 period, fell sharply to −7.1 per cent of GDP in 2008, the highest budget deficit in the Eurozone (Central Statistics Office, various years). This economic downturn has depressed rents and house prices, but the full extent of its impact on the housing market is as yet unclear. The most robust house-price data available indicate that prices nationally fell by 26 per cent between December 2007 and August 2009 (Permanent TSB/ESRI, various years). However, several commentators have suggested that these data radically underestimate the true extent of price decline.

This chapter examines the implications of this boom and bust for housing wealth, debt and stress in Ireland, and in particular its impact on different age and income groups, housing tenures and regions of the country. The discussion of this issue presented here is prefaced by an outline of the methods used to compile the data on which this analysis is based and followed by a discussion of the implications of this analysis that draws on the international literature on trends in housing policy, stress debt and asset accumulation.

RESEARCH METHODS

This chapter draws on a number of data sources. The core of our analysis is based on data from the Irish module of two EU-wide longitudinal social surveys – the European Union Survey on Income and Living Conditions (EU-SILC), conducted annually from 2003 to date, and its precursor, the European Community Household Panel (ECHP), which was conducted between 1994 and 2002. As part of these surveys, interviews were conducted with large representative samples of Irish households and the anonymized microdata on their results were made available to the authors via the Irish Social Science Data Archive.

Here we analyse data from the 1994, 2000 and 2007 iterations of these surveys. The first of these years marks the period prior to the Celtic Tiger boom, the second its height and the third its end and the beginning of the current severe economic downturn. The objective of this exercise is to explore the impact of the boom and bust on housing wealth, debt and stress among different household types. In this chapter housing wealth is assessed with reference to outright ownership of principal residences and second-homeownership. Mortgaged principal residences and rent or mortgage arrears during the last 12 months are employed as indicators of housing debt and subjective indicators (difficulty making ends meet and burdensome housing costs) are used to examine housing stress. In order to assess variations in the experiences of different household types, these indicators are disaggregated according to: housing tenure, the age of the household head, income quartile and also whether they live in Dublin (the capital and by far the largest city), the Mid-East region (effectively the commuter belt surrounding Dublin which has grown dramatically in recent years) or in the rest of Ireland.

The data from these EU surveys are supplemented by data from the Irish census of population and an Irish sample survey – the Quarterly National Household Survey (2007 Q1 and 2009). In addition, administrative data on the following issues are employed: house prices; mortgage lending; supports for unemployed mortgage holders, and repossessions of lands, dwellings and premises collected by the courts.

HOUSING WEALTH

Table 5.1 details trends in housing wealth in 1994, 2000 and 2007 as indicated by outright ownership of dwellings and second-homeownership. It identifies a marked increase in housing wealth between these years among most of the social groups under examination, but indicates that this increase is distributed unevenly among the different age and income groups, regions and asset types examined.

Of the two indicators of housing wealth examined, outright ownership of principal residences expanded most dramatically between 1994 and

Table 5.1 Indicators of housing wealth in Ireland by age, location and income, 1994, 2000 and 2007

Indicator of housing wealth		25–49 years (% within age)			% change 1994–2007	50–64 years (% within age)			% change 1994–2007	65 years plus (% within age)			% change 1994–2007
		1994	2000	2007		1994	2000	2007		1994	2000	2007	
1. Principal residence owned outright		17.9	18.4	24.7	6.8	51.6	56.3	69.1	17.5	79.4	85.4	87.8	8.4
Location	Dublin	9.4	12.2	16.0	6.6	38.6	44.7	58.6	20.0	74.4	81.9	85.2	10.8
	Mid-East	9.3	13.5	19.9	10.6	46.8	57.5	68.3	21.5	90.6	83.3	94.4	3.8
	Rest of Ireland	23.7	22.4	30.4	6.7	59.6	62.1	73.3	13.7	80.3	87.5	87.9	7.6
Income	Quartile 1 (lowest)	23.8	27.1	19.8	-4.0	60.3	60.6	56.9	-3.4	77.3	86.9	82.3	5.0
	Quartile 2	21.1	23.6	26.3	5.2	49.6	51.8	69.9	20.3	80.7	78.8	90.3	9.6
	Quartile 3	17.6	15.4	25.8	8.2	52.0	63.2	69.3	17.3	91.0	83.6	95.4	4.4
	Quartile 4 (highest)	10.9	13.2	23.9	13.0	45.1	50.7	74.8	29.7	84.7	96.9	90.8	6.1
2. Second-home ownership		5.4	10.1	8.4	3.0	7.2	14.9	9.1	1.9	3.0	5.8	3.6	0.6
Location	Dublin	6.8	13.5	11.7	4.9	10.4	19.0	17.5	7.1	4.3	6.6	5.7	1.4
	Mid-East	9.0	6.0	5.8	-3.2	4.8	10.8	3.7	-1.1	1.6	5.8	3.3	1.7
	Rest of Ireland	4.2	9.1	7.2	3.0	5.7	13.3	6.5	0.8	2.7	5.5	2.9	0.2
Income	Quartile 1 (lowest)	3.6	4.2	4.7	1.1	4.9	5.4	1.1	-3.8	1.4	2.4	1.6	0.2

Table 5.1 (continued)

Indicator of housing wealth	25–49 years (% within age)			% change 1994–2007	50–64 years (% within age)			% change 1994–2007	65 years plus (% within age)			% change 1994–2007
	1994	2000	2007		1994	2000	2007		1994	2000	2007	
Quartile 2	4.8	9.1	1.3	−3.5	5.3	15.8	3.0	−2.3	4.4	6.8	2.1	−2.3
Quartile 3	5.3	10.7	5.0	−0.3	6.0	12.7	5.6	−0.4	9.9	14.0	6.2	−3.7
Quartile 4 (highest)	7.5	13.4	14.9	7.4	12.1	23.9	20.0	7.9	9.2	17.1	17.3	8.1

Note: Data refer to households.

Source: Generated by the authors from the EU-SILC (2007) and ECHP (1994, 2000) surveys.

2007 and most consistently across most of the social groups under review. It grew among all age groups, but expanded most dramatically among households headed by an individual aged 50–64 (up 17.5 per cent) and least dramatically (up 6.8 per cent) among younger households (under 50 years of age). The greatest proportionate expansion in outright ownership took place in Dublin and the Mid-East. The rest of Ireland saw a much more modest expansion in outright ownership, albeit from a higher base.

Between 1994 and 2007, levels of outright ownership fell among households in the lowest income quartile headed by individuals aged 25 to 64, whereas the opposite trend is evident among household heads in this age group with incomes in quartiles 2–4. This relationship between higher income and rising outright ownership does not pertain among older households (headed by individuals aged 65 years plus). However, levels of outright ownership are very high among all households in this age group, irrespective of income.

Table 5.1 indicates that trends in second-homeownership are less uniform, both over time and among the different social groups under examination. Although second-homeownership grew rapidly among all age groups between 1994 and 2000, it declined again slightly by 2007. Furthermore, the rise in second-homeownership is concentrated principally in Dublin and among households in the top income quartile.

The rising rate of outright ownership of primary dwellings and second homes among Dubliners is surprising in view of the trends in house prices since the mid-1990s. Between 1996 and the peak of the house-price boom in 2006, prices in Dublin grew by 363 per cent and in the Mid-East region by 321 per cent, whereas prices in the rest of Ireland rose by 260 per cent (Permanent TSB/ESRI, various years). As a result, the differential between prices in Dublin and the country at large, which stood at around 10 per cent for many decades, increased to 38 per cent by 2007 (Bacon and McCabe, 1999). The scale of inflation in Dublin has been linked to inadequate housing supply, as until 2003/04 new housing output lagged behind other regions to significant extent (Norris and Shiels, 2007; Berry et al., 2001). However, this inflation is also strongly related to the concentration of economic growth in this region during the Celtic Tiger period.

The distinctive nature of economic growth in Dublin also explains why high housing costs did not diminish the pace of housing-asset accumulation here. Economic growth led to higher-than-average incomes and income growth in this city. In 1994, 29.8 per cent of Dubliners had incomes in the highest quartile compared to just 16 per cent of residents of the rest of Ireland, whereas the equivalent figures for 2007 are 44.1 and 22.5 per cent.[1] The available evidence also indicates that higher housing costs in Dublin and the Mid-East pushed some households into the rented sectors, particularly lower-income and younger residents. This trend is less acute than would be expected in view of the pace of regional house-price inflation. Census data indicate that between 1996 and 2006 the proportion of renting households grew from 25 to 27 percent in Dublin, from 14 to 16 per cent in the Mid-East and fell from 16 to 13 per cent in the rest of Ireland (Central Statistics Office, 1996, 2006).

Trends in the intergenerational distribution of income in Ireland during the last decade are also pertinent. Between 1994 and 2007, the growth in households in the top income quartile was concentrated among younger households (headed by individuals aged 25–49 years), whereas the number of high-income households headed by middle-aged and older people increased only marginally between these years.[2] Thus, unlike the case in many other European countries, intergenerational inequalities in housing wealth in Ireland are to a significant extent counterbalanced by intergenerational inequalities in household incomes (see Fahey et al., 2004 for a more detailed discussion).

The high level of outright homeownership among older household heads in Ireland, irrespective of household income, reflects the particularly generous government subsidies for this tenure. For instance, sales of social housing to tenants at a significant discount from market value commenced on a large scale in the 1930s, and played a central role in driving the high rate of outright ownership among older, low-income households (Fahey et al., 2004). Two-thirds of the dwellings built originally for social renting have been sold to tenants, and these accounted for approximately 16.6 per cent of the total owner-occupied stock in 2006 (Central Statistics Office, 2007b). From the mid-1980s, however, direct universal supports for homebuyers (such as grants for first-time homebuyers) were gradually scaled back and ultimately abolished, and the availability and value of indirect universal subsidies, made up principally of tax relief on mortgage interest, was radically reduced (Norris and Winston, 2004). These universal supports were replaced by targeted supports for low-income homebuyers such as the shared ownership and affordable housing scheme. Norris et al. (2007) suggest that due to inadequate design and housing market inflation, these programmes have suffered from low take-up. Take-up of the right-to-buy social housing scheme has also fallen radically since the 1990s as the social-housing sector has contracted and become increasingly dominated by low-income households who lack the financial resources to purchase (Norris et al., 2007).

A sharp drop in house prices from December 2006 has obviously reduced housing wealth in Ireland. Between then and August 2009 house prices in Dublin fell by 28 per cent while house prices in the rest of Ireland declined by 23 per cent (Permanent TSB/ESRI, various years).

House-price data for the Mid-East are not available for 2009, but the 2008 data suggest that prices in this region have experienced a stronger correction than elsewhere. Several commentators and property industry surveys have suggested that these data, based on mortgage draw-downs that may lag developments in selling prices, radically underestimate the true level of house-price falls and that in fact prices fell by between 30 and 50 per cent between 2007 and 2009 (see Duffy, 2009).

HOUSING DEBT

Table 5.2 disaggregates trends in housing debt, as revealed by mortgaged principal residences, by age group, location and household income. As would be expected, in view of the rising levels of outright homeownership highlighted above, this table reveals that the proportion of households with mortgaged principal residences fell between 1994 and 2007 among all the social groups under examination. However, mortgage holding was unevenly distributed among these groups in 2007. Mortgages remain much more common among households headed by individuals aged between 25 and 49 years, residents of Dublin and the Mid-East and households in the highest income quartile. Furthermore, the decline in mortgage holding is concentrated strongly in the period after 2000, which coincides precisely with the height of the house-price boom and less directly with the aforementioned withdrawal of public subsidies for homeownership. Most notably, this table highlights a particularly marked fall in mortgages held by younger households with incomes in the lowest quartile during this period. Only 5.8 per cent of such households had mortgaged principal residences in 2007. This development is most likely related to high-house price inflation, which largely priced this group out of the market at this time. However, it is also related to the rolling back of the universalist supports for homebuyers in the 1990s and to the aforementioned shortcomings in the plethora of supports for low-income homebuyers that replaced them.

Developments in mortgage lending that are pertinent to these housing-debt trends are sketched in Table 5.3. This table highlights historically low and declining mortgage interest rates during most of the years between 1996 and 2006 coupled with a radical increase in mortgage debt per capita in the post-2000 period. The latter trend was driven both by a sharp increase in the number of mortgage loans drawn down by borrowers and in the size of these loans – mortgages of over €250000 increased from 2.3 per cent of the total in 2000 to 41 per cent of the total in 2007. This development was in turn facilitated by extensive financial product 'innovation' among mainstream lenders, rather than in the sub-prime sector,

Table 5.2 *Indicators of housing debt by age, location, income and tenure, 1994, 2000 and 2007*

Indicators of housing debt		25–49 years (% within age)			% change 1994–2007	50–64 years (% within age)			% change 1994–2007	65 years plus (% within age)			% change 1994–2007
		1994	2000	2007		1994	2000	2007		1994	2000	2007	
1. Mortgage on principal residence		56.6	62.9	46.2	–10.4	37.9	32.1	16.1	–21.8	7.2	7.2	2.1	–5.1
Location	Dublin	68.2	72.7	53.1	–15.1	48.0	44.1	21.6	–26.4	14.5	14.8	3.6	–10.9
	Mid-East	70.1	68.9	58.5	–11.6	48.2	31.0	20.0	–28.2	3.0	1.8	1.7	–1.3
	Rest of Ireland	48.6	56.9	39.9	–8.7	30.8	26.0	13.3	–17.5	4.8	3.9	1.7	–3.1
Income	Quartile 1 (lowest)	18.9	23.6	5.8	–13.1	20.8	9.5	4.7	–16.1	6.4	3.5	1.0	–5.4
	Quartile 2	45.5	53.0	21.2	–24.3	32.9	35.0	13.7	–19.2	8.1	13.0	1.9	–6.2
	Quartile 3	69.8	72.6	44.4	–25.4	43.5	32.6	18.4	–25.1	7.1	16.3	2.6	–4.5
	Quartile 4 (highest)	80.5	78.0	64.5	–16.0	52.9	48.3	22.1	–30.8	15.3	3.4	9.1	–6.2

Note: Data refer to households.

Source: Generated by the authors from the EU-SILC (2007) and ECHP (1994, 2000) surveys.

Table 5.3 Trends in residential mortgage lending in Ireland, 1996–2008

	1996	1997	1998	1999	2000	2001	2002	2003	2004	2005	2006	2007	2008
Representative interest rates on new mortgage loans (%)	7.10	7.50	6.00	4.38	6.17	4.72	4.69	3.50	3.47	3.68	4.57	5.07	n.a.
Residential mortgage debt per capita ('000s)	3.83	4.70	5.65	7.02	8.62	10.00	12.11	14.98	19.12	24.08	29.29	32.20	n.a.
Mortgages paid ('000s)	56.0	57.9	61.4	70.8	74.3	66.8	79.3	84.7	98.7	107.6	111.3	84.3	n.a.
Loans > €250 000 (%)	n.a.	n.a.	n.a.	1.4	2.3	4.6	5.9	9.1	18.0	27.0	37.0	41.0	41.0
100% loans (%)	n.a.	n.a.	n.a.	n.a.	n.a.	n.a.	n.a.	n.a.	4.0	7.0	14.0	10.0	12.0
Loan term > 30 years (%)	n.a.	n.a.	n.a.	n.a.	n.a.	n.a.	n.a.	n.a.	10.0	23.0	31.0	35.0	39.0

Note: n.a. means not available.

Source: European Mortgage Federation (various years) and Department of the Environment, Heritage and Local Government (various years).

which has remained small in Ireland compared to the USA, for instance (Coates, 2008). For instance, 100 per cent mortgages first became available around 2004 and between then and 2008 rose from 4 to 12 per cent of all mortgages granted, and mortgages with a term of more than 30 years rose from 10 to 39 per cent of mortgages concurrently (Department of the Environment, Heritage and Local Government, various years).

Trends in mortgage lending can be disaggregated according to the characteristics of borrowers, thereby allowing for the identification of the social groups in greatest housing debt. As would be expected in view of the trends in house-price inflation outlined earlier in this chapter, those in greatest debt are recent first-time buyers, particularly those living in Dublin. In 2006, 74 per cent of this group drew down mortgages of over €250 000 compared to 38 per cent of first-time buyers in the country as a whole, and 64 per cent of repeat homebuyers and property investors in Dublin (Department of the Environment, Heritage and Local Government, various years). In the same year, 31 per cent of first-time buyers in Dublin took on 100 per cent mortgages, as did 34 per cent of first-time buyers in the country at large and just 5 per cent of repeat buyers/investors in Dublin. Also in 2006, 70 per cent of mortgages drawn down by first-time buyers in Dublin had terms of over 30 years, compared to 20 per cent of loans granted to repeat buyers/investors in this city and 60 per cent of those granted to first-time buyers in the country as a whole.

This increased concentration of high housing debt among first-time buyers in Dublin was followed by a sharp downturn in house prices in late 2006, which raises the possibility of negative equity, where house values are lower than the value of related debt. Drawing on the same house-price data employed in this chapter, Duffy (2009) has recently assessed the extent of negative equity in the Irish housing market. He estimates that 9.1 per cent of mortgage holders were in negative equity by the end of 2008. This rose to 18 per cent by the end of 2009 and it is estimated will rise to 29.6 per cent by the end of 2010. Given the higher loan-to-value ratios for first-time buyer mortgages, he estimates that negative equity is more common among this group and also more severe – they make up the vast majority of households whose dwellings are worth more than 10 per cent less than the associated mortgage. Duffy's estimates indicate that the 2008 figure for negative equity in Ireland is similar to those in the USA and the UK. Hellebrandt et al. (2009) estimate that between 7 and 11 per cent of owner-occupier mortgage holders in the UK were in negative equity in spring 2008, for instance, and estimates for the USA indicate that 10 per cent of mortgages in single-family dwellings were in negative equity at this time (cited in Ellis, 2008). However, the full extent of negative equity is likely to be greater than he suggests for a number of reasons. His estimates do not include mortgage top-ups or interest-only mortgages, which he suggests accounted for 15 per cent of mortgages approved in 2008. In addition, they are based on the, widely contested, assumption that house prices fell to 15 per cent below their peak by December 2008. Furthermore, in view of the particularly high levels of debt among recent first-time buyers in Dublin, which were outlined above, negative equity is likely to be particularly common among this group.

HOUSING STRESS

Table 5.4 disaggregates trends in one objective and one subjective indicator of housing stress for the years 1994, 2000 and 2007. These indicators are: mortgage arrears during the previous 12 months; and burdensome housing costs. It reveals that trends in both are differentiated over time and by age group and household income.

For the most part, both mortgage arrears and the perceived burden of housing costs declined significantly among those under 65 years of age between 1994 and 2000, but they increased again by 2007. Notably this trend was more marked among households in the bottom half of the income distribution and also among younger household heads. In 2007, 47.1 per cent of household heads aged between 25 and 29 years with incomes in the bottom quartile stated that they found housing costs a heavy burden, while 13.2 per cent of the same cohort reported that their mortgage had been in arrears during the last 12 months. Conversely, despite their higher levels of housing debt, younger homeowners in Dublin reported similar levels of burdensome housing costs to their counterparts in other parts of Ireland, although mortgage arrears were higher in this section of the population.

Thus the data presented here indicate that, rather than housing debt, levels of housing stress in Ireland are driven primarily by household income, specifically by the adequacy of income compared to housing costs. For many younger residents of the Dublin and Mid-East regions, their higher incomes largely compensate them for their higher housing costs.

As mentioned in the introduction to this chapter, the post-2007 economic crisis has effected a sharp decrease in the incomes of many households principally as a result of rising unemployment. This may have in turn led to a mismatch between housing costs and income and therefore to changes in the distribution of housing stress and the frequency of mortgage defaults. Furthermore, the extensive international literature on negative equity also indicates that its presence increases the likelihood of mortgage default, but it does not necessarily result in repossession (see

Table 5.4 Indicators of housing stress by age, location and income, 1994, 2000 and 2007

Indicators of housing stress		25–49 years (% within age)			% change 1994–2007	50–64 years (% within age)			% change 1994–2007	65 years plus (% within age)			% change 1994–2007
		1994	2000	2007		1994	2000	2007		1994	2000	2007	
Mortgage arrears during the last 12 months		9.0	2.9	3.2	−5.8	6.5	1.5	5.5	−1.0	3.4	0.0	5.8	+2.4
Location	Dublin	8.6	3.3	5.2	−3.4	5.7	0.2	2.0	−3.7	1.3	0.0	15.9	+14.6
	Mid-East	8.5	0.1	0.6	−7.9	2.7	9.6	0.0	−2.7	3.8	0.0	0.0	−3.8
	Rest of Ireland	9.5	3.2	2.6	−6.9	8.1	1.4	9.7	+1.6	5.3	0.0	0.0	−5.3
Income	Quartile 1 (lowest)	30.5	4.0	13.2	−17.3	9.0	2.8	9.0	0.0	2.4	0.0	25.9	+23.5
	Quartile 2	17.1	7.4	23.3	+6.2	7.9	0.2	9.6	+1.7	4.9	0.0	0.0	−4.9
	Quartile 3	6.3	2.2	2.7	−3.6	10.1	4.5	10.3	+0.2	0.0	0.0	0.0	0.0
	Quartile 4 (highest)	3.3	0.5	0.7	−2.6	2.3	0.3	1.5	−0.8	10.6	0.0	0.0	−10.6
Housing costs a heavy burden		23.7	13.8	16.7	−7.0	17.0	13.6	13.6	−3.4	17.0	11.4	7.8	−9.2
Location	Dublin	24.5	8.8	15.9	−8.6	14.9	12.9	13.6	−1.3	15.0	8.9	6.6	−8.4
	Mid-East	30.4	9.6	15.5	−14.9	16.2	15.7	11.8	−4.4	13.1	24.1	6.4	−6.7
	Rest of Ireland	22.3	17.3	17.4	−4.9	18.3	13.2	13.9	−4.4	18.1	11.3	8.3	−9.8

Income												
Quartile 1 (lowest)	29.7	31.8	47.1	+17.4	24.4	21.8	21.9	−2.5	20.2	12.9	9.1	−11.1
Quartile 2	33.9	20.8	34.7	+0.8	19.6	15.5	13.9	−5.7	13.7	7.9	9.4	−4.3
Quartile 3	21.1	12.8	16.1	−5.0	15.8	17.7	16.9	+1.1	5.9	11.3	4.2	−1.7
Quartile 4 (highest)	17.0	5.4	11.6	−5.4	10.7	4.6	8.4	−2.3	8.7	11.6	1.2	−7.5

Note: Data refer to households and homeowners only.

Source: Generated by the authors from the EU-SILC (2007) and ECHP (1994, 2000) surveys.

Foote et al., 2008). Households most at risk of repossession are those that are both in negative equity and experience a fall in income.

The extent of housing stress and the potential for widespread repossessions of property is not as great as might be expected in view of the sharp fall in employment in Ireland since 2007. This is because the employment contraction is concentrated in industries such as construction and manufacturing, and among those 15 to 25 years, who have below-average levels of mortgage holding (Central Statistics Office, 2007b, 2009). For those in public and private sector professions (such as finance and business administration, public administration, education and health and social work), which are associated with above-average levels of mortgage holding, employment actually expanded between 2007 and 2009.

However, there is a high risk of mortgage default among some sections of the population. Specifically, there have been marked contractions in employment among Dubliners (−7.0 per cent between 2007 and 2009) and among those aged 25–44 years (−4.1 per cent concurrently) (Central Statistics Office, 2007b, 2009). Both of these sections of the population are likely to be highly indebted and in negative equity. The vulnerability of these groups is confirmed by data on take-up of mortgage-interest supplement, the principal, means-tested government support for unemployed homeowners, which subsidizes the interest portion of their mortgages. Take-up of this benefit grew from 3318 households in 2004 to 8091 in 2008. Data for the latter year indicate that claimants are strongly concentrated in Dublin (28 per cent of claimants) and among the 25–49 year age group (78.9 per cent of claimants) (Department of Social and Family Affairs, various years).

The recent increase in take-up of mortgage-interest supplement and in unemployment does not yet seem to have translated into very widespread repossessions of dwellings, although repossessions have risen. Data from the Courts Information Service (various years) indicate that court cases for the possession of lands/dwellings/premises (disaggregated data for different types of property are not available) rose from 140 in 2004 to 490 in the first half of 2009. Industry sources indicate that this relatively low level of repossessions is the result of short-term factors – specifically a 12-month moratorium on the repossession of dwellings on the part of the major Irish banks, which was agreed as part of the government recapitalization of these institutions (Duffy, 2009). Repossession rates are likely to rise after the moratorium ends and also if, as expected, Eurozone interest rates rise from their current historic low; unlike the norm elsewhere in Europe, most Irish mortgages are variable rather than fixed (Duffy, 2009).

CONCLUSIONS

This chapter has examined developments in housing wealth, debt and stress before and after Ireland's recent economic boom. It has revealed that the Celtic Tiger period is characterized by contradictory trends. On the one hand, housing wealth – as measured by outright homeownership and second-homeownership – increased markedly among most social groups. On the other hand, low-income households, particularly in urban areas, were priced out of owner-occupation and forced into rented accommodation; among the mainly urban and younger households left servicing mortgages, debt levels increased radically, although the perceived burden of these debts (housing stress) did not rise in parallel because many indebted households have higher-than-average incomes.

This period could also be characterized as one during which Ireland's traditionally distinctive housing policy and distribution of housing assets converged with the international norm, or at least with the norm in other developed, anglophone countries (see Forrest, 2008). Ireland has long had high levels of homeownership, but before the 1990s, this was underpinned by both low house prices and what amounted effectively to a socialized system of homeownership. As part of the latter, generous, universalist indirect and direct subsidies for homebuyers were provided by government, the public sector was also a major provider of mortgages (and very rarely repossessed dwellings in arrears), and substantial levels of sales of social rented dwellings to tenants, at a large discount from the market value, helped lower-income households to access homeownership (see Norris et al., 2007 and Norris and Fahey, 2009 for a fuller discussion). As a result, homeownership was relatively evenly distributed across income groups and this remains the case among older households in Ireland, particularly those headed by individuals aged 65 and over. From the 1990s, however, these generous universalist homeownership supports were rolled back and the housing market boomed, particularly in the capital and largest city (Dublin), to the extent that effectively a separate market operated here. Both of these developments reflect contemporary international norms, and the house-price boom is also directly related to the globalization of housing-finance markets, specifically to the entry of UK-based banks into the Irish mortgage market after 2000, which led to increased competition for borrowers, lower borrowing costs and financial product innovation. As a result of these developments, the distribution of housing assets in Ireland has begun to converge with the international norm and among younger households has become increasingly concentrated among higher-income earners.

Since 2007 the Irish economy and housing market have declined both suddenly and sharply, leading to rising unemployment and negative equity. To date this bust has had less widespread negative impacts on home-owners than would be excepted because outright homeownership rates remain relatively high in Ireland and job losses have been concentrated among those social groups less likely to have mortgages. Ironically, then, Ireland's 'transitional' homeownership system seems to have afforded it some protection from the global financial crisis. Older households, who bought their homes with the help of generous government supports, have high rates of homeownership, and among younger people, homeowner-ship is concentrated among higher-income households, who can best afford to service large mortgages.

However, our analysis also points up a high risk of mortgage unafford-ability and default among some sections of the population – principally younger homeowners in Dublin, who have recently suffered high rates of job losses, negative equity and indebtedness. These developments have not yet translated into radically increased repossessions of owner-occupied dwellings, but they probably will do so in the near future. This is because mortgagors in Ireland are highly exposed to interest-rate fluctuations and these rates are expected to rise in the near future; the lack of repossessions to date is due chiefly to a time-limited moratorium on repossessions by the major banks, which is due to lapse in the near future and arrangements for supporting struggling mortgage holders in Ireland, which were designed in the context of low housing debt, high government subsidization of house-purchase costs and widespread use of government-provided mortgages, are likely to be inadequate in the context of high debts and overwhelming dominance of commercial lenders in the mortgage market. Mortgage-interest supplement is a discretionary benefit rather than an entitlement, and is also stringently means-tested and therefore not generally avail-able to households with any earned income (Norris and Winston, 2004). Furthermore, this is currently the only support available to households at risk of mortgage default in Ireland, where for instance the publicly guaranteed mortgage-refinance arrangements that have been employed successfully in the USA (the Home Affordable Refinance Program and the Home Affordable Modification Program) and the UK (the Mortgage Support Scheme and Mortgage Rescue Scheme), do not currently exist (Duffy, 2009). The analysis presented in this chapter indicates that the Irish government should explore the establishment of a more comprehen-sive and inclusive range of supports for mortgage holders at risk of default as a matter of urgency.

NOTES

1. These figures were generated by the authors from the EU-SILC (2007) and the ECHP (1994) surveys. They refer to households.
2. These data refer to households and were generated from the EU SILC (2007) and ECHP (1994) surveys.

REFERENCES

Bacon, Peter and Fergal McCabe (1999), *The Housing Market: An Economic Review and Assessment*, Dublin: Stationery Office.
Berry, J., S. McGreal, S. Stevenson and J. Young (2001), 'Government intervention and impact on the housing market in Greater Dublin', *Housing Studies*, **16** (6), 755–69.
Central Statistics Office (1996), *Census, 1996: Housing and Households*, Dublin: Stationery Office.
Central Statistics Office (2006), *Census 2006: Housing*, Dublin: Stationery office.
Central Statistics Office (2007a), *Census 2006: Principal Demographic Results*, Dublin: Stationery Office.
Central Statistics Office (2007b), *Census, 2006: Housing and Households*, Dublin: Stationery Office.
Central Statistics Office (2009), *Quarterly National Household Survey, Quarter 1, 2009*, Dublin: Stationery Office.
Central Statistics Office (various years), *Measuring Ireland's Progress*, Dublin: Stationery Office.
Coates, D. (2008), 'The Irish sub-prime residential mortgage sector: international lessons for an emerging market', *Journal of Housing and the Built Environment*, **23** (2), 131–44
Courts Information Service (various years), *Courts Service Annual Reports, 2000–2007*, Dublin: Courts Information Service.
Department of the Environment, Heritage and Local Government (various years), *Annual Housing Statistics Bulletin*, Dublin: Department of the Environment, Heritage and Local Government.
Department of Social and Family Affairs (various years), *Statistical Information on Social Welfare Services*, Dublin: Department of Social and Family Affairs.
Duffy, David (2009), *Negative Equity in the Irish Housing Market*, Dublin: Economic and Social Research Institute Working Chapter No. 319.
Ellis, L. (2008), 'How many in negative equity? The role of mortgage contract characteristics', *Bank of International Settlements Quarterly Review*, December, 81–90.
European Mortgage Federation (various years), *Hypostat*, Brussels: European Mortgage Federation.
Fahey, Tony, Brian Nolan and Bertrand Maître (2004), *Housing, Poverty and Wealth in Ireland*, Dublin: Institute of Public Administration.
Foote, C., K. Gerardi and P. Willen (2008), 'Negative equity and foreclosure: theory and evidence', *Journal of Urban Economics*, **64** (2), 234–45.
Forrest, R. (2008), 'Globalization and the housing asset rich: geographies, demographies and policy convoys', *Global Social Policy*, **8** (2), 167–87.

Hellebrandt, T., S. Kawar and M. Waldron (2009), 'The economics and estimation of negative equity', *Bank of England Quarterly Review*, Quarter Two, 110–21.

Honohan, P. and B. Walsh (2002), 'Catching up with the leaders: the Irish hare', *Brookings Chapters on Economic Activity*, Spring, 1–77.

Kemeny, Jim (1981), *The Myth of Homeownership: Private Versus Public Choices in Housing Tenure*, London: Routledge.

Kennedy, Kieran, Thomas Giblin and Deirdre McHugh (1988), *The Economic Development of Ireland in the Twentieth Century*, London: Routledge.

Norris, Michelle and Tony Fahey (2009), 'From asset based welfare to welfare housing: the changing meaning of social housing in Ireland', Dublin: School of Applied Social Science, University College Dublin, Working Chapter, WP09/05.

Norris, M. and P. Shiels (2007), 'Housing affordability in the Republic of Ireland: is planning part of the problem or part of the solution?', *Housing Studies*, **22** (1), 45–62.

Norris, Michelle and Nessa Winston (2004), *Housing Policy Review: 1990–2002*, Dublin: Stationery Office.

Norris, M., D. Coates and F. Kane (2007), 'Breaching the limits of owner occupation? Supporting low-income buyers in the inflated Irish housing market', *European Journal of Housing Policy*, **7** (3), 337–56.

O'Connell, C. (2005), 'The housing market and owner occupation in Ireland', in Michelle Norris and Declan Redmond (eds), *Housing Contemporary Ireland: Policy, Society and Shelter*, Dublin: Institute of Public Administration, pp. 21–43.

O'Connell, C. and T. Fahey (1999), 'Local authority housing in Ireland', in T. Fahey (ed.), *Social Housing in Ireland. A Study of Success, Failure and Lessons Learned*, Dublin: Oak Tree Press, ch. 3.

Permanent TSB/ESRI (various years), *Permanent TSB/ESRI House Price Index*, Dublin: Economic and Social Research Institute.

6. Housing in the Netherlands before and after the global financial crisis

Richard Ronald and Kees Dol

Since 1990, and particularly after 2000, housing marketization has been a core policy in the Netherlands. Housing commodification in this context has had, however, a particularly Dutch complexion featuring numerous state interventions, guarantees and controls rather than simple deregulation and marketization (see Stephens et al., 2008). Despite a much higher proportion of national mortgage debt and a greater prevalence of non-amortizing housing loans compared to its neighbours, even the more economically liberal ones, the Dutch institutional framework appears to have held up well to the most recent global financial crisis. At least, few households have yet felt the impact of the crisis through the housing system. None the less, house prices are in decline and housing transactions have dropped dramatically, impacting substantially on the construction industry. Greater danger lies, especially in the longer term, with the broader impact of the downturn on the real economy. Official predictions estimate zero growth in 2010 and unemployment to almost double to 8 per cent by 2011 (CPB, 2009). Further degradation of economic conditions may exacerbate housing-market conditions, cyclically feeding back into the real economy. This danger is more acute as intensive housing commodification in recent decades, notwithstanding government guarantee measures, has inevitably made the housing market more vulnerable.

This chapter examines the position of the Dutch housing system with regard to recent global economic turmoil, government responses to housing-market downturn and the impact upon Dutch households. This first requires an examination of the pre-crisis development of Dutch housing, which reflects, on the one hand, the influence of globalized networks of capital and neo-liberal restructuring of public provision, and, on the other, the localized influence of institutional and sociopolitical frameworks that have defined a rather particular 'pathway' in Dutch housing commodification. The outcome has been a reorientation in recent decades away from socialized approaches and towards more privatized and market-focused operations. At the same time, key housing regulatory practices and, significantly, the synergies of these practices in symphony have left Dutch households relatively insulated from economic vicissitudes. These include, most notably, The National Mortgage Guarantee (Nationale Hypotheek Garantie, NHG), the Mortgage Interest Tax-Deductibility Scheme (Hypotheekrenteaftrek), commercial housing-loan practices and the characteristics of a mature and relatively successful social-rental housing sector.

The chapter goes on to set out how the global financial crisis has been played out in the Netherlands, how it has affected households and how the government has reacted. Direct interventions in the housing sector have progressively escalated as the coalition government has sought to compensate for downturn in the market. The focus has been on measures to invigorate home purchase and thus reverse the decline in housing construction and transactions. In the past, housing associations have been central in anticyclical responses to market downturns. However, while they still control over 32 per cent of housing stock, with the effective privatization of the sector since 1995, housing associations have been constrained in their abilities, or desire, to offset falling private supply and demand by escalating rental housing development. In the longer term, while the effects on households have been limited by housing-system arrangements, decline in the real economy and rising unemployment will constitute an increasing threat to the overall sustainability of stability.

GOING GLOBAL OR GOING DUTCH

In the 2000s it became increasingly apparent that local housing systems were interconnecting with a global financial architecture, locked in with worldwide flows of capital and investment markets (Forrest, 2008; Aalbers, 2008, Ronald, 2008). Similarly, debates on neo-liberalization pointed to trends in governance across national boundaries characterized by retrenchment in social housing policy in favour of market-disciplinary regulatory restructuring (Brenner and Theodore, 2002; Doling and Ford, 2003). While neo-liberalism was unevenly embedded in the Netherlands, government approaches to housing had, since the end of the 1980s, become increasingly orientated towards more commodified forms of provision and consumption, with the market rather than the state seen as the most capable authority in the coordination of the housing sector.

Deregulation and marketization advanced rapidly during the 1990s and 2000s. On the one hand, social housing associations (which then controlled 38 per cent of all housing stock) became autonomous, self-financed organizations in 1995 with obligations to fulfil social objectives in regard to low-income households (see Priemus, 1996; Salet, 1999, Boelhouwer, 2002). On the other hand, deregulation and reregulation facilitated greater production of, and finance for, housing for sale, as well as rapid increases in both demand for, and prices of, owner-occupied homes (Boelhouwer, 2000). The result was a significant growth in the rate of owner-occupation from 40 per cent of households in 1980 to 57 per cent by 2008. This was accompanied by a massive expansion in mortgage debt from 60.8 per cent of GDP in 1998 and 99.1 per cent in 2008 (EMF, 2009), one of the highest rates in the EU and well beyond those of neighbouring countries with higher homeownership rates and more liberalized mortgage sectors.

Although shifts in Dutch housing reflect the logic of globalization and neo-liberalization, housing practices and institutional relationships have remained distinct. On the one hand, a key housing commodification strategy has been the deregulation of the social-rental sector, rather than wholesale tenure transfer. Meanwhile, even though lending has advanced rapidly and mortgage products have diversified, the mortgage sector has so far proved comparatively robust as system mechanisms are focused on offsetting potential risk. Thus, while homeownership has increased more than a third and mortgage debt has more than quadrupled in 20 years, the housing system in the Netherlands appears to have been more resistant to the global financial crisis than similar economies with much smaller aggregate housing debt. This resilience is arguably bound up with a specific path-dependence originating with the institutional transformations by which Dutch housing has been commodified. The following sets out the features of the Dutch transformation, which has had substantial consequences for the housing market and the security of households in the recent period of economic upheaval.

DUTCH APPROACHES TO HOUSING

Broadly speaking, in the course of the late twentieth century, housing policy in the Netherlands shifted away from a focus on public health to a concern with the economy. Prewar housing was a matter for local municipalities, but after 1945, with the emergence of major housing shortages, housing became a responsibility of central government (see van der Schaar, 1987). While reconstruction was emphasized in housing policy until the end of the 1960s, in the 1970s attention to standards and ensuring good-quality housing across all segments of society became the rationale for strong state intervention and subsidization of both social and private housing sectors. In order to facilitate universal improvements in housing quality, the state introduced housing allowances – allowing rents to increase at the same time as remaining affordable for low-income households – as well as land and cost subsidies for construction of housing for rent and for sale.

The 1980s marked a period of significant reorientation. Governments began to face major budgetary difficulties and also started to question whether there was too much state responsibility for housing. Subsequently, although the physical quality of housing remained a subject of policy, lower-income groups became the target of housing subsidies rather than the entire housing sphere.

In the government memorandum, '*Housing in the 1990s*', (Heerma, 1989), new thinking was translated into policy rhetoric. The memorandum reflected a departure from a planned approach to the economy, which had been influenced by social-democratic circles since the war, and a (re) discovery of the market. Reflecting both new economic realities and international (de)regulatory experiments and policy transfers, it was assumed that the private market would succeed the state in solving housing issues. In 2000, another memorandum, '*People, Wishes, Housing*' (*Mensen, Wensen, Wonen*), reaffirmed the state's intentions to advance the extension of the owner-occupied housing market ahead of all other tenures, to reach 65 per cent by 2010. The advance of homeownership fell far short of this. None the less, housing governance and policy structures were radically overhauled.

MEASURES AND OUTCOMES OF HOUSING COMMODIFICATION

In the most recent housing-policy era, subsidies for the provision of housing have dried up, with direct public expenditure on housing reduced, between 1970 and 2006, from 12 per cent of total budget expenditure to 3 per cent (including housing allowance but excluding tax relief on mortgages). Considerable responsibilities were handed over from the central government to local authorities, and, eventually, independent housing associations and market agents. While there are a number of key policy measures that sought to advance the share of private housing, these strongly reflected institutional conditions that had previously prevailed. Moreover, while direct subsidies have been reduced, costs have essentially been restructured around the new, more segregated regime.

Homeownership schemes in the 1990s offered low-income families home-purchase subsidies. These initiatives were eventually incorporated in 2000 into the 'Promotion of Homeownership Act' (Bevordering Eigen Woningbezit, or BEW) synthesizing two related bills: 'Stimulating

Homeownership', 1998, and 'Individual Purchase Contribution', 1999. The main task of the BEW was to regulate the 'purchase grant' for first-time buyers. There have been rather limiting conditions, as subsidies were for homes with a maximum sale price of €123 500 (including additional costs) while mortgages could not exceed €98 775 (indexed 2003), well below market averages. In the mid-2000s the government upped the rate to €150 000 and increased the total budget for this programme to €25 million. Another scheme offering low-income first-time buyers special low interest loans with a total €40 million budget was also introduced by municipalities. Conditions vary by municipality and the maximum loan remains below market averages.

As in the UK, the transfer of housing stock from public housing associations featured in the commodification of Dutch housing. None the less, the context, characteristics and scale of this shift was very different from the UK experience. Until the early 1990s the selling of social housing was 'virtually unheard of' in Dutch politics (Aalbers, 2004, Boelhouwer, 2002). Attempts had been largely ineffective as numerous conditions to sales were necessitated politically. The Partij van de Arbeid (PvdA), the leading social-democratic party, did eventually accept sales of social-rental units, but as part of a package of 'stimulation to purchase' rather than a 'right to buy'. Even so, the scale of sales envisioned by policy makers was far from what has been realized. Meeting the original targets necessitated the sale of 700 000 rental units; 162 000 private (21 per cent reduction) and 538 000 social-rented ones (25 per cent reduction) (see Aalbers, 2004). Initially, housing associations agreed to collectively sell off 50 000 dwellings annually, but the actual figure has been closer to 20 000. Housing associations were not so keen to sell off so much existing stock (and thus diminish their size) and prices were not substantially reduced to attract buyers. Meanwhile, social tenants were also reluctant to leave the protection of social-rental housing.

For many social renters the advantages of buying simply do not outweigh the costs in terms of the difference between cheap rents and mortgage costs, even after special deductions. Meanwhile, building new units for sale has been a more accepted strategy for social landlords than simply selling off their stock. Shared homeownership schemes have been popular, especially as homeownership preferences among low-income households are often not matched by the ability to pay. For homebuyers, the catch has been that capital gains have to be shared with the housing association (Kleinhans and Elsinga, 2010).

Despite government attempts to get renters into homeownership, it has made more sense for low-income households to go on renting and for higher earners to buy. On the one hand this has been advantageous as a relatively attractive and good-quality social-rental sector subdued the need for sub-prime borrowing and constrained the growth of marginal or risky homeowners in the 2000s. On the other, as policy measures have exaggerated tenure advantages to different types of household, it has intensified forms of divided citizenship between private buyers and social renters. Increasingly, the division has led to an accumulation of social and economic problems in some parts of the social-rental sector. In this context, specific neighbourhoods have been identified that require attention (*Vogelaar Wijken*) and large-scale urban renewal, led by housing associations, has been forwarded as the solution (van Gent et al., 2009).

Another key outcome of Dutch housing privatization has been increases in prices. In both owner-occupied and rental sectors real housing costs increased approximately 33 per cent (in terms of real income) between 1989 and 2006 (Neuteboom and Dol, 2008). However, the causes in each sector differ. The rental sector is dominated by housing associations, which have increasingly followed a more market approach to setting rents. Even though maximum rent levels are set and there are restrictions on price hikes for sitting tenants, there has been plenty of room to increase rates. In the European context, Dutch rent levels used to be low but are now average. This has led to the government spending more on housing allowances. This is still considered better than providing object subsidies, as means-based subject subsidies are more 'efficient'.

In the owner-occupied sector, economic growth in the 1990s and 2000s was accompanied by historically low interest rates and increases in income and household demand for owner-occupied homes, fuelling price increases. On the supply side, with the shift in emphasis from social-rental to private owner-occupied housing construction, the output of housing has decreased while the number of housing transactions has increased. House prices subsequently rose by 371 per cent (in real terms 216 per cent) between 1985 and 2006. Figure 6.1 illustrates both house-price increases and the shift from rental housing to owner-occupied housing output. Housing-policy transformations have thus not necessarily negated the financial cost for the government, but, rather, restructured it. There remain constituencies of homeowners and renters that require ongoing flows of public spending via housing allowances and mortgage-interest tax relief (a *de facto* cost for the state), which increase with rents and house-price inflation. Nevertheless, there are few households who find housing unaffordable and – until the global financial crisis and to a large extent after it – numbers of households in arrears have been relatively small (1.2 per cent in the rental sector and 0.8 per cent in the owner-occupied sector in 2006, Eurostat, 2008).

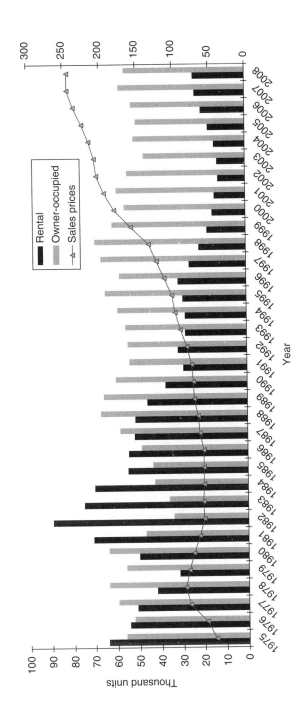

Source: VROM (2010).

Figure 6.1 Historical house-price index and housing output by tenure

A HOUSE OF CARDS?

Despite mass housing privatization in recent decades – involving substantial growth in household investment in the housing market and massive increases in individual and aggregate mortgage debt – many households have remained insulated from market downturn and global financial turmoil. There are, arguably, four key features of the Dutch housing system that have, in combination, both contributed to the rapid expansion in prices and mortgage debt in the Netherlands and, so far, provided system stability.

One critical driver in the growth of mortgage lending has been the (so-called) 'privatization' of mortgage guarantee practices. The current Mortgage Guarantee Fund (NHG) is the successor of local government schemes, which were consolidated and privatized in 1995 in order to enhance the fund structure and create greater transparency (see Elsinga et al., 2009). While previously each municipality could set its own conditions, after the last housing-market crash in the early 1980s the Dutch government sought to control risks by introducing premiums to build up funds that could offset potential losses. After 1995, borrowers could buy into the NHG guarantee scheme, which promises the full repayment of the principal plus interest to the lender should the borrower default. Mortgagees pay 0.4 per cent on top of the outstanding loan, but also receive an interest rate discount up to 0.5 per cent. While a private fund was chosen, as it was argued to be more efficient, it is effectively backed by a 'fall-back' agreement with national and municipal governments. The Dutch national bank thus considers the NHG a government guarantee and loans covered are exempt in the calculations of solvency required of lenders.

Between 1995 and 2006 the market share of loans with NHG support grew to cover more than one-third of borrowers – and now covers most new purchases, as will be discussed below. Individual households receive on average €533 discount on mortgage interest paid (around €70 million in total). The NHG has a discretionary right to hold the defaulting borrower liable for any difference between the cost of the repayment to the lender and the reimbursement from the sale of the house. Past demands on the fund have been limited and, in 2007, of the €95.6 billion outstanding mortgage guarantee, defaults amounted to only €24.3 million (0.025 per cent) (NHG, 2010).

A second important factor in the growth of borrowing has been the Mortgage Interest Tax-Deductibility Scheme (MITDS), or *Hypotheekrenteaftrek*. This facility means that homebuyers can deduct all mortgage interest paid against income tax, so that real costs compared to income are low. As the highest Netherlands tax rate is 52 per cent (with average tax deductibility at 37 per cent), servicing mortgage debt has been relatively attractive, with many people taking the maximum loan for as long as possible. Indeed, mortgaged households will often maximize tax relief in the short run rather than minimizing costs over the total lifespan of the mortgage. In recent years this has encouraged the proliferation of interest-only mortgages, which advanced from 3 per cent of all mortgages in 1994 to 44 per cent by 2006. Investment mortgages that also maximize the potential tax relief for owner-occupiers have advanced from 0 to 20 per cent over the same period, while repayment-type mortgages declined from 93 to 34 per cent. MITDS has thus played a role in expanding and prolonging household mortgage debt, although this has been considered less risky because of the advantages of savings made (mortgagees are less exposed, in terms of the real value of their debt, to increases in interest rates). Almost nine out of ten homeowners benefit from this kind of tax relief, although high-income households – with higher taxes and, typically, more expensive homes – benefit most.

While the reduced risk facilitated by MITDS is arguably demonstrated by a very low repossession rate in the Netherlands, it also poses a challenge to the mortgage system. This homeownership subsidy cost the Dutch government €12.5 billion in 2007, up from €6 billion in 1995. This is more than four times all other direct subsidies for housing put together. There is also a risk to the government from interest-rate increases: a rise of as little as 1 per cent could cost the state upwards of €2.5 billion. Although advisory councils to the Housing Ministry (VROM-Raad) have mooted the withdrawal of this tax benefit (subsidy), this has been so far resisted politically as it would make the debt-to-service ratio unmanageable for the majority of mortgaged homeowners (see Neuteboom and Dol, 2008). The government has sought in recent years to encourage households to repay their debt: by taking into account the surplus value of the sold property when a household moves on to a new home; by limiting the qualifying period to 30 years. This approach to mortgage debt has intensified since the economic crisis of 2008.

An environment encouraging the maximization of household mortgage debt has also been reflected in and reinforced by a third factor: private-sector loan practices. NHG and MITDS mean that homebuyers and housing loans appear less risky to lenders as long as mortgage payments are within household repayment capacity. This has promoted lending practices with both high loan-to-income and loan-to-value ratios. Indeed, first-time buyers may often put no savings in and take an LTV as high as 1.25 (or 125 per cent of purchase price). However, most mortgages are fixed rate, for 6–10 years on average, providing some stability over time. The reason for the acceptance of high debt lies in the focus of the mortgage system on capacity to pay rather than creditworthiness or collateral (Neuteboom and Dol, 2008). In the past there was a tendency to lend more loosely to households with expectations of earning higher incomes in the future, but there has been more formal, but non-binding regulation since 2007 (Code of Conduct Mortgage Lending). This agreement specifies a set of standards that includes how much, as a percentage of income, may be spent on housing at a certain rate of interest. Using these standards, lenders calculate acceptable borrowings limits. Banks, for example, do not normally award mortgages if the debt-to-service ratio exceeds 30–35 per cent. It appears that the Code of Conduct has limited risky lending and may even have discouraged the introduction of sub-prime loans. Still, many banks give higher loans to young households with good prospects.

A final factor that has contributed to stability in the Dutch housing system has been the continued presence of a large and attractive social-housing stock of 2.2 million units (32 per cent of housing). As discussed earlier, many households, even those with better incomes, have been reluctant to leave the protection of low rent and secure tenure (Aalbers, 2004). This has meant that the proportion of low-income marginal homebuyers has remained modest, and even those who do transfer out of private and social-rental housing into owner-occupation are cushioned by NHG and MITDS, and sometimes BEW purchase subsidies (which are now being phased out) and shared ownership programmes in which there is a guaranteed option to sell back to the housing association at a fixed price. This has both inhibited the emergence of sub-prime or predatory lending, and reduced the number of vulnerable homeowners.

THE TIDE TURNS

Ostensibly, measures to advance mortgage lending and homeownership in the Netherlands are not characteristically risky and although the language of privatization and marketization has prevailed, deregulation has been cushioned by government-backed schemes or explicit guarantees to support private and independent organizations like the NHG and housing associations. It is not surprising, then, that the global financial crisis has, as yet, had a limited impact on the housing system. None the less, the strength of the housing system is based upon a level of stability in the market and real economy. As economic conditions continue to deteriorate, there is a real danger that one or more of the pillars of the system could collapse. To be more specific, increasing economic pressure on highly mortgaged households could drive a cycle of mortgage default and repossessions, fuelling house-price deflation and undermining the mortgage-guarantee system, necessitating drastic state financial intervention. Growing unemployment and continued housing-market stagnation pose considerable threats in this regard.

While the housing system has held up during the financial downturn, the private housing market and wider economy have been far from immune. In the 2000s, the banking sector in the Netherlands began to invest, albeit more cautiously than in the UK, for example, in what would become a mire of toxic loans and assets associated with the expansion of US subprime lending and mortgage-backed securities (the majority of Dutch mortgages, however, were not financed via securitization). The banking sector featuring large banks connected intimately with global investment networks was thus strongly affected by the credit crisis. Specifically, ING, ABN-AMRO and SNS Reaal, as well as Dutch insurers like Aegon and Fortis, all entered a crisis period in late 2008. Dutch state intervention was substantial and comprehensive. The government had to directly take over ABN-AMRO, which had only just been acquired by a consortium including the Royal Bank of Scotland Group and the Dutch–Belgian giant Fortis (the twentieth largest business in the world by revenue at the time) at the end of 2007. State intervention was deemed necessary as key lenders no longer had the resources to provide long-term loans. To sustain the flow of lending, the government set aside €200 billion for interbank lending guarantees and spent over €30 billion on capital injections and bank nationalizations.

In December 2008 official estimates predicted a mild recession, with GDP shrinkage of 0.75 per cent in 2009. In June 2009, however, this estimate was increased to a 3.5 per cent decline and by August the figures had been revised again to 4.75 per cent shrinkage in 2009 and zero growth in 2010 (Central Plan Bureau, 2009). There was also concern that by 2011 unemployment could exceed 8 per cent. These estimates became the basis for the National Budget for 2010. In response to the shock figures, measures were developed by a coalition of political parties during the course of 2009 that specified necessary spending cuts. The final agreement ('Working for the Future') included an extra €3 billion financial injection for 2009 with another €3 billion earmarked for 2010. While this injection appears substantial, it represents a much smaller figure than the cuts in public spending that have been set out in order to cope with the shift in economic conditions. The national debt has begun to accelerate and is expected to reach €35 billion in 2010, and may well reach €92 billion by 2018 unless deficits decline substantially before then (de Kam, 2009).

HOUSING CONDITIONS

The housing market has proved a relatively effective barometer of both shifting economic expectations and of changing fiscal conditions. After the credit crisis hit, the average selling price of homes dropped approximately 10 per cent: from €259425 in 2008 Q3 to €233608 in 2009 Q3. The quality-adjusted price index shows a decline of about 5 to 6 per cent. Subsequently, house-price declines have levelled out. The average house price at the end of 2009 stood at €237755. A more significant concern has been the more dramatic drop in housing-market transactions. In 2009 there were 127532 transactions among the existing stock of housing in the Netherlands compared to 182392 in 2008 and 202401 in 2007. There has, however, been a sharper drop in sales of new-build housing, which fell by more than 50 per cent between the end of 2007 and the end of 2009 (Figure 6.2). This more significant fall is largely a result of reticence among potential buyers of new builds who typically agree a purchase price well before the completion of the unit. While this can advantage advance buyers when prices are increasing rapidly, in a climate of falling prices and economic uncertainty potential buyers have been reluctant to agree to buy a home that may have already dropped several per cent in value by the time it is complete.

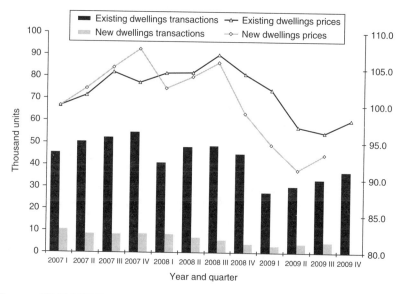

Source: VROM (2010).

Figure 6.2   Pre- and post-crisis house-price index and housing transactions

With speculative building strongly implicated in the late 1970s housing bubble, Dutch developers adopted a regime in the 1980s whereby construction does not begin until 70 per cent of units are sold. More recently, however, as households have been increasingly reluctant to buy new units, many developers have been unable to sell enough units to proceed with development, and have, in some cases, in light of increasing economic pressures and unavailability of credit, indefinitely abandoned projects. For those who have bought units on suspended projects, there are guarantees that the buyer will be compensated or the unit will be built by another developer. However, construction companies themselves have suffered considerably from market conditions leading to increasing numbers of bankruptcies and layoffs (according to the Central Bureau of Statistics, around 18 000 jobs were lost in the construction sector between mid-2008 and the end of 2009). It has been estimated that another 50 000 jobs in construction are under threat (Priemus, 2010). While new-build regulations may have been a nightmare for builders in the recent economic climate, a more positive corollary is that as there are few unsold completed dwellings, supply should quickly adjust to decline in demand, which may explain the relative shallow and short-lived house-price decline.

Many developers have responded by fragmenting development and reducing the size of projects from 50, for example, to about 15 dwellings per project. This has allowed them to proceed with development on a smaller scale, but is likely to affect housing output later on (Dol and van der Heijden, 2009). Housing production in the Netherlands has proved inelastic in recent years, and a political concern has been the inadequacy of supply and the need to increase output. The total housing output in 2009 actually showed a marginal increase of around 4000 units (to a total of 83 000) – largely as a result of projects started in 2007 and 2008 – but the industry is experiencing a declining workload. If sales do not increase substantially, production in 2010 may easily fall to around 60 000 (VROM, 2010; CBS, 2010).

HOUSEHOLD IMPACTS

As yet, the impact of changing economic and housing-market conditions on individual households has been limited. Indeed, it is evident that some have benefited from the housing-market downturn and while, according to Cadastre figures, there has been a sharp drop of more than one-third in housing transactions overall (Figure 6.2), this is much less pronounced among younger buyers (only a one-quarter decline among the under 30s). It seems that first-time buyers in particular may be taking advantage of the drop in prices. Although lending conditions have tightened up in the Netherlands, those with secure employment have continued to access more than 100 per cent mortgages and high loan-to-income rates, partly as a result of the mortgage guarantee. Although the overall housing market has declined, lower-end housing units typically associated with market entry have actually been more resistant to economic trends. Meanwhile, higher-end properties have suffered even more than averages would indicate (de Vries, 2009).

Another social outcome of housing-market change has been a decline in residential mobility, which, it is suggested, slowed down more than 10 per cent in 2008 and 2009 (van Hoek, 2008). Market declines have thus been associated with a fall in divorces and new households being formed. There has also been a shift in demand from owner-occupied housing to renting (Priemus, 2010; van den Eerenbeemt, 2009). Considering the size and quality of the rental sector in the Netherlands, the non-purchase option is still a viable alternative for Dutch households seeking to sit out the financial storm. Rental tenants enjoy considerable protection in the Netherlands, and while social-rental tenants pay sub-market rents and have secure tenure (with low-income ones receiving housing allowances), sitting private tenants are also protected by government controls on rent increases.

Perhaps the most fundamental marker of continued household stability in contradiction to changing macroeconomic fortunes is the low level of home repossessions in the Netherlands. A key indicator there is the number of involuntary auctions of repossessed homes. While the annual number of such forced sales was 1504 in 2004, the rate had already increased to 1811 by 2007, reflecting growing pressures of increasing prices on homeowners. The rate increased further to 1961 in 2008 and 2256 in 2009 reflecting the change in market conditions, but not a national crisis among households. As discussed earlier, mortgage conditions are considerably more stable in the Netherlands than in neighbouring market liberal economies, and Dutch increases in repossessions appear relatively minor in comparison. For example, in the UK (with around four times the population of the Netherlands) 46 000 homes were repossessed in 2009 (official predictions had estimated 75 000) and the current estimate for 2010 is 53 000 (CML, 2010). UK repossessions have more than doubled from 22 400 in 2006 and in 2003 there were as few as 8500.

Repossessions, of course, are only one indicator of stress upon households and tend to be delayed until well after the economic triggering event. Many Dutch households are likely to struggle with arrears for years before finally being repossessed. Moreover, considering the prevalence of fixed-rate mortgages as well as the generosity of unemployment benefits in the Netherlands (which are typically 70 per cent of final salary for the first year), it could be a long time before the effects of the economic crisis become manifest in the housing market. While there have been dramatic predictions of escalating unemployment, so far increases have been marginal, with unemployment rates under 3 per cent at the end of 2008 and under 4 per cent in 2009. Following the last major recession beginning in 1980, there were a mere 1527 repossessions in 1981. This had reached 5864 by 1983 and 11 305 by 1985. By 1990, the figure had dropped back to 3032 (WEW, 2010). Arguably, there are now more guarantee mechanisms insulating households and the current housing market, not least the NHG. In 2008 and 2009 purchases using the NHG advanced rapidly, with around 80 per cent of mortgages within the guarantee price range now being covered. Moreover, claims against the NHG have been relatively stable and while there was an increase from a total of 757 claims in 2007 to 927 in 2008, in 2009 there were only 763 claims. The NHG estimates that one in three claims were the outcome of divorce compared to one in ten because of unemployment (NHG, 2010).

GOVERNMENT RESPONSES

Although households seem to be weathering the financial storm, the government has been quick to act in the housing market in order to compensate for worsening conditions in the real-estate sector. One of the first reactions was to raise the limit of the NHG for homebuyers from €265 000 to €350 000. The measure was introduced to stimulate banks to provide 100 per cent loan-to-value loans to a broader market segment. This was proposed at the end of 2008, but not enacted until the middle of 2009, when declining market conditions become more evident. Even though this was not considered a large financial risk, the Cabinet reserved €9 million to offset unexpected adversity. This intervention also sought to compensate for the more extreme downturn in the middle to upper end of the market, encouraging both buying and lending, and thus production. In addition, the conditions of the NHG facility for households with payment problems (introduced in 2005) have been relaxed since July 2009. Essentially, this facility provides a partial payment holiday for a maximum of three years, but this money has to be paid back (WEW, 2010).

An open letter by Minister van der Laan (Minister of Housing) on 30 Janurary 2009 setting out the government's position on housing and the emerging crisis emphasized the responsibilities of individual housing-market players. Measures were consequently announced to stimulate the sector by supporting non-government agents. Thus, in addition to the increase in the NHG limit for homebuyers, there was a temporary increase in the guaranteed borrowing limit for housing associations. The objective was to encourage housing associations to take over commercial projects that had ground to a halt. The assumption has been that housing associations are better placed to realize such projects as either temporary or permanent rental housing (Priemus, 2010).

In the past, when under government control, housing associations had been used in anticyclical measures to compensate for downturn in the private market. This is evident in Figure 6.1, which illustrates the increase in rental-housing production stimulated largely by housing-association development in the mid-1980s. In the present crisis housing associations are independent non-profit organizations and have often been more concerned with their own preservation, acting along with government imperatives to the extent that it serves their own interests. According to Van Heuven, Director of Aedes (the umbrella organization representing housing associations), 'associations will only consider taking over commercial building projects, as the Cabinet suggests, if this fits in with their business operations and the local building remit' (Harms, 2009, p. 13).

Associations have been hurt by the financial crisis, with difficulties in unloading property built for sale reducing capacity to invest in new construction, along with continuing restrictions on rental revenue from national rent policy. The crisis also hit on top of the recent introduction of corporation tax for housing associations. In early 2009 Aedes reported that housing-association liquidity was under pressure, and by mid-2009 about one quarter of housing associations were accorded B status by the Central Housing Fund (Centraal Fonds Volkshuisvesting), meaning that they are 'financially vulnerable'. It has been public banks that have compensated for the erosion in conditions for housing associations, with the Municipalities Bank (BNG) and the Water Boards Bank (Waterschapsbank) becoming the biggest investors with their stakes rising to 60 per cent and 90 per cent in 2008 and 2009.

Due to the considerable support from public institutions, and in light of the substantial asset wealth housing associations inherited from their public deregulation, some working groups of civil servants, politicians and economists have recently proposed that in order to reduce the public deficit, housing associations should take on the economic burden for housing allowances (*Financiële Dagblad*, 2009). Such a notion, if realized, could cost housing associations up to €2.4 billion a year – requiring them to increase rents and sell off more properties – but would also reduce government spending on housing to a small residual. Nothing is yet set regarding how housing associations can or will take on more of the financial burden for Dutch housing, although, in the context of the scale of government debt brought on by the crisis, the advantageous position associations have enjoyed in the last decade and a half will surely be reconsidered.

In a second letter on 15 May 2009, Minister van der Laan set out further emergency measures for the private house-building sector. The package provided more than €700 million for 2009 and 2010. More than half of this was targeted at boosting the construction sector, with the rest in energy-investment allowances to stimulate sustainable investment by tenants and owner-occupiers. A third letter on 12 June identified another €245 million (€395 million total) for temporary incentive schemes for new-build projects aligned with the Urban Renewal Act. The intention is to regalvanize projects that have been delayed or postponed. It allows developers, housing associations and municipalities to build more, but at their own risk. In addition, while there has been less concern with private rental construction – with increasing movement towards that sector in reaction to changing conditions in the owner-occupied market – since July greater subsidies have been available for units that fall under the rent-regulation limit. Projects are submitted in the name of municipalities, many of which have oversubscribed to the scheme. In August 2009, €100 million had been allocated for a total of 15 000 units. In principle, if construction did not start before January 2010, the subsidies had to be paid back.

CONCLUSIONS

As elsewhere, in recent decades housing privatization and marketization have advanced rapidly in the Netherlands. None the less, massive growth in homeownership and mortgage debt has not necessarily made the housing system unstable, and it appears, notwithstanding some market volatility, substantially more robust than other countries in the current economic crisis. Controls applied to speculative development after the last housing-market downturn seem to be working, as are mortgage checks and guarantees. Changes in the social housing sector have also been considerable, although this sector is unlikely to be able to compensate for system volatility as effectively as in the past. Arguably, the strength of Dutch social-rental housing has inhibited the rise of vulnerable home-owners and risky lending, but associations themselves, as autonomous self-interested institutions, are now more concerned with riding out the financial storm than with committing their resources to risky projects in order to help out the government and private sector. Inevitably, financial-stimulation measures will be less effective than a return of real confidence. Banks and other lenders have become more cautious and are increasingly insisting on NHG guarantees for borrowers.

The perceived scale of the crisis and the emerging size of public deficits are also facilitating a renegotiation of the role of the state in the housing system. It has become evident that housing associations will need to take on greater responsibilities for housing overall as the state seeks to reduce spending on housing allowances and squeeze more from housing associations in terms of fulfilling social obligations. At the same time, there has been a surprising development in the debate over the MITD. A survey by a leading newspaper, *De Volkskrant*, in the spring of 2010 revealed that an increasing number of people (approximately 64 per cent) are open to the idea of cutting back entitlements to mortgage-interest tax deductions, specifically for the wealthiest households (*De Volkskrant*, 29 March 2010). This ostensibly opens the door for a political debate on reducing what is effectively the largest state-housing subsidy and arguably one of the largest pillars of policy support for homeowning households.

In speculating on future developments in Dutch housing and their implications for households, while arrears among mortgaged homeowners have been limited, as unemployment grows, repossessions are likely to escalate. This will not only intensify economic and political stress, but also threaten to undermine an integrated network of government financial guarantees. The greatest danger to Dutch households is thus a deep and prolonged recession rather than the housing market itself. The nation is particularly vulnerable to global conditions in this regard, as the economy is strongly orientated towards international trade. The Netherlands is ranked fifth in the world by the WTO (in 2009) as an export-orientated nation, despite its small population of 16 million.

Priemus (2010) argues that European countries are divided in terms of the effects of the crisis. He identifies one group of countries including the UK and Ireland where the decline in the housing market is causing an economic recession. In the other, which includes the Netherlands and Norway, it is the economic recession that is causing decline in the housing market. This statement rather overestimates the influence of the housing market over the larger economy in countries like the UK, which stands out against Ireland (and Spain) in terms of housing demand and reliance on the construction sector as a driver of GPD. However, the Netherlands does illustrate how guarantee mechanisms and a more diversified housing system can inhibit the impact of fluctuating global economic conditions on individual households.

REFERENCES

Aalbers, M.B. (2004), 'Promoting home ownership in a social-rented city: policies, practices and pitfalls', *Housing Studies*, **19** (3), 483–95.
Aalbers, M.B. (2008), 'The financialization of home and the mortgage market crisis', *Competition & Change*, **12** (2), 148–66.

Boelhouwer, P.J. (2000), 'Development of house prices in the Netherlands: an international perspective', *Journal of Housing and the Built Environment*, **15** (1), 11–28.

Boelhouwer, P.J. (2002), 'Trends in Dutch housing policy and the shifting position of the social rented sector', *Urban Studies*, **39** (2), 219–35.

Brenner, N. and N. Theodore (eds) (2002), *Spaces of Neoliberalism: Urban Restructuring in North America and Western Europe*, Oxford, Wiley-Blackwell.

CBS (2010), *Statistics Netherlands*, Statline online database, http://statline.cbs.nl/statweb/, accessed 7 July 2010.

Central Plan Bureau (CPB) (2009), *Centraal Economisch Plan 2009*, The Hague: CPB.

CML (2010), 'Arrears and repossessions down, but vulnerability remains', Council of Mortgage Lenders, http://www.cml.org.uk/cml/media/press/2612, 13 May.

de Kam, F. (2009), 'Overheid zakt weg in moeras van schulden', *NRC Handelsblad*, 12 July.

De Vries, P. (2009), 'De impact van de kredietcrisis op de koopwoningmarkt', *Economisch-Statistische Berichten*, **94** (4568), 571.

Dol, K. and H. van der Heijden (2009), *Knelpuntenmonitor Woningproductie 2008: integrale samenvatting*, OTB Research Institute for the Built Environment, Delft University of Technology.

Doling, J. and J. Ford (2003), *Globalisation and Home Ownership: Experiences in Eight Member States of the European Union*, Amsterdam: IOS Press.

Elsinga, M., H. Priemus and L. Cao (2009), 'The government mortgage guarantee as an instrument in housing policy: self-supporting instrument or subsidy?', *Housing Studies*, **24** (1), 67–80.

EMF (2009), *HYPOSTAT: A Review of Europe's Mortgage and Housing Markets*, Brussels: European Mortgage Federation.

Eurostat (2008), European Union: Eurostat, Community Statistics on Income and Living Conditions, http://epp.eurostat.ec.europa.eu/portal/page/portal/essnet/eu_silc.

Financiële Dagblad (2009), 'Huurtoeslag betaalbaar voor corporaties door op grote schaal woningen te verkopen', available at http://www.fd.nl/artikel/13753235/huurtoeslag-betaalbaar-corporaties-grote-schaal-woningen-verkopen, accessed 7 December 2009.

Forrest, R. (2008), 'Globalization and the housing asset rich: geographies, demographies and policy convoys', *Global Social Policy*, **8** (2), 167–87.

Harms, E. (2009), 'Hoe staat de woningmarkt ervoor?', *Tijdschrift voor de Volkshuisvesting*, **15** (3), 11–15.

Heerma, E. (1989), *Volkshuisvesting in de jaren negentig* (Housing in the Nineties), The Hague: Sdu.

Kleinhans, R. and M. Elsinga (2010), '"Buy your home and feel in control." Does home ownership achieve the empowerment of former tenants of social housing?', *International Journal of Housing Policy*, **10** (1), 41–61.

Neuteboom, P. and K. Dol (2008), *Housing Policies in a Rapidly Changing World: Government Financial Measures to Promote Homeownership and Housing Affordability in the Netherlands*, Report, Stockholm: Statens Bostadskreditnamd.

NHG [Nationale Hypotheek Garantie] (2010), 'Voorlopige NHG-Jaarcijfers 2009: Meer NHG's; minder gedwongen verkopen', available at http://www.nhg.nl/organisatie/publicaties/nieuwsbrief-overzicht.html, accessed 18 January 2010.

Priemus, H. (1996), 'Recent changes in the social rental sector in the Netherlands', *Urban Studies*, **33** (10), 1891–901.

Priemus, H. (2010), 'The credit crunch: impacts on the housing market and policy responses in the Netherlands', *Journal of Housing and the Built Environment*, **25**, 95–116.

Ronald, R. (2008), *The Ideology of Home Ownership: Homeowner Societies and the Role of Housing*, Basingstoke, UK: Palgrave Macmillan.

Salet, W. (1999), 'Regime shifts in Dutch housing policy', *Housing Studies*, **14** (4), 547–57.

Stephens, M., M. Elsinga and T. Knorr-Siedow (2008), 'The privatization of social housing: three different pathways', in K. Scanlon and C. Whitehead (eds), *Social Housing in Europe II: A Review of Policies and Outcomes*, London: LSE, pp. 105–30.

van den Eerenbeemt, M. (2009), 'Huizenmarkt staat overal op instorten', *De Volkskrant*, 2 January.

van der Schaar, J. (1987), *Groei en bloei van het Nederlandse volkshuisvestingsbeleid*, Delft: Delft University Press.

van Gent, W.P.C., S. Musterd and W.J.M. Ostendorf (2009), 'Bridging the social divide? Contemporary Dutch neighbourhood policy', *Journal of Housing and the Built Environment*, **24** (3), 357–68.

van Hoek, T. (2008), *De Vastgoedlezing 2008: Crisis op de Nederlandse woning- en vastgoedmarkt?*, Amsterdam: Amsterdam School of Real Estate.

De Volkskrant (2010), '63 procent voor aanpak hypotheekrenteaftrek', available at http://www.volkskrant.nl/binnenland/article1363698.ece/63_procent_voor_aanpak_hypotheekrenteaftrek, accessed 29 March 2010.

VROM (Ministry of Housing, Spatial Planning and the Environment) (2010), *Monitor Nieuwe Woningen*, Den Haag, available at http://www.vrom.nl/infowonen/docs/MNW%202009-4%20TAB.pdf, accessed 9 May 2010.

WEW (Stichting Waarborgfonds Eigen Woningen) (2010), 'Crisismaatregelen NHG gaan vandaag in', press release www.nhg.nl, accessed 9 May 2010.

7. Housing policy and the economic crisis – the case of Hungary

József Hegedüs

INTRODUCTION

The world economic crisis has also reached the new member states of the EU, resulting in a serious economic shock for some of them because of the fiscal mismanagement at the beginning of 2000 (Mitra et al., 2010). These countries are the 'weakest links' of the extended EU. Hungary was one of them, which in 2002 and 2003 introduced measures to improve the living standards of the population without a strong economic foundation. By 2006, the public-sector deficit went above 9 per cent of GDP, the external debt increased to 65 per cent of GDP and the current account deficit was 7.4 per cent, because of these massive imbalances. Thus the Hungarian economy had become very vulnerable to the global financial crisis, and Hungary needed an IMF US$ 25 billion special loan to manage the attack against its national currency. Housing policy has contributed to the economic problems through the immense homeownership support started in 2001/02, which resulted in an exceptionally fast increase of the housing-mortgage sector and households' indebtedness. As a consequence of the economic crisis, a sharp drop in housing investment took place, house prices decreased and a mass of housing evictions has been forecast, entailing serious social conflicts. Will it indeed happen, and, if yes, what consequences will it have for the new housing system that has emerged since the great political transition of 1989/90?

Beyond this direct social issue there is a more theoretical question related to the discussion on typology of the welfare systems and housing regimes (Hegedüs and Tosics, 1996). What happened to what was termed the 'Eastern European Housing Model', what kind of housing regime replaced the socialist housing system? Will the global economic crisis have an effect on the future trends in housing-policy developments in the region?

To answer these questions, in the first part of the chapter I shall develop a conceptual framework for understanding housing regimes in the transitional countries. The second part will focus on the question of how housing policy contributed to the vulnerability of the economy in Hungary. The third part will analyse the different measures taken by the government to alleviate the social effect of the crisis. In the last part of the chapter I shall draw some conclusions about the future trends of housing regimes in Hungary.

HOUSING AND WELFARE REGIMES IN THE POST-SOCIALIST SYSTEMS – A FRAMEWORK OF ANALYSIS

The East European Housing Model (Hegedüs and Tosics, 1996) summarizes the main characteristics and elements of the housing system in the centrally planned economy, which was a social-economic system with high job security,[1] low – heavily subsidized – housing costs, and small income differences. In this housing system, a vast majority of services was provided 'in kind' or at an under-cost/market price allocated according to 'merits' (Kornai, 2000). The main characteristics of this model were single-party political control over the housing sector, the subordinate role of market mechanisms, lack of competition among housing agencies (bureaucratic coordination), and broad control over the allocation of housing services (huge, non-transparent subsidies). However, under this model several 'sub-models' (versions) emerged as responses of the individual countries to challenges in the process of developing the socialist economy (Turner et al., 1992). While the main characteristics of the model could be explained as a consequence of the centrally planned economy (priority of industrialization, socialist capital accumulation, controlled urbanization, etc.) through a hard structuralist approach, the divergences of the model were considered theoretically as 'policy options' taken by individual societies through the interaction of agencies under the control of the Communist Party.[2] The structural conflicts ('cracks' in the model, such as housing shortage, inefficiency of central planning, quasi-market processes, existence of informal economy) were managed by different methods, for example introducing strict control mechanisms (Bulgaria, Russia, East Germany) or allowing quasi-market processes (Yugoslavia, Hungary). These variants of the model were different from each other in terms of tenure structure (state-owned rental, cooperative housing, private rental and owner-occupied sector) or in terms of housing-finance schemes provided by state banks. Despite differences, the common structural features have left their imprint on the housing systems (e.g. controlled urbanization, housing estates, poorly maintained public housing, and rationed 'elite' houses for the nomenclature).

The mainstream theories of welfare regimes had difficulties in theorizing socialist countries before the transition (1989/90), because the 'typical welfare theory' was looking for the social mechanisms by which the state intervenes in market processes to manage inequality and conflicts in different spheres of public life (education, old-age provision, pension system, family policy, etc.). This is why classifications such as the 'Industrial Achievement–Performance model' or 'authoritarian welfare state' (Wilensky, 1975, Aidukaite, 2009) do not take us closer to understanding the welfare regimes of the socialist countries. In the socialist system, social policy was merely the extension or continuation of state dominance aimed at providing basic services. Consequently, social policy allocated public services on a merit basis, more as an act of rewarding various social groups than as a means of compensating inequalities in the society. The 'socialist welfare system' created a society where practically there was no unemployment, income differences were small, public services (education, health, etc.) were free, housing costs were low and free/cheap holidays were offered to those who had 'positional advantages' in the social/political structure.[3]

The socialist society went through a transformation process. Hungary in the 1980s, as a response to the economic difficulties caused partly by the energy-price increase of 1970, moved towards a hybrid system, in which the political hegemony of the Communist Party was combined with quasi-market elements, and the state started to build up social policies to manage the problems of households with disadvantages both in the state and the quasi-market sphere.[4] The critical sociology of the existing socialist system focused on the roles of the state, market and 'reciprocity' in creating and levelling social inequalities (Szelényi, 1983, Manchin and Szelényi, 1987 and in housing; see Hegedüs, 1987).

The regime change created a totally new situation where real (frequently unregulated) market forces and democratic political institutions shocked society, and large social groups had no chance to adjust to the new social and economic conditions. Social policy, in a broader sense, became a crucial element to alleviate social conflicts and pacify society (Vanhuysse, 2006). In reaction to the social conflicts and tensions, a new welfare system was built up step by step through uncoordinated measures in various areas (income benefit programmes, education, pension system, etc.). There is no consistent model that would guide the individual solutions in different areas; there are no masterminds of the welfare-regime builders. This type of 'trial-and-error' approach was more or less a general phenomenon in the region. The policy changes – a result of compromises among different social forces (bureaucracy, interest groups, non-profit sector, international donor agencies, etc.) – were conditioned by constant fiscal pressure on the governments and the extremely high influence of the informal economy.

THE HOUSING REGIME AFTER THE TRANSITION

The Transitional Recession and Crisis in the Housing System

As a result of the transitional recession, GDP fell by 15 per cent in the first part of the 1990s, and as a result of the closed-down state-owned companies, the employment rate (share of those employed in the working-age population) decreased from 76.3 per cent (1990) to 61.4 per cent (2000), and real household income in 2000 was lower in real terms than in 1990 (see Table 7.1).

Table 7.1   Macroeconomic indicators (1990–2009)

Year	Estimated house price increase (previous year = 100)	Consumer price index (previous year = 100)	GDP (previous year = 100)	New construction	Building permit
1990	136.8	128.9	96.7	43 771	42 913
1991	111.9	135.0	88.1	33 164	29 896
1992	112.8	123.0	96.9	25 807	28 659
1993	103.3	122.5	99.4	20 925	23 848
1994	112.0	118.8	102.9	20 947	27 152
1995	116.1	128.2	101.5	24 718	39 053
1996	109.1	123.6	101.0	28 257	30 462
1997	108.8	118.3	104.3	28 130	30 474
1998	123.0	114.3	105.2	20 323	23 442
1999	129.6	110.0	104.2	19 287	30 577
2000	144.9	109.8	104.9	21 583	44 709
2001	114.3	109.2	104.1	28 054	47 867
2002	115.5	105.3	104.4	31 500	49 000
2003	117.8	104.7	104.3	35 543	59 241
2004	107.7	106.8	104.9	43 913	57 459
2005	102.9	103.6	103.5	41 084	51 490
2006	105.2	103.9	104.0	33 864	44 826
2007	103.3	108.0	101.0	36 159	44 276
2008	101.3	106.1	100.6	36 075	43 862
2009	91.7	104.2	93.7	31 994	28 400

Source: Central Statistical Office, FHB house price index.

After 1990, market mechanisms replaced state control in the housing sector. The housing privatization, started in 1986, speeded up, and by 2000 only 4 per cent of the housing stock was owned by local governments (in 1989, 23 per cent of the stock was in state ownership). The housing management of multi-unit buildings (typically housing estates) had been transformed, and private management companies dominated the market. State-housing construction companies were privatized or went bankrupt, and land policy was taken over by the decentralized local governments, while the majority of urban land was transferred to private ownership. The housing-finance system had become technically bankrupt by 1990 because of the long-term state-housing loans issued in the 1980s with a fixed low interest rate (1–3 per cent). The state-owned housing bank was first consolidated, and – together with other banks – privatized. Housing subsidies amounted to 7.5 per cent of GDP in 1989 and decreased to 0.8 per cent of GDP by 1998 (World Bank, 1991). As a consequence, by the end of the 1990s a deep crisis could be detected in the housing sector. New construction diminished to 20 per cent of its 1980s levels, around 0.5 per cent of the existing stock, and the deterioration of the housing stock accelerated. The housing mortgage market basically vanished: while outstanding loans were 16–17 per cent of GDP in 1989, they fell to 1–1.5 per cent by the end of the 1990s (Hegedüs and Várhegyi, 2000). Access to social housing shrunk, because construction of new social housing was stopped.

New Housing Programme from 2000 – Oversubsidizing Homeownership

As a result of the austerity programme of 1995–96, economic performance improved. Real GDP grew at an average rate of 4.4 per cent over the period of 1997–2002, and had reached the level of the pre-transition period by 2001. Unemployment had been falling from the middle of the 1990s, and stabilized at 5–7 per cent at the turn of the century, although the employment rate remained low. Inflation stabilized and the interest rate decreased at the end of the 1990s as a clear sign of macroeconomic stabilization (see Table 7.2). A new housing programme was introduced in 2000, which had three main objectives: (1) introduction of mortgage finance; (2) increase of the social housing stock; and (3) improving housing quality through refurbishment of housing estates. There was a consensus among different political forces and governments on these objectives, although in terms of housing-policy measures there were big differences, influenced less by political values and more by the interplay of different lobbies and the constraints of fiscal pressure on the government.

Transition countries faced another critical social problem tied to the housing system. Housing expenditures (cost of energy and public services

Table 7.2   Share of the housing policy public budget

Year	Rental sector programme (%)	Home ownership (%)	Rehabilitation, modernization (%)	Housing allowances (%)	Total (%)	(in billion HUF)	As a % of GDP
2000	7	73	13	7	100	49	0.4
2001	15	70	10	6	100	62	0.4
2002	23	66	7	4	100	101	0.6
2003	14	79	5	2	100	194	1.0
2004	7	85	5	2	100	245	1.2
2005	7	83	6	4	100	270	1.2
2006	2	51	5	42	100	399	1.7
2007	2	54	8	36	100	351	1.4
2008	3	55	11	32	100	283	1.1
2009	3	59	9	29	100	280	1.1

Source: Estimates based on government's reports.

but not rent) increased faster than household incomes, and income inequality increased. The ratio of average income in the lowest percentile to the average in the highest percentile increased from 4.6 in 1987 to 7.6 in 2004 (Keszthelyiné Rédei and Szabó, 2006), which caused a huge affordability problem for low-income groups. The share of households who had housing arrears reached 6 per cent in 2003 (CSO, 2003). However, housing affordability had not been addressed by housing policy, and remained the responsibility of social policy, because of the weak cooperation among the ministries responsible for housing and social issues. Moreover, housing allowance programmes had not been integrated under the social ministries. Rent allowance, national and local government housing allowance, utility allowance and energy allowance programmes operated in parallel, without any coordination (Hegedüs and Teller, 2007).

The right-wing government (1998–2002) introduced major changes in housing policy in 2000. The most significant element of the programme was support to housing mortgages. Two interest-rate subsidies were introduced beyond the already existing demand-side construction grant for families with children: (a) an interest-rate subsidy to mortgage bonds (supported by the 'bank lobby') and (b) an interest-rate subsidy for loans connected to new construction (supported by the 'construction lobby').[5] The third element in the subsidy programme was the personal income tax (PIT) mortgage payment allowance.

In the original proposal (in 2000) the size of the mortgage subsidies and the PIT allowance were at a low level, which gave a fiscally manageable impetus to the development of mortgage finance. However, the government had been under constant pressure by lobbying groups, and the conditions and eligibility criteria for the two interest-rate subsidy schemes had been relaxed between 2000 and 2002. Additionally, in the spring of 2002 (before the election) the PIT deduction was expanded to loans for buying existing housing units as well as opening up a huge market for mortgage banks. By the end of 2002 it had become clear that the volume of housing loans had increased very fast as a consequence of the subsidies. In 2002 the outstanding loans more than doubled, reaching 4.5 per cent of GDP. There were two important drawbacks to the programme: fiscal consequences and the equity effect.

First, the fiscal effects of the mortgage programmes were not projected correctly. In October 2002, one of the prominent economic research institutes estimated (Molnár and Pichovsky, 2002)[6] the future cost of the two mortgage subsidy programmes at 42 billion HUF for the year 2005, while in fact it reached 153 billion HUF by 2003. It was clearly fiscally unsustainable. The socialist government (2002–06) – for political reasons – kept postponing decisions to cut the subsidies. The leading political parties got into a 'game' promising more and more support to the housing sector without understanding the fiscal and social consequences of the proposed programmes.

Second, the social consequence of the housing subsidy programme had a regressive income redistribution. The net value of the mortgage subsidy in 2002–04 was 50–70 per cent of the loan (taking into calculation the two interest-rate subsidies and the PIT allowance), which could be accessed without means testing. The regressive equity effect of the mortgage programme is shown clearly by the allocation of the PIT allowance in 2004, where the upper 20 per cent of households in the income distribution got 60 per cent of the total subsidy, and the upper 40 per cent received 80 per cent (Hegedüs and Somogyi, 2005, pp. 199–202).

After a long political debate, the government changed the conditions of the mortgage programme in 2004. The interest-rate subsidies were decreased and tax exemptions in PIT for mortgage repayments had been first cut severely, and then abolished in 2007.

Housing credit grew very fast in Hungary between 2000 and 2004, and the cut in subsidies did not halt the expansion of the market, because foreign exchange (FX) dominated loans successfully replaced the subsidized HUF loans. Their share went from close to zero in 2004 to 90 per cent in 2008. There were no direct fiscal burdens in relation to the loans issued in FX. The availability of cheap funds and the exceptionally wide spread gave a wide motivation for the banks and mortgage brokers to expand the market to consumer loans.

Failure of Social Housing Policies After 2000 – Lack of Political and Institutional Support

The social-rental sector has shrunk and it has become a residual sector, in which are concentrated the most vulnerable groups of society. In almost every country in the region, politicians and government officials emphasized the need for social housing after mass privatization and the recovery of the economy at the end of 1990s (Hegedüs, 2007). The housing policy launched in 2000 included a grant programme for local authorities to support the expansion of the social-rental sector. Local authorities were eligible for a grant of up to 75 per cent of the cost of investments for social-rental housing, and between 2000 and 2004, several hundred local governments took part in the programme. The programme had several weaknesses. Average costs were considered to be very high, the allocation criteria for new tenancies were not regulated, and local politics played a role in discretionary allocation. Moreover, during the period of operation of the scheme, the privatization process continued: thus local authorities privatized 25 000 units, but built, bought or renewed only 8800 rental units.

In 2004, the government stopped the social rental programme due to fiscal pressure, citing the high cost per unit. However, the importance of the social-rental sector was never questioned in government documents. In 2005 a new rent allowance programme was finally introduced, which aimed to use the private rental sector for social purposes. Local governments could apply for a rent allowance for low-income families with children who had private-rental contracts. The programme has failed because it required landlords to be registered with the tax authority. As the majority of private landlords do not pay tax, they did not change their attitude for the sake of participating in this programme. A second problem was that the income limit for eligible households was too low (cautious budgetary planning), and eligible households were not able to pay the rent. In 2006, another new loan programme was launched, giving local governments access to subsidized loans from the Hungarian Development Bank for investment in the public-rental sector. However, interest by local governments was very limited.

Housing Policy Support for Rehabilitation Programmes

The rehabilitation programme (under the housing-policy objective to improve housing quality) became important after 2004, especially the 'panel' programme, the programme of rehabilitation of buildings built by prefabricated technology. The housing estates represent 30 per cent of the urban housing stock in Hungary, the majority of which was built in the 1970s and 1980s, and served mainly the housing needs of first-generation intellectuals and the lower middle class (Szelényi, 1983; Hegedüs and Tosics, 1986). After the housing reforms in 1980, and especially as a consequence of housing privatization, housing estates started to deteriorate. Politically it was a popular programme as it reached a wide strata of society and was relatively cheap from a fiscal point of view. A constant expansion of the 'panel' programme has taken place since 2004, as a result of which 25 per cent of this stock (190 000 housing units) has been renovated to some degree. There are more serious social problem areas in segregated housing estates and run-down urban areas with a high share of Roma population, which require more social attention and fiscal resources. Some programmes started in 2006, but mostly on a pilot scale. Urban rehabilitation programmes started slowly after 1990 under the control and support of the local governments, but in most cases the urban poor were forced to move out of the renewed neighbourhoods. The first urban rehabilitation programme aimed at improving the living conditions of the 'sitting poor' started in 2006.

Housing Allowance Programmes

Housing affordability (paying the housing-related cost) for low-income groups became the most important social problem after 1990. The social safety net had not developed with the growing need of those unemployed (including not only the official unemployed) and increasing income inequality and poverty. The explicit housing allowance programmes were very weakly financed by local governments until 2006, when the Ministry of Social Affairs introduced a national (called 'normative') scheme that reached 8 per cent of the most vulnerable social groups. From 2000, the increase in energy prices regulated by the Office of Energy under the control of the central government created a large budgetary burden. For political reasons, gas prices had not been increased and the privatized energy companies had been compensated by an across-the-board price subsidy (the cost of which reached 120 billion HUF). However, in 2007 the fiscal burden of the price subsidy was too high, therefore the government had to increase gas prices and at the same time introduced a special, means-tested gas price allowance programme managed by the Treasury. The cost of the programme was 150 billion HUF in 2006, ten times more than the housing allowance programme (Hegedüs and Teller, 2007). Beside these programmes, other specialized lower-cost programmes operate to compensate the households' housing expenditures. In the water sector, the water companies, which had an extremely high production cost, received a price subsidy managed by the Ministry of Environment (Hegedüs and Papp, 2007). The local governments operate special utility and rent-subsidy programmes; the most important of these is the Utility Fee Compensation Fund set up in 1995 (Győri, 2003; Hegedüs and Somogyi, 2006).

To summarize, housing affordability is one of the most important social issues. The post-socialist welfare regime, however, was not able to build up an integrated safety-net system, due to a 'targeting failure'. Because of the difficulty of measuring incomes, safety-net programmes (for the unemployed, low-income groups, family support, etc.) put the level of support below subsistence level, which means that households without other sources of income cannot survive at a socially accepted level. However, the government would not be able to pay the adequate amount for the needy households based on the official income because of the scarcity of resources. Households that have only the official low income supplemented with income benefits tend to live in deep poverty without recourse to family networks. Without help from relatives, they are unable to pay the cost of housing, and they will be forced to rely on illegal income sources (stealing, usury, etc.). A long, sharp debate among economists and sociologists has been devoted to across-the-board programmes and to 'targeted' programmes. But this is a false debate, because without reliable measurement of income it is very difficult to move towards a more efficient, targeted system. It is important to emphasize that the targeting issue is not just a technical difficulty, but it is, to a large extent, due to failures in structural changes of the public sector (education, health system, etc.).

THE WORLD ECONOMIC CRISIS AND ITS CONSEQUENCE ON THE HOUSING SYSTEMS

Macroeconomic Mismanagement

In 2002 and 2003, the Hungarian government started a loose fiscal policy, which led to an increase in household consumption by 9.8 per cent (2002) and 7.9 per cent (2003), much above the level that the productivity increase would have justified. GDP grew by 4.4–4.7 per cent (between 2002 and 2004), but the postponed austerity measures led to a high deficit with a peak at 9.3 per cent in 2006 and increased the gross foreign-debt-to-GDP ratio from 57 per cent in 2002 to 73 per cent in 2008. In 2004 Hungary joined the European Union, which created an optimistic view of the prospects for the economy. The debt-to-GDP ratio increased after 2004 as residential mortgage finance was fuelled by cheap international credit

(FX-denominated loans mainly in Swiss francs and Japanese yen). Direct foreign investments continued to come to Hungary, which, with the increase in EU funds, maintained the growth of the economy.

The 2008 worldwide economic crisis hit Hungary, which had to take emergency loans from multinational institutions. The new interim Hungarian government introduced an austerity programme that consolidated the budget and by 2010 brought down the deficit to 3.8 per cent of GDP from nearly 9 per cent in 2006.

Vulnerability of the Housing Finance System

Because of the fiscal effect of the housing programme, in 2004 the government reduced the size of the subsidy and tightened the eligibility criteria. However, the banks introduced FX-denominated loans based on cheap international credit, which maintained the growth of the residential mortgage market. Actually, the FX-denominated loans had already existed in the market before 2004, but because of the high interest-rate subsidy they could not compete with the Hungarian currency loans. After the subsidy cut, the non-subsidized FX loans became cheaper for households than the subsidized HUF loans; however, the interest-rate risk and exchange-rate risk were borne by the borrower. By 2008 the ratio of outstanding loans in GDP had increased to 24 per cent and the share of FX loans to 74 per cent of the total stock (see Table 7.3).

The competition in the banking sector was one of the most important

Table 7.3   Outstanding housing and consumer loans backed by mortgage

Year	HUF housing mortgage loans (%)	FX housing mortgage loan (%)	FX equity withdrawal loan (%)	Total (%)	(In billion HUF)	As % of GDP
2000	98	2	0	100	191	1.4
2001	98	2	0	100	327	2.1
2002	98	2	0	100	795	4.6
2003	99	1	0	100	1 532	8.1
2004	84	7	9	100	2 140	10.3
2005	67	19	14	100	2 732	12.4
2006	51	28	21	100	3 545	14.9
2007	38	35	28	100	4 548	17.9
2008	26	41	33	100	6 156	24.0
2009	24	42	33	100	6 304	24.2

Source: Hungarian National Bank.

factors in the expansion of the mortgage sector after the interest-rate subsidy was cut. Banks started to use financial intermediaries (brokers) from 2006, and the mortgage brokers' business expanded very fast. There were 45000–50000 agents by 2006. The competition among the banks had not led to a lower interest rate (no real price competition took place), but banks competed with each other in relaxing the underwriting criteria offering loans with higher loan-to-value ratios and offering loans without a strict income test (Banai et al., 2010). As a consequence, the traditional mortgage loans were increasingly replaced by general loans with real-estate collateral used for consumption, not for housing (mortgage equity withdrawal) and their share had increased to 33 per cent by 2008 (see Table 7.3).

One possible explanation for why the spread was kept very wide is that, in an effort to expand the market, banks wanted to reach households whose income derives from the informal economy, in which case lower interest rates would not have generated substantially more loans. Banks have relied more and more on the intermediary services of brokers (offering higher fees covered by the wide spread) and loosened the underwriting criteria. There were products that did not involve a proper income test or value test. Some banks relaxed the procedures even more by using, for example, the selling price in a contract, instead of the properly assessed property value.

Until 2007, the macroeconomic parameters seemed to justify the expansion. It is true that wages did not increase, but there was not any decrease either, unemployment rates were stable, inflation was under 4 per cent and even the house-price increase was not conspicuous. Everybody seemed to be pleased with the expansion of the market: clients, banks, brokers, developers, even the politicians – and it was a profitable business as the EURIBOR was 2.5 per cent, while the mortgage loan interest rate was 6–6.5 per cent.

Housing-sector Consequences of the Financial Crisis

The mortgage market changed dramatically after September 2008. The weakening Hungarian currency (HUF) caused a radical 30–40 per cent increase of the mortgage repayment for borrowers of FX-denominated loans, which increased the probability of arrears. The majority of the mortgage loans were at variable rates (85 per cent of the loans issued between 2004 and 2008), the payment burden has increased not only by the exchange rate, but because the banks also priced the increased credit risks. The other important factor for the growing number of defaults was increasing unemployment. Due to the general economic recession, increasing unemployment and decreasing household income, the probability of arrears is growing.

The number of clients in the Central Adverse Credit Database (KHR)[7] more than doubled over 2008–9. The stock of the non-performing mortgage loan portfolio (overdue more than 90 days) has increased to 6.3 per cent of the total stock from 2.6 per cent between 2008 and 2009. The share of NPL is 2.5 times higher among the general-purpose mortgage loans than among the housing mortgage loans.

By the end of 2009 there were 46 225 properties (120 per cent more than in 2008) where foreclosure procedures had started or which had been sold to companies that specialized in the management of non-performing loan portfolios ('factor houses'). In 2008, banks started and managed foreclosure procedures in 360 cases per month, while 520 contracts were sold to the NPL management companies. In 2009 the banks started fewer cases by themselves, but sold 850 contracts per month to the NPL management companies.[8] The process of starting foreclosures has slowed down because the real-estate market is frozen, and there is a very limited number of transactions. The danger is that if the market recovers, a mass eviction process will start.

After September/October 2008 banks started to tighten the underwriting criteria; some banks stopped issuing loans in underdeveloped areas (where house prices and the number of transactions are low). Banks typically ceased issuing FX loans from November 2008 onwards. However, only one bank announced that they were not going to issue FX loans, but because of the competition among banks, they withdrew the announcement. The conditions of the different types of loan have also been changed; HUF-based loans with a mortgage-rate subsidy have again become the cheapest. However, the demand for loans has plummeted as well. Banks issued 7 per cent fewer mortgage loans in 2009 than in 2008.

House prices increased just before the new housing policy was implemented as a correction to the downward trend in the 1990s. The mortgage boom had an effect on house prices but did not lead to a house-price bubble. From 2008 to 2009, house prices declined by 12 per cent. Housing transactions have decreased by 40 per cent in 2009 (according to experts' view). Housing construction has fallen since 2008: it decreased by 11 per cent in 2009, but the number of building permits decreased by 36 per cent (see Table 7.1). The expected tightening of the housing-subsidy scheme in 2009 brought forward some housing investments in that year.

Policy Responses to the Housing Crisis

The Hungarian government's response to the crisis focused on managing the fiscal deficit, which was a condition for the IMF loan. The drastic cut in the housing subsidies was part of the fiscal adjustment programme announced in 2009, under which both the interest-rate subsidy and the homeownership demand-side cash grants were suspended, although the cut will be effective in 2010. The government introduced several programmes to lessen the hardship on households caused by the economic recession.

According to a programme introduced in early 2009, the government gives a guarantee for a bridging loan for two years with a reduced payment to households that have difficulty paying their loan because they have lost their job. However, the eligibility criteria are so tight that very few people can take part in the programme. The government was very cautious when it decided about the eligibility criteria in order not to take over the risk of the 'bad loans' issued by the banks. The conditions are the following: (1) unemployment started after 30 September 2008; (2) the loan was taken for their property, which is their principal residence; (3) they do not have another property; (4) the loan is less than 10 million HUF.

From the 24 000 restructured loans, only 3000 were eligible for the government programme. Bank experts argue that the banks offer better solutions for defaulting clients. However, banks reacted to the government model by developing their own solutions, partly because it is administratively simpler for them and financially more advantageous. Consequently, the banks persuaded the clients to choose their workout products for troubled loans, which were received positively by government circles as they wanted more cases to be solved without government fiscal commitments.

There were also other initiatives aimed at easing the hardship caused by the economic crisis. One of them was the setting up of a crisis fund, to which well-off individuals and companies can contribute. The crisis management fund will provide one-off assistance to some 30 000 of Hungary's most disadvantaged families, who lost their job after 1 October 2008, or for whom the loan payment increased more than by 20 per cent.

An 'anti-bank' civil movement has started and has tried to ban the banks' unilateral practice to set the cost of the variable-rate loans and to repossess the defaulted properties. The Lobbying Association of Entrepreneurs (VÉSZ) organized actions against banks and blocked auctions held for repossessed properties. The government put a moratorium on foreclosure in September 2009 until 15 April 2010. However, even the banks have put a lot of effort into their own special workout programmes to reduce the number of foreclosures, but the mortgage brokers, who typically bought the stock of the outperforming loans, wished to continue the foreclosures. The government introduced another programme for local governments that offers preferential loans for them to buy repossessed homes and let the original owner remain as a tenant in the property. Local governments, however, have typically rejected the possibility as there is no long-term guarantee of the central government's support of this newly created rental stock.

In September 2009, banks, as a response to 'anti-bank sentiment', accepted the Code of Conduct under the government's guidelines, in which they introduced more consumer-friendly procedures. This included, for example, stopping the abusive practice of unilateral change of contracts, giving 115 days for the defaulted borrowers to sell their home before it is foreclosed; and placing more emphasis on better information for borrowers.

The government has strictly regulated the mortgage market since March 2010, setting the maximum loan-to-value for HUF loans to 70 per cent, for loans in euros to 60 per cent, and for other foreign-currency loans to 45 per cent, and it has stipulated that the payment ratio of the FX loans should be lower than that of the HUF loans.

CONCLUSION

The president of the Bank Association in a TV report[9] (9 September 2009) argued that the Code of Conduct will solve three problems: first, lack of transparency, that is, banks' procedures for changing the interest rate and the associated fees will be transparent; second, lack of credibility; that is, the bank procedures and rules will not be changed unilaterally after the contract has been signed; and third, lack of symmetry, which means that if the conditions improve, banks will be willing to make appropriate changes favourable to the consumers in time. This announcement indirectly supports the weak-state thesis (Hegedüs, 2009), that is, the private-sector interest dominates the social and economic relations in society. The economic crisis has shown how much the consumers were at the mercy of the banks. The banks realized extra profit in the credit boom of 2002–08 by keeping the spread extremely wide, and introducing innovative loan products, which increased the vulnerability of the economy. In 2004, the government, facing a fiscal deficit, levied an extra tax on the banking sector, which was accepted by the banks without major resistance. The government, the Hungarian Financial Supervisory Authority (HFSA) and the Hungarian National Bank were unable to regulate the market in order to reduce the risk of the portfolio, although it was clear to everybody that expanding borrowing leans on the unpredictable and unseen informal economy.

Very similar processes have taken place in the energy sector, where the privatized energy companies were able to capture the regulatory agency, and have an extraordinary influence on the price-setting process. Recently, as a part of the election campaign (spring of 2010), there was an attack on the regulatory agency because of the unjustified price increase. In the banking sector, the HFSA started to investigate why the banks did not reduce the interest rates when the HNB lowered the base rate, which has been the first attempt by the government to try to improve the efficiency of the regulations in April 2010.

The consequences of the 2008 crisis are more serious, and the government introduced a regulation that, provided it is enforced, will definitely limit the possibility of borrowing on the informal economy in the future. But mass evictions and repossessions have not yet started, and the housing system is not prepared for the management of this social problem, especially due to the lack of a transparent rental and social-rental sector. The safety net is not able to manage the economic hardship caused by the crisis, and those who can not find support from the family and jobs in the informal economy will sink into poverty and homelessness. The fiscal deficit of the government leaves limited possibility for improving the social safety net (expanding the social-rental sector, and increasing the unemployment benefits and income support).

Twenty years after the regime change in the region, housing research is still studying the transformation of the EEHM. There is no simple conclusion to be drawn concerning the nature of the housing system in transitional countries. The concepts of 'weak state', 'targeting paradigm' and the ongoing integration of these countries into Europe define the wide scope of the recently emerged housing regimes, making any generalized typology uncertain. The basic question is when the state will grow strong and will be able to regulate the private sector efficiently in accordance with the needs of a market society. When will we leave non-functioning targeting behind and push back the informal sector in order to improve the operation of the safety net?

NOTES

1. To be unemployed was considered a 'crime', which led to high 'internal unemployment' (meaning many jobs were kept in the companies with low salary and almost 'no work').
2. This approach could be conceived as a 'soft structuralist' approach, which combines 'rational choice' (policy choice or agency choice) with structural elements. In our earlier work we followed this argumentation, for example, in the explanation of 'self-help' housing in Hungary (Hegedüs, 1992).
3. Unemployment was considered a version of crime. Rationing free public services caused social inequalities. It was, however, not only the nomenclature (political elite) that enjoyed 'positional advantages', but people in different key positions at lower levels of the hierarchy could also have access to some of these privileges.
4. The socialist Yugoslavia followed a similar model, combined with self-management of

the state-owned companies. Interestingly enough, China has successfully implemented a model that had several common elements with the pre-transition Hungarian one (see Wang, 2010).

5. See the social aspect of the programmes in Hegedüs and Somogyi (2005), and the technical description in Szalay and Tóth (2003).

6. The Hungarian National Bank report in 2004 (HNB, 2004) evaluated the changes of the mortgage-subsidy programme in the spring of 2002 as unsustainable. However, this was not indicated in the financial report of 2002 (HNB, 2002), which had a section on the role of housing.

7. Borrowers who are late with a loan payment, which is higher than the minimal wage (69 000 HUF/month) for more than 90 days. But people who cheated in the underwriting process can be put on a 'blacklist' of the Central Adverse Credit Database. They are kept in the database for five years.

8. Source: http://index.hu/gazdasag/magyar/2009/11/09/nem_kell_az_allami_segitseg/, accessed 17 January 2010.

9. Source: http://www.noltv.hu/video/1834.html, accessed 17 January 2010.

REFERENCES

Aidukaite, Jolanta (2009), 'Old welfare state theories and new welfare regimes in Eastern Europe: challenges and implications', *Communist and Post-Communist Studies*, **42** (1), 23–39.

Banai, Á., J. Király and M. Nagy (2010), 'End of the golden age in Hungary' (Az aranykor vége Magyarországon), *Közgazdasági Szemle*, **LVII** (2), 105–31.

CSO (2003), 'Housing Survey Database', Central Statistical Office.

Győri, P. (2003), 'A budapesti díjkompenzáció rendszere' (Public utility allowance in Budapest), in Katalin Pallai (ed.), *The Budapest Model: A Liberal Urban Policy Experiment*, Budapest: Central European University Press, pp. 253–60.

Hegedüs, J. (1987), 'Reconsidering the roles of the state and the market in socialist housing systems', *International Journal of Urban and Regional Research*, **11** (1), 79–97.

Hegedüs, J. (1992), 'Self help housing in Hungary', in Kosta Matey (ed.), *Beyond Self-Help Housing*, Profil Verlag, pp. 217–31.

Hegedüs, J. (2007), 'Social housing in Hungary', in Christine Whitehead and Kathleen Scanlon (eds), *Social Housing in Europe*, London: London School of Economics, pp. 105–18.

Hegedüs, József (2009), 'How does "path dependency" explain changes in the Eastern-European Housing Model (EEHM)?', plenary presentation at ENHR Conference in Prague.

Hegedüs, József and Mária Papp (2007), 'Impact of decentralization on public service provision (Case of water sector)', manuscript, MRI.

Hegedüs, J. and E. Somogyi (2005), 'Evaluation of the Hungarian Mortgage Program 2000–2004', in J. Hegedüs and R.J. Struyk (eds), *Housing Finance: New and Old Models in Central Europe, Russia and Kazakhstan*, Budapest: LGI, pp. 177–208.

Hegedüs, J. and E. Somogyi (2006), 'The governance of costs: condominiums mediating conflicts around water affordability', manuscript, Metropolitan Research Institute.

Hegedüs, J. and N. Teller (2007), 'Managing risks in the new housing regimes of the transition countries – case of Hungary', in John Doling and Marja Elsinga (eds), *Home Ownership: Geting In, Getting From, Getting Out*, Amsterdam: IOS Press, pp. 175–200.

Hegedüs, J. and I. Tosics (1996), 'The disintegration of the East European Housing Model', in David Clapham, József Hegedüs, Keith Kintrea and Iván Tosics (eds), *Housing Privatization in Eastern Europe*, Westport, CT: Greenwood Press, pp. 15–56.

Hegedüs, József and Eva Várhegyi (2000), 'The crisis in housing finance in Hungary in the 1990s', *Urban Studies*, **37** (9), 1619–41.

HNB (2002), *Report on Financial Stability*, December.

HNB (2004), *Report on Financial Stability*, April.

Keszthelyiné Rédei, M. and Zs Szabó (2006), 'The level and distribution of incomes in the last one and a half decades in Hungary' (A jövedelmek színvonalának és elosztásának alakulása Magyarországon az elmúlt másfél évtízedben), in *Incomes and Income Distribution*, Budapest: Central Statistical Office.

Kornai, J. (2000), 'What the change of system from socialism to capitalism does and does not mean', *Journal of Economic Perspectives*, **14** (1), 27–42.

Manchin, R. and I. Szelényi (1987), 'Social policy and state socialism', in Gosta Esping-Anderson, Lee Rainwater and Martin Rein (eds), *Stagnation and Renewal in Social Policy*, White Plains, NY: Sharpe, pp. 102–4.

Mitra, Pradeep, Marcello Selowski and Juan Zalduendo (2010), *Turmoil at Twenty (Recession, Recovery, and Reform in Central and Eastern Europe and the Former Soviet Union)*, Washington, DC: World Bank.

Molnár, László and Kristóf Pichovsky (2002), 'Cost of the interest rate subsidy in housing finance and its feasibility' (A kamattámogatási rendszer költségei és finanszírozhatósága a lakáshitelezésben), manuscript, October. Economic Research Institute (Gazdaságkutató Intézet).

Szalay, György and Gyula Tóth (2003), 'A lakásfinanszírozás gyakorlata, kapcsolódó kockázatok és azok kezelése a Magyar bankrendszerben' (The practice of the housing finance, its risk and risk management in the Hungarian bank system), manuscript, Hungarian National Bank, December, accessed 10 May 2010, available at http://www.mnb.hu/Root/Dokumentumtar/MNB/Penzugyi_stabilitas/mnbhu_penzugyi_stab_tanulmanyk/lakasfinanszirozas.pdf.

Szelényi, Iván (1983), *Urban Inequalities under State Socialism*, Oxford: Oxford University Press.

Turner, B., J. Hegedüs and I. Tosics (eds) (1992), *The Reform of Housing in Eastern Europe and the Soviet Union*, London: Routledge.

Vanhuysse, Pieter (2006), *Divide and Pacify: Strategic Social Policies and Political Protests in Post-Communist Democracies*, Budapest: CEU University Press.

Wang, Y.P. (2010), 'The new social housing provision system in China: which welfare regime does it fit?', paper presented at the International Conference on Comparative Housing Research – Approaches and Policy Challenges in a New International Era, Delft, 24–25 March 2010.

Wilensky, H. (1975), *The Welfare State and Equality: Structural and Ideological Roots of Public Expenditures*, Berkeley, CA: University of California Press.

World Bank (1991), *Housing Sector Reform in Hungary*, Washington, DC: World Bank.

8. The impacts of the global financial crisis on housing and mortgage markets in Australia: a view from the vulnerable

Mike Berry, Tony Dalton and Anitra Nelson

INTRODUCTION

By most accounts, the Australian economy and housing sector have been spared the worst effects of the global financial crisis (GFC) that broke out in the USA in 2008 and spread rapidly through most developed economies (IMF, 2009a). What has turned a seemingly localized default crisis in the US residential mortgage markets into 'The Great Recession' has been the combination of low interest rates in the wake of the dot.com boom and 9/11, and the increasing interlinkages and fragility of the financial systems in the USA, Europe and Japan. This meant that many more people than defaulting mortgagor households were negatively affected by the GFC. Economic contraction, rising unemployment and mortgage defaults have reinforced each other in a downward vicious circle. Failures in the banking and shadow banking sectors have spilled out into the real economy, most notably in the US automobile industry, resulting in unprecedented monetary interventions and fiscal stimulus policies by national governments, including those in the large emerging nations (for example China).

Australia, almost alone among the developed economies, has not (yet) gone into 'technical recession'. Although growth has slowed significantly, it was positive in 2009, unlike the forecast 3.9 per cent contraction for developed economies as a whole (IMF, 2009b). The 'credit crunch' that has hamstrung other economies has emanated from the pervasive insolvency threat hanging over commercial and shadow banking institutions, which saw their balance sheets shredded by accumulated investments in 'toxic assets', financial instruments backed by sub-prime mortgages, and heavy involvement (on both sides) in the trade of opaque instruments like credit default swaps. Conversely:

The Australian financial system has, throughout the crisis period, remained resilient. In aggregate, the Australian banks have experienced only a modest decline in profitability. While there has been some diversity of performance across banks, bank losses and impairments across the banking system to date have been lower than in many other countries. The banks are well capitalised and have strengthened their balance sheets further with significant new equity raisings during the past year. (Reserve Bank of Australia, 2009, p. 1)

Nevertheless, as argued below, increasing mortgage arrears and default (albeit from a very low base) have characterized Australia's housing system over the past two years. Moreover, the impacts of these developments fell unequally across the population and (ominously), if global conditions tip the major economies into a second-dip recession or Chinese growth falters, unemployment will rise in Australia, inevitably rebounding in local housing markets and pushing default and repossession rates higher.

This chapter is divided into four sections. First, the relative strengths in Australia's financial system and housing market are examined. Second, we look at the trends in mortgage arrears and possessions, based on both official and market data. Third, we present the results of our primary research by drawing on a survey of and interviews involving a sample of mortgagors threatened with repossession through claims made by mortgagees in the Supreme Courts in the largest states of New South Wales and Victoria. Finally, some comments are made regarding policy developments.

THE AUSTRALIAN CONTEXT

The four largest commercial banks in Australia account for over 80 per cent of outstanding mortgages and initiated over 90 per cent of new mortgages since the GFC began. Mortgage loans represent over half of the on-balance-sheet loan assets of these banks (Reserve Bank of Australia, 2009), which are among a handful of large banks worldwide with a AA or AAA rating from large credit agencies. The main impact of the GFC on Australia's large and small banks, building societies and credit unions (together referred to as 'authorized deposit-taking institutions' or ADIs), was via the wholesale market for funds. Like most banks, Australia's borrowed aggressively in this global market for short-term funds to meet burgeoning domestic demand for mortgage finance that had fuelled a long house-price boom (1997–2007). Borrowing short and lending long left the banks exposed. In 2008 interest-rate spreads rose sharply in these markets and some froze. However, the Australian government moved quickly to guarantee wholesale borrowings of all Australian ADIs, including local subsidiaries of overseas banks. This meant that even during the most intense period of the crisis (late 2008–early 2009), Australian ADIs maintained reasonable access to these financial markets and kept lending. Nevertheless, as Garnaut (2009) argues, for a short period in September 2008, before the government guarantee, Australia's large banks were technically bankrupt due to the global freeze in debt markets. The government also gave a blanket guarantee of all deposits in ADIs (charging a fee only on deposits above A$ 1 million).

The stability of the Australian banking system was also aided by unintended consequences of a competition policy imposed over 20 years ago. From the mid-1980s, successive national governments signalled that they would disallow any mergers between the big four banks in order to preserve competition in lending, especially in mortgage markets. This left big banks free of takeover threats and pressure to grow in order to stave off predators. Consequently, their exposure to the main source of further banking growth – highly risky credit derivatives – was not excessive.

That Australian banks held significant (and growing) mortgage loans on their balance sheets was much less risky than in many other countries, given the chronic undersupply in domestic housing markets, due to very strong underlying demand fundamentals driven by high population growth (and falling household size). Australia did not face the large US housing supply overhang in the wake of the US housing bubble. Strong demographic focus on growing capital cities, notably Sydney and Melbourne, also placed a prop under housing prices in those regions. Although average house prices levelled off in 2007, falling slightly in some sub-markets during 2008, they began rising strongly again in 2009. This trajectory was reinforced by the boost in first homeowners' grants, part of the federal government's fiscal stimulus package. To the extent that housing markets slowed, the main result was fewer transactions, rather than downward price corrections. Hence Australia's financial system has not experienced the shock to bank solvency and lending felt elsewhere in the world.

Although domestic consumption and investment fell, this was not due to any negative wealth effect from house-price changes, but rather to the 54 per cent drop in the stock market (at its worst in mid-2009) and uncertainty and loss of confidence brought on by global economic developments. As a highly open economy, Australia is heavily dependent on export earnings from natural resources and the domestic economy is heavily dependent on its major trading partners' fortunes. In addition, a strong Australian dollar threatens export competitiveness throughout the economy, increasing pressures on import-competing local businesses. This dependence, as noted below, raises the risk of future housing-related problems for marginal homeowners.

MORTGAGE ARREARS AND DEFAULTS IN AUSTRALIA

The relative strength of the mortgage loan books of Australian banks is evident in the fact that non-performing loans rose only slightly to 0.62 per cent as at June 2009, compared to double-digit results for US banks.

Several factors, in addition to those noted above, are responsible for this outcome:

- Lending standards were not reduced to the same extent as elsewhere in the developed world; 'no-doc' or sub-prime loans formed a much less significant part of the Australian market.
- Interest rates did not fall as far as elsewhere, meaning less pressure to lend to potential borrowers with poor repayment capacity.
- Around 80 per cent of residential mortgage loans were variable interest-rate loans, falling by almost 400 basis points in 2008 Q4, reducing repayment stress.
- Australian mortgages are 'full recourse'; after a court-imposed possession order, lenders can claim against all assets of defaulting borrowers.
- Legal requirements on lenders to lend responsibly are more stringent in Australia and the key regulatory agency (the Australian Prudential Regulation Authority) actively supervises the main ADIs.

This rosy picture needs to be qualified: in the very small 'non-conforming mortgage' market, arrears have climbed towards 10 per cent from 2 per cent in 2004; loans originated by wholesale intermediaries also climbed (Berry et al., 2009). Moreover, arrears were higher in some sub-regions, notably Western Sydney.

However, it is clear that these statistics do not reveal a complete picture of the degree of financial stress and the range of effects on households affected by difficulties arising from fallout from the GFC. The consulting firm Fujitsu (2009) tracks mortgagor distress through a rolling Australia-wide sample of 26 000 homebuyers. Mortgagors are classified as being in mild or severe stress, as follows:

- *Mild mortgage stress*: households who are maintaining current mortgage repayments but, in order to do so, re-prioritizing expenditure, borrowing more (e.g. on credit cards or other loans) and/or refinancing existing mortgages.
- *Severe mortgage stress*: households who are in mortgage arrears, are trying to sell their house or refinance, or are facing foreclosure.

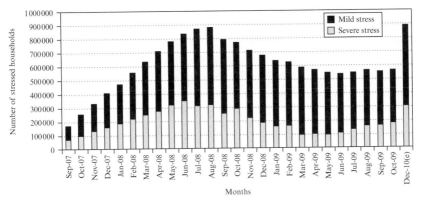

Source: Fujitsu Consulting (2009, p. 13).

Figure 8.1 Mortgage stress over time, Australia

Figure 8.1 summarizes results of this survey.
Several key points can be made here:

- Total estimated mortgage stress peaked in August 2008 at over 800 000 households. Thereafter, due in large part to falling mortgage-interest rates, total and especially severe stress fell.
- The trend turned back up in 2009 Q2 as unemployment crept up towards 6 per cent (from 4.4 per cent in 2007).
- Looking ahead, Fujitsu Consulting forecasts a significant rise in both mild and severe stress by the end of 2010.

This last point is important. Although official unemployment is expected to peak at around under 6 per cent (instead of the 8.5 per cent estimated in the 2009–10 Federal Budget), underemployment is expected to continue rising. Full-time jobs are being replaced by part-time jobs and average hours worked are falling (ABS, 2009). If this trend continues, more households will suffer income losses that will impact negatively on mortgage repayment capacity. Fujitsu Consulting (2009, p. 1) concludes:

> The outlook remains uncertain for homeowners, but it all hinges on unemployment levels through the next few months and expected rises in interest rates later in the year. We now estimate stress by June 2010 will be just over one million households, and those in severe stress perhaps as high as 294,000. There are a number of risk factors linked to higher interest rates and falling net incomes which explain this.

In the year to August 2009, the main perceived causes of mortgage stress were fear of unemployment, drop in income and poor investment returns. However, looking ahead, one quarter of households surveyed expressed concern about future interest-rate-rises, reducing their ability to meet repayments. This proportion rose to half for recent first-time buyers. In October 2009, the RBA raised official interest rates by 25 basis points, the first country to begin to tighten monetary policy. Official rates were raised by a further 50 basis points by the end of 2009. The four large banks passed on more than this rise to mortgagors.

The impacts of changing mortgage stress fall unequally across different social groups and over space. Fujitsu Consulting has identified and tracked a number of categories of mortgagor households.

Focusing on households in severe stress, the Fujitsu data suggest that most came from three categories:

- *Suburban mainstream*: mid-life-course households mainly employed in lower-to-middle income, routine white-collar or blue-collar jobs, living within the major metropolitan regions.
- *Disadvantaged fringe*: households with low-paid blue-collar or service-sector jobs, living in peripheral metropolitan or country regions, with relatively low educational levels, and most of non-Anglo ethnic background.
- *Battling urban*: these younger households are concentrated in lower-socioeconomic, higher-than-average-density suburbs, employed in casual jobs, vulnerable to recurrent unemployment or reduced-hours employment.

Together, these three categories account for over 60 per cent of households estimated to be in mortgage stress. Although less numerous, it is still worth noting that a number of other household types are experiencing stress. This includes small numbers of older and retired higher-income mortgagors, facing repayment difficulties in the wake of the global economic downturn.

Also affected are lower-income seniors, still paying off their mortgages and suffering significant income losses due to the sharp decline in equity markets and other investment areas. Highly geared younger moderate-income households, particularly first-time buyers concentrated on the urban fringe, will likewise face repayment difficulties, given the near certainty of interest-rate rises during 2010. The Reserve Bank Governor, Glenn Stevens (2009), has stated in evidence before the Australian Parliament that official interest rates will be increased towards trend level (some 200 to 300 basis points above the current level) as the economy continues to recover. The Bank's head of research, Anthony Richards (2009) underscored this point by noting that mortgage rates would have to increase to forestall another episode of domestic house-price inflation.

As implied above, mortgage stress across different sub-groups has a definite geographical dimension. Figure 8.2 maps the incidence of total stress (mild and severe) across Melbourne. Broadly speaking, stress is concentrated in lower socioeconomic suburbs in the outer north-west and outer south-east sub-regions; conversely, low levels of stress are concentrated in the more affluent inner-city, bayside suburbs, Mornington Peninsular, outer north-east and middle eastern suburbs.

This map matches well another representing an 'employment vulnerability index'[1] (EVI) developed by the Centre of Full Employment and Equity at the University of Newcastle – see Figure 8.3. Areas with high levels of mortgage stress also house people facing insecure employment prospects.

LIFE AT THE SHARP END: A STUDY OF MORTGAGE POSSESSIONS

Among the small proportion of Australian mortgagors who fall into default, some end up facing legal action by lenders seeking possession of the mortgaged dwelling. Figure 8.4 presents relevant data from the Supreme Courts of NSW and Victoria.

Possession numbers clearly rose in both states over the periods in question. These cases exclude the many more households who faced possession but 'chose' to sell or vacate the dwelling without going through the full legal process. Nevertheless, it could be argued, those households that did lose their houses in this manner are likely to be among those most adversely affected. In order to explore both this process and its impacts on people's lives, we secured the permission of the Chief Justices in both jurisdictions, and the assistance of their staff, in drawing a sample of 90 households to whom we administered a questionnaire survey; all but four respondents were homeowners (rather than investors). In addition, in order to 'drill down' into the issues and problems experienced, we subsequently interviewed 19 survey respondents and nine other mortgage-stressed households (on an individual basis) accessed through community financial advocacy organizations in Melbourne.[2] It should be noted that the survey was indicative only. It is not possible to achieve a representative sample of repossessed mortgagors, given the sensitivities, lack of information and privacy requirements

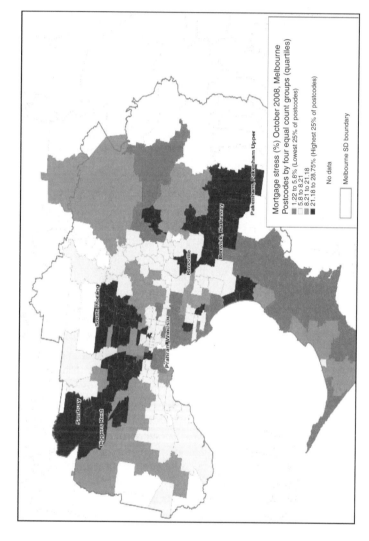

Source: Fujitsu Consulting (2009), special calculation.

Figure 8.2 Mortgage stress in Melbourne

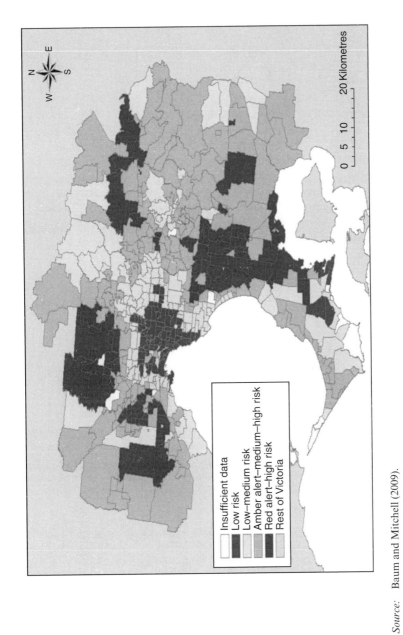

Legend:
Insufficient data
Low risk
Low–medium risk
Amber alert–medium–high risk
Red alert–high risk
Rest of Victoria

Source: Baum and Mitchell (2009).

Figure 8.3   Employment insecurity in Greater Melbourne

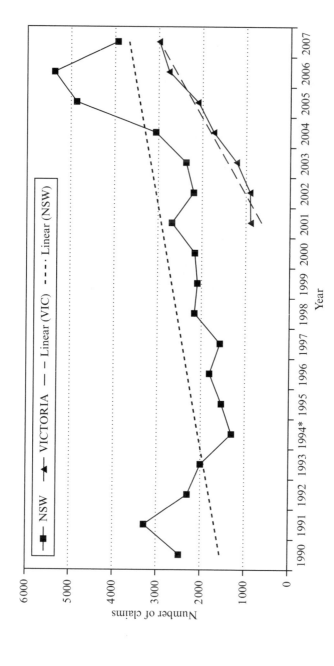

Source: Personal communications with Supreme Court of NSW and Supreme Court of Victoria.

Figure 8.4 Number of applications for claims of possession

involved in this sphere; this limitation must be kept in mind in what follows.

The main survey findings are detailed below, followed by two brief case examples:

- Two-thirds of respondents had annual incomes under the national average (around A$60 000); only 10 per cent had incomes in excess of A$100 000.
- The mean initial mortgage value was A$202 966 and the mean non-housing debt held at the time of the survey was A$43 154 (including average credit card debt of A$6034).
- Two-thirds of respondents had remortgaged their dwellings at least once, a quarter three times or more.
- Two-thirds of respondents had begun to experience mortgage repayment difficulties within three years from purchase, a third between six months and two years.
- The main reason given for falling into arrears was loss of income, either from unemployment or other reasons (63 per cent of cases). A third of respondents as well, or instead, noted high interest rates and other debts as significant trigger factors. Significant numbers pointed to relationship breakdown and/or illness or accident.

Key Themes

Attempting to change the terms of the loan

For respondents who fell into repayment difficulties due to loss of income, 59 per cent attempted to change or renegotiate the terms of their loan with their lenders. Only 7 per cent of attempts were successful. Where other triggers were involved, a similarly low rate of successful renegotiation resulted; in the case of default triggered by high interest rates and other debt burdens, the success rate fell to 4 per cent. Eighty per cent of these respondents attempted to resolve their difficulties by selling their houses; 13 per cent vacated and rented to tenants. Of those who sold up, 35 per cent were still left with unpaid debts. Seventeen per cent of respondents who attempted to change the terms of their loan chose to be considered or were declared bankrupt.

Seeking advice

Fewer than one in five respondents had sought initial financial or related advice before taking out their loans. Conversely, more than half did seek advice once they fell into repayment difficulties; interestingly, the exceptions were borrowers whose main descent into difficulties was sparked by illness or accident (less than one-third). What is not clear is *why* the latter sub-group was less likely to seek advice; did the factor of illness or accident reduce the ability or willingness of people to do so? Where they did seek advice, family or friends figured prominently.

Loan refinancing

Higher-income respondents were much more likely to have refinanced their mortgage loans than lower-income borrowers. Almost half the respondents with annual incomes in excess of A$60 000 refinanced more than once, compared to around a quarter of respondents receiving incomes less than A$40 000 or dependent on unemployment or social security benefits. Conversely, higher-income respondents were less likely than others to consolidate their other debts through refinancing, as were single-person households.

Timing of repayment difficulties

Respondents in receipt of benefits were more likely than those with earned incomes to get into difficulties within six months of taking out the loan. Of those households getting into difficulties between two and three years, two-thirds had incomes in excess of A$60 000.

Main causes of default

Three-quarters of respondents on benefits and 61 per cent of those earning less than A$40 000 nominated loss of income as a cause of their repayment difficulties. This trigger was particularly prevalent in the 45–54 age group (80 per cent in this cohort reported this factor). Higher-income earners were most likely to suffer difficulties due to high interest rates, underestimating the cost of monthly repayments or bearing the burden of other debts. Illness and relationship breakdown were particularly prevalent in borrowers earning more than A$100 000 per annum and in the 35–44 age group. Three-quarters of couples with children faced difficulties because of lost income or unemployment. Almost 40 per cent of single-parent families were struggling due to illness or accident.

Financial coping mechanisms

Both higher-income households and those on benefits relied on greater credit-card use to get by; these households were concentrated in the 35–54 age range. Benefit recipients and middle-income borrowers were most dependent on borrowing from friends and family, as were younger borrowers in the 25–34 range. Couples, both with and without children, and blended families were most reliant on credit cards.

Type of lender

Higher-income respondents were most likely to have borrowed from banks. Conversely, two-thirds of those on benefits or earning less than A$40 000 borrowed from non-bank lenders or 'other' sources. This latter finding might suggest the application of less stringent credit assessment and/or higher interest rates facing more vulnerable households. Banks were most likely to lend to middle-aged-borrowers. Both younger and older respondents were most likely to have taken out loans with non-bank and 'other' lenders.

Selected Interviews

The data presented below are drawn selectively from two of the follow-up interviews conducted with survey respondents who had agreed to be interviewed. All names are fictitious, in order to preserve anonymity. The interviews were aimed at further exploring the triggers and consequences of mortgage default and contrasting the very different circumstances that defaulting households face. For a fuller analysis of all the interview data see Berry et al. (2010).

James's case

James is a doctor working in an Australian country town. He was married with children when taking out a mortgage loan of A$620 000, with a deposit (initial equity) of A$100 000. He also had a business debt of A$450 000 and an investment property (rental house) with another A$400 000 mortgage on it. His other debts, including to the Australian Taxation Office, totalled around A$100 000.

James describes what happened:

> I put all my assets into my ex-wife's name, ex-ex now. And our accountant had, I guess along with everyone else's advice advised us to take out a big debt to avoid tax, etc. So we were right up to the hilt. I'd been working out bush in [NSW country town] for eighteen months, getting up [at 02:30] and running. I'd see the family three days every three weeks. Things started to fall apart, teenage boys, etc. The marriage had been difficult. And [it] came to a situation where I felt I had no financial control, you know? I was being assured by my ex-accountant and ex-wife that all was well, and I'm saying 'I can't keep working 80–100 hours a week'. And so I pulled the pin, basically, and one thing led to another and ended up being that the company was insolvent. So the only way we could have extricated ourselves from the situation was to sell a property, which might have been worth 1.2 [million dollars], eventually being sold for 976 [thousand dollars]. And I'm still going through with the liquidators and the tax office and yeah, that's how it stands at this stage.

James was hit by the perfect storm. His heavily indebted business faced bankruptcy at the same time as his marriage was failing and he was forced to cut back on his medical practice. He and his ex-wife sold the family house in a slow real-estate market to reduce debt that was largely in James's name. In answer to whether he was in bankruptcy proceedings, he replied:

> No, I'm trying to avoid that. What's happened is that it was an acrimonious separation, a delay in property sales eventually forced the bank to take action on me because the debt was all in my name. Well I think we probably lost 10–15 per cent. We sold in a recession in January of this year [2009], well February actually. And I'd been trying to persuade the ex-wife to sell it two years ago before the crash started, because I could see it was coming but I had no control of my assets. I sabotaged myself by putting all my assets in my ex's name.

In answer to where he was currently living, he replied:

> Well at the moment I'm living in a A$100 a week bed sitter until my situation clarifies. I'm still earning about A$2–3000 a week. But yeah I have no credit. I don't have a credit card, I can't borrow, I'm all tied up in debt.

James falls within the Fujitsu 'exclusive professionals' category of at-risk groups. His complex situation demonstrates that a relatively high income is no guarantee against the incidence and impact of severe mortgage stress. He did not initially seek professional advice on his housing-related borrowings, beyond family and friends. The causes he ascribed to his difficulties were: reduced employment income, relationship breakdown and too many other debts. With respect to the last point, he noted that he depended on credit card borrowing once he initially went into mortgage arrears.

Jennifer's case

Jennifer, married with three children, purchased a house jointly with her husband for A$280000. The mortgage was around A$240000. Her husband worked full time in the construction sector, earning about A$1200 per week for long hours worked. As a result of recurrent episodes of domestic violence, associated with her husband's alcohol and other substance abuse, Jenny eventually left the family home and moved into temporary rental accommodation. Her husband ceased making mortgage repayments, while spending several periods in gaol and rehabilitation programmes. The mortgagee gained possession and sold the house for A$30000 less than the original purchase price.

Yeah, so anyway I then left, after counseling and that sort of thing, I took him back in regards to living separately under one roof. So that we wouldn't lose the house and we could separate in a more mature way and organize the finances and the house and all that sort of stuff. At the time it sounded like a fantastic idea, but it just went absolutely horrific. There was violence and you know, I had to leave the house. I could only take one of the kids, the police were involved, he had two kids, I had one for a week, it was just messy. The police wouldn't get involved because they thought it was a Family Court issue which [ignored the fact that the] Family Court wasn't [yet] involved. Then it was [an] AVO [apprehended violence order against husband] and I eventually got a house to rent, several months later, and then the violence continued by him stalking, slashing my tyres, burning my fence, he'd turn up at places that I was at, you know. He was hiding in my backyard and would make appearances in the middle of the night, and so it goes on. So then he went to gaol at one point for four to six weeks, then he went to rehab for, I think it was three months and then he came out and did the same things again, so he went inside for I think it was nearly three months or something, and came out, did the same stuff again and to save himself from going back to gaol he's, I found out today, he's just got out of six months rehab in Sydney.

Well initially he left so I had the house and he continued to pay for a month, he continued to pay the mortgage and then when he moved back in he continued to pay, then I left and he said he was going to pay it and I said 'well that's fine'. I don't want anything from the house. I don't want, I didn't want his superannuation. All I wanted for him to do was sign me out of the mortgage so I could walk away. He didn't do that and he didn't pay the mortgage through all that period of time. So unfortunately, I'm left with whatever debt is now left because it's only just been auctioned off. It was taken over by [prominent mortgage lender named] and it was only auctioned two weeks ago for much less than what we bought it for back in the day. Yeah.

Although Jennifer was co-owner and joint signatory on the mortgage documentation, she has found it virtually impossible to get assistance or even information from her lender. Other debtors have, however, found their way to her door.

Honestly, I have not seen one piece of paperwork. No one has seen me. The only people I have seen are debt collectors coming and saying, you know, 'why haven't you paid?' and that's it. I don't have any bank statements. It was not coming out of my account. I have no connection to the account it's coming out of. It was done through his side of things and unfortunately I was the only contact they could find.

No, I didn't have any help. Just sort of, the bank didn't really help me out. I tried to contact them a couple of times and they weren't helpful because I didn't have a password, and I didn't, you know, it was under his account so I couldn't, had no control over what happened there. In relation to, you know, even finding out if he was actually paying the mortgage. And I didn't have any money. I left the relationship with no money. And three kids, and you know, they were at that stage, 18 months, four and six or nearly seven. So, you know they, I couldn't exactly dump them all and go an' get a high paying job. It's not that easy.

Jennifer, at the time of the interview, was renting a house with her three children, dependent on social security benefits and studying to complete a nursing degree. She was being pursued for outstanding amounts owing to her bank, the local council and other debtors. She received little or no information or assistance from her lender and did not seek or receive any financial or legal advice during the period of mortgage distress. In terms of the Fujitsu analysis, her case probably best fits the 'battling urban' category, but clearly her particular personal circumstances were heavily affected by the nature of an abusive marriage, limited employment opportunities and the pressing nature of child-care responsibilities. The absence of adequate advice and advocacy resources and the lack of onus on the lender to provide either adequate information or timely assistance for someone in her position were also prevalent factors in intensifying the impacts.

POLICY DEVELOPMENTS

The House of Representatives Inquiry into Home Loan Lending Practices and Processes instigated by the Standing Committee on Economics, Finance and Public Administration (House of Representatives, 2007, pp. xv–xvi) resulted in a report with three main recommendations to improve home mortgage lending and ameliorate risks of defaults, that is for:

- the Australian Bureau of Statistics (ABS) to expand data collection on repossessions of homes, requiring more detailed information from lenders and the courts;
- the federal government to take over responsibility and expand the regulation of credit to all lenders and mortgage brokers in order to simplify and unify legislation and supervision;
- comprehensive access to external dispute resolution to address complaints, easing current eligibility limits and specifying the lifting of the Banking and Financial Services Ombudsman's limit of A$280 000 to A$500 000.

With the change of government at the October 2007 federal election, the Treasury prepared a Green Paper, *Financial Services and Credit Reform* (Australian Treasury, 2008), advocating Commonwealth control of credit, especially home mortgages. This reform was expected to overcome widely agreed-upon deficiencies relating to the complexity, lack of uniformity and duplication of effort under distinct state and territory rules. The Green Paper (ibid., p. 9) advanced a national agenda to unify and simplify the sector by dealing with gaps in the regulation of consumer credit and protect all consumers with external debt resolution, to license providers of credit and require minimum standards of conduct. During 2009 a start was made to implement these measures in the form of national consumer credit regulation (ASIC, 2009).

Plans to bring mortgages under uniform national legislation subjecting mortgage brokers, non-ADI and ADI lenders to consistent licensing requirements, and minimum standards of conduct based on advice provided to borrowers have been implemented relatively quickly. On 27 April 2009 a draft bill was released providing a national licensing system, with minimum standards for education, qualifications and training, and requirements that lenders only offer loans appropriate to the borrowers' debt-servicing capacity (Woolrich, 2009). The Australian Securities and Investment Commission (ASIC) has increased its staff by 200 to register the 10 000 suppliers of credit to the 5.7 million Australian households that have debts, including 2.9 million with mortgages. Similarly, legislation long in development took effect in late 2009, introducing mandatory licensing throughout the sector of broking activities, attempting to ensure transparency, minimum qualifications, greater responsibility for objectively assessing debt-servicing capacities of borrowers (evidence of income and so on) and reasonable fee structures. In May 2009 the government announced that ASIC would start to regulate margin lending by categorizing it as a financial product under the Corporations Act. 'New laws to provide national regulation of the A$21 billion margin loan industry will place curbs on investors using the family home as security for taking on risky levels of debt to buy shares,' stated the Australian Broadcasting Corporation (Ryan, 2009). Disclosure of fees, appropriate advice and assessment of debt-servicing capacity are now required of lenders as well as improving borrowers' access to external debt resolution.

Berry et al. (2010) present detailed discussion of other relevant policy options.

CONCLUSION

To the extent that they are implemented, it remains to be seen how effective the measures outlined above will be. If forecasts of rising mortgage distress provided by market analysts such as Fujitsu Consulting prove accurate, policy in this area will be severely tested. Impacts will vary across households, dependent on a range of socioeconomic, demographic and individual factors. The trend to increasing economic inequality, expressed spatially and in changing labour-market structures, also reinforces the pattern of uneven impacts identified in our research. At the very least, government regulators and policy makers will need to more closely monitor actual patterns of mortgage distress on the ground and be prepared to revise and develop appropriate policies to mitigate the most extreme adverse outcomes, even in a country that to date has escaped the worst economic fallout from the global financial crisis and 'Great Recession'.

NOTES

1. This index is a weighted average of three indicators: the proportion of people employed in occupations vulnerable to employment loss; the proportion of people employed who do not have post-secondary educational qualifications; and the proportion of people working full time (for details see, Baum and Mitchell, 2009, Appendix A).
2. Details of the survey and interviews are presented in the final report of the project funded by the Australian Housing and Urban Research Centre (see Berry et al., 2010).

REFERENCES

Australian Bureau of Statistics (2009), *Labour Force Australia, September 2009* (cat. no. 6202.0, Canberra).
Australian Securities and Investment Commission (2009), 'National consumer credit regulation', available at http://www.asic.gov.au/credit, accessed 28 July 2009 and 15 August 2009.
Australian Treasury (2008), *Financial Services and Credit Reform: Improving, simplifying and standardising financial services and credit regulation* (Green Paper, June), Canberra: Commonwealth of Australia.
Baum, Scott and Bill Mitchell (2009), *Red Alert Suburbs: An employment vulnerability index for Australia's major urban regions*, Newcastle, NSW: Centre of Full Employment and Equity, University of Newcastle.
Berry, M., T. Dalton and A. Nelson (2009), 'Mortgage default in Australia: nature, causes and social and economic impacts', positioning paper, Melbourne: Australian Housing and Urban Research Institute, available at http://www.ahuri.edu.au.
Berry, M., T. Dalton and A. Nelson (2010), 'Mortgage default in Australia: nature, causes and social and economic impacts', final report, Melbourne: Australian Housing and Urban Research Institute, available at http://www.ahuri.edu.au.
Fujitsu Consulting (2009), 'Anatomy of Australian mortgage stress: October 2009 stress-o-meter update', Sydney: Fujitsu Consulting, available at http://www.fujitsu.com.au.
Garnaut, Ross (2009), *The Great Crash of 2008*, Melbourne: Melbourne University Press.
House of Representatives (2007), *Home Loan Lending: Inquiry into Home Loan*

Lending Practices and Processes Used to Deal with People in Financial Difficulty (September report), Standing Committee on Economics, Finance and Public Administration, Canberra: Parliament of the Commonwealth of Australia.

International Monetary Fund (2009a), *Global Financial Stability Report: Responding to the Financial Crisis and Measuring Systemic Risk*, July, Washington, DC: International Monetary Fund.

International Monetary Fund (2009b), *World Economic Outlook April 2009: Crisis and Recovery*, April, Washington, DC: International Monetary Fund.

Reserve Bank of Australia (2009), *Financial Stability Review*, Sydney: Reserve Bank of Australia.

Richards, A. (2009), 'Housing market developments', paper presented to Committee for the Economic Development of Australia, Housing Forum, Sydney, 29 September.

Ryan, P. (2009), 'Government announces margin lending crackdown', available at http://www.abc.net.au/news/stories/2009/05/07/2562989.htm, accessed 7 May 2009.

Stevens, G. (2009), 'Opening statement to Senate Economic Reference Committee, Parliament of Australia', available at http://www.rba.gov.au/Speeches/2009/index.html, accessed 28 September 2009.

Woolrich, N. (2009), 'Govt to establish consumer credit laws', Lateline (Business) ABC, available at http:// www.abc.net.au/lateline 27 April 2009, accessed 7 May 2009.

9. Rebuilding housing policies in response to the current crisis. Is homeownership the solution?

David Thorns

INTRODUCTION

Understanding the current housing crisis requires a focus on both economic and social changes. The predominant mode of analysis has focused on the economic determinants of the collapse of the financial and housing markets, first in the USA and then flowing into global markets and causing house prices to fall. As a consequence there have been mortgagee sales and housing stress accompanied by a threat to, and decline in, rates of homeownership in a number of countries. The social consequences of the crisis, and the impact on the attitudes and values that underpin housing investment, have been less prominent in the analysis. The chapter begins from the position that housing is a set of services, a cluster of activities both material and non-material, which means that sentiments and feelings, along with calculations as to the economic value of a house, are central to an understanding of the place of housing within the economy and society more generally. Further, recent research and theory have drawn attention to understanding housing within a framework of ecosystems that are complex, contextualized and exhibit multiple equilibrium states (see Crabtree, 2009; Olsson et al., 2004).

To understand the social interaction and mediation around the development of housing forms that now occur increasingly within global and local processes requires a comparative analysis of housing that is situated within a close analysis of the context in which meaning is created. To fully appreciate this we need to recognize the influence of cultural, social, economic, environmental and spatial relationships. Such an approach draws our attention to an understanding that 'What constitutes a house and or a home points to different but overlapping interpretations of the nature, function and purpose of this significant domestic space' (Mangin et al., 2008, p. 6).

Research and analysis must thus develop a more nuanced and subtle approach to enable us to unravel these relationships and allow the creation of a new understanding in what is a fluid and changing central 'space' where our everyday life is engaged. Thinking this way, we see that a 'house is much more than just a physical structure placed on a piece of land – it is a home – and as such constitutes a core institution of many societies (for example, Britain, US, Canada, NZ, Australia)' (ibid.).

This shift in understanding allows us to appreciate the great variety of housing and home spaces – from the homeless through to residual state/ public tenancies often on welfare benefits and with multiple social and other problems/challenges through a variety of ownership submarkets, to gentrifying urban areas and new and older forms of restrictive entry through covenants and zoning practices through to gating (Dupuis and Thorns, 2008). In addition there is a variety of forms of tenure including private and public rental, institutional mortgage arrangements for individual purchase to forms of cooperative and not-for-profit forms of ownership often associated with institutional structures such as not-for-profit housing associations and other cooperative and co-ownership schemes.

An approach that opens us to an understanding of the experience of home/housing by various household members is not necessarily constant and unchanging but is likely to be affected by the age, stage in the life course/cycle, gender, social class and ethnicity of the individuals and households. For housing to be translated into home, a social process occurs that consists of relationships between household members in which services are provided and received and reciprocities established. Such relationships may be the product of mutual agreement or may be arrived at through a mixture of agreement and domination and exploitation (Perkins and Thorns, 2003).

THE NATURE OF THE CRISIS – CONTEXT, ORIGINS AND EFFECTS

The current crisis originated in the USA. It was not just a consequence of the sub-prime failures although this was critical to the most recent collapse of the US housing bubble. The origins lay in a system that encouraged people to take on mortgage payments and debt that increased both their and the financial system's vulnerability. The increased income inequality over the 1980s and 1990s created affordability problems and a growing gap between those who could afford owner occupation and those in the lower income bands who were increasingly forced to rent. The shift from seeing housing as shelter to seeing it as a source of capital gain and thus a speculative good, and the encouragement to 'extract' capital through remortgaging on the basis of the assumed capital gain allowed debt to rise and thus increased vulnerability to losses if a downturn occurred (Stone, 2009). Further, the reorganization of the banking and finance industry to an industry increasingly dominated by global players rather than by locally based institutions that had both knowledge of, and commitment to, the local community had significant consequences for households and communities. The distancing of decision-making from the local setting assisted in eroding trust in the system as it moved judgements and responsibilities from local to more globally oriented players, breaking a bond between the lenders and the local community within which bankers were significant and largely trusted citizens. In New Zealand, with financial deregulation in the late 1980s, the banking system has been restructured from a range of small and locally connected institutions into one dominated by four major banks, all currently Australian owned. A survey in late 2009 showed wide public loss of trust in the banks, which were seen as more focused on profits than on their customers. The loss of trust and confidence in the financial system and other institutions is a very important aspect of the current crisis that has been identified as a systemic failure of late modernity (Beck, 1992a, 1992b, 1996a, 1996b).

The way that the housing finance and property market operated between 2000 and 2007 thus contributed to increases in debt that then flowed into a credit crisis, as when the slump occurred and the 'debts' were called in it was shown that much of this was speculative and thus there were no realizable assets to cover the 'debt' (Case, 2009). Financial institutions, as they were unable to meet their obligations, began to fail. Individuals and countries were living beyond their means on credit and spending against future growth in values that, when disrupted by the ending of the boom, created havoc in the financial and housing markets. The increase through this period in the number of individuals and households routinely using wealth extraction for managing ongoing expenditure both increased their risk and exposure to downturns in the market and had major implication for savings, asset growth and retirement provision.

The outcomes this crisis generated were financial failures that spread rapidly across the globe and led to a recession and financial and banking failures requiring considerable intervention by governments to bail out the sector and prevent further collapses. The recession has pushed up unemployment rates, with the EU and US average now over 9 per cent. The collapse of purchasing power that this has created can be seen in weaker consumer 'confidence' and spending, which has led to a global crisis in many industries, with consequent job losses. In the housing and property markets prices have declined, with loss of equity, an increase in mortgagee sales and a significant decline in new housing construction that is likely to put pressure on house prices and so stimulate another upswing as the recession recedes. One of the current consequences is to reduce affordability as both a higher deposit and a tightening of lending criteria are now being required, and there is a squeeze on savings with low interest rates. Increased pressure on the rental market could push up prices, so expanding the number of those who are captured or trapped renters – those currently trying to enter markets.

NEW ZEALAND EXPERIENCE

In settler societies such as New Zealand and Australia, housing policies and construction have been driven by migration rather than rural–urban internal movement of the population. Homeownership was seen in these societies as part of the 'nation-building' process and the creation of stable engaged citizens. In New Zealand parliamentary debates around the 1919 Housing Act suggested that 'home ownership would create "better sentiment in the people" . . . kill discontent and disloyalty, and lead people to be moral and self denying' (NZ Parliamentary Debates, 1919, 371–4). Commitment to individual homeownership thus has a long history of support (Thorns, 2009; Davidson, 1994; Ferguson, 1994). A strong ideology of homeownership has been consistently supported by politicians. Owner occupation is the tenure of choice, as it has been seen as a good way to encourage citizenship as well as to provide shelter (Thorns, 2008). Homeownership is still seen as a central part of growing up and becoming an adult and successful member of New Zealand society (Ansley, 2001, pp. 18, 20).

Such a view is encouraged by a real-estate industry, development lobby and from data that show that housing has consistently returned as good as if not better rates of return than other forms of investment activity. The Real Estate Industry of New Zealand house price index shows that this has more than tripled since 1992, which represents a 11.8 per cent annual return over the last 17 years. This rate is despite fluctuations caused by booms and busts. In contrast, the share market has returned only an average of 7 per cent over the last 20 years (*The Press*, 16 September 2009).

A further indication of the economic importance of housing assets within the New Zealand economy is to look at the size of the asset value relative to other aspects of the economy. This shows that the housing asset value as at December 2008 was $617 billion, over three times New Zealand GDP, while at the same date merchandising trade exports were valued at around $40 billion. Housing assets at this time were 15 times the annual value of exports. The NZX share market was at $52 billion, managed funds were at $74 billion and the Reserve Bank estimated that corporate assets were $300 billion (PricewaterhouseCoopers 2009).

House prices appreciated on average around 50 per cent during the 1990s and then during the most recent boom at around 200 per cent between 2000 and 2007. The last time this rate was achieved was in the 1970s. This was the period when the property bubble really began to have a significant impact on how some, at least, viewed their property. High inflation rates increased the nominal values, encouraged speculation and redistributed wealth, opening up greater gaps between those who owned and those who rented (Grimes et al., 2007).

The pattern over the past two decades is one of two booms and two slumps. The first boom was from 1994 to 1998 and the second from 2002 through to 2008. Housing speculation fuelled inflation and was not significantly affected by the attempts by the Reserve Bank to cool the market through increasing the official cash rate (OCR). Increases in the OCR pushed up mortgage interest rates but, due to the number of two- and three-year mortgages, was limited in its affects. Similarly, the cutting of the OCR by the Reserve Bank in mid-2008 to 2.5 per cent did not have an immediate impact on pulling the economy out of its recession. However, the New Zealand recession has been shorter than in many of New Zealand's trading partners and was declared to be over after a year in mid-2009. But interest rates in New Zealand have attracted speculative money and pushed the exchange rate up from 50 cents to the US dollar at the beginning of 2009 to around 72 cents in December 2009 (Government House Prices Unit, 2008; Macfie, 2009).

Significant increases in housing wealth over the last 12 years have occurred, with transfers into housing of wealth especially for existing owners from the new entrants to the market and those migrating to New Zealand and entering the local market for the first time. The impact on wealth distribution has thus been uneven and has contributed to the widening of the income and wealth distribution rather than a narrowing (Arcus and Nana, 2005). One of the consequences of the increasing value in housing assets is that although household debt has increased from 33 per cent to 149 per cent of household disposable income, net wealth has grown from 219 per cent of disposable income in 1982 to 403 per cent by 2002 and 604 per cent by 2007 (Henderson and Scobie, 2009). This has meant that those deemed 'vulnerable' as their debt servicing is greater that 30 per cent of gross income was 6.2 per cent for non-partnered households in 2004 rising to 12.1 per cent in 2008 and for partnered 7.9 per cent to 18.4 per cent. The proportion that had both negative net wealth and 30 per cent debt servicing was only 1.8 per cent and 1.1 per cent in 2008. In both cases 'vulnerability' has increased by 2008 but only by a relatively small percentage (approximately 5000 extra households in each case) due to the positive impact of net wealth growth). A prolonged and steep decline in house prices and values would be needed to significantly increase overall vulnerability. However, the figures tend to underestimate the impact on recent entrants to the market and the impact of high loan-to-value ratios, which were a feature of the most recent lending during the latest housing boom (Henderson and Scobie, 2009).

In New Zealand, one trigger for the downturn was the collapse of finance companies that had invested in residential apartments being developed by property developers as investments. Many of these started to have problems because they were unable to generate cash flow as buyers became fewer and the market began to unravel. In some cases this was exacerbated by the finance companies also being exposed to high-risk loans that failed in the consumer finance market. As the recession occurred in late 2008 the number of people unable to meet loan repayments increased and mortgagee sales occurred, but numbers are still small. In New Zealand the major trading banks are Australian owned and were not significantly affected by the sub-prime failures as they had not invested in the 'toxic loans'. However, they had been lending money for housing with minimal levels of security, so feeding the boom. They have now tightened lending to require 20 per cent deposits rather than 5 per cent, and so contributed to a slowing of new construction. There has been a 50 per cent decrease of lending for new housing starts during the latest boom and this is now starting to be reflected in a rising market where shortages are contributing to rising prices. Falling house values and the consequent loss of equity have resulted in some homeowners experiencing negative equity.

A fall of around 10 per cent in house prices has been sustained since the height of the boom but recent market movements are showing that much of the fall by the end of 2009 has been regained. Unemployment has risen, but off a low base of 3.3 per cent in the middle of 2008 to 5 per cent at the end of 2009. It is predicted to continue to rise to around 6.5 per cent in 2010 depending on the rate of recovery. This is despite the Reserve Bank indicating that New Zealand was officially out of recession by October 2009. However, the impact of the rising government deficit and debt repayments, both public and private, create the need to borrow money on the global market and show that the impacts of the global recession could be felt over the next five to ten years. This is due to the level of repayment of public and private debt. The response from the current government is a programme of fiscal austerity and the cutting of government expenditure, which has already resulted in redundancies within the state sector and moves to increase competition and potentially the privatization of some areas of government activity and services.

The current revival in house-price levels is fuelled by shortages of supply, and migration. Building activity from mid-2008 to 2009 has fallen by 6.5 per cent to its lowest level in seven years. There are now some signs of revival as the rate of building consents is increasing. Commercial building also declined, but at a slower rate with a 2.5 per cent fall. Migration has surged during the recession, in part boosted by returning New Zealanders due to the rise in unemployment overseas which has lifted demand for housing at a time when building was low and fewer houses were being offered for sale.

SOCIAL AND CULTURAL ASPECTS

One of the central social and cultural understandings is that homeownership is about more than simply the accumulation of wealth. Homeownership is linked to 'ontological security'. This concept, originally developed by Laing (1969), refers to an individual's sense of safety and well-being, a feeling of reassurance in an uncertain world. Giddens (1990) picks this up in his work and sees it referring to an individual's sense of certainty and continuity in their social and material worlds. Dupuis and Thorns (1998) use this concept to explain the strength of the homeownership sentiment. It gives people a sense of having a place where they feel secure in an increasingly uncertain and less secure world. In property-owning countries this sense of security is invariably linked with ownership of land and house, and reflects a sentiment that one's home is one's castle! Homeownership is seen to bring stability, pride in the local area and commitment to neighbourhood activity, which can generate and sustain social capital (Ansley, 2001). Thus a decline in this tenure status is often viewed as a cause for concern by political parties and governments, as shown by the New Zealand Labour Government's *Housing Strategy* (2005) and the present Centre Right Coalition Government's housing policies.

The New Zealand rate of homeownership reached 66.7 per cent by the mid-1950s as a result of strong government support through State Advances Corporation loans to homeowners buying their first home and their ability to capitalize the family benefit to contribute towards the deposit. The rate climbed further through the 1970s and 1980s, to peak finally at 72.9 per cent in 1991. Since then the rate has continued to fall, reaching 62.7 per cent in 2006, and is predicted to reach 61.3 percent by 2016. The pattern of decline is not even across the country, with a faster rate of decline in the Auckland region, where the rate in 2001was 64.8 per cent. This is predicted to fall to 58 per cent by 2016 (DTZ, 2005, 2007). These falls are creating a rising demand for rental accommodation.

Complicating the picture somewhat is the fact that in 2006 family trust ownership was identified, previously these arrangements would have been hidden within the owner-occupation category. This form of ownership represented 12 per cent of all tenure in 2006, showing how they have grown in popularity as a way of protecting the family asset base accumulated mostly from house ownership (Thorns, 2008).

Property owning for investment purposes expanded during the most recent boom; this form of investment became popular for baby-boomers with spare cash as they moved into the cash-rich and empty-nest stage of their life course, having discharged the mortgage on their family home. A by-product of this shift was that rents rose more slowly than the cost of owning, so did not become as unaffordable as buying a house (Thorns, 2008, 2009). A significant gap between the costs of renting and buying opened up and contributed to the decline in homeownership. A further factor affecting the cost of new construction was that it concentrated in the middle to upper levels of the market rather than the low-cost starter homes. With the average size of households falling but average floor area and number of bedrooms increasing, the demand for housing space from middle- to upper-income dual-earning households was a factor driving up the price of new housing (Statistics New Zealand, 2007a, 2007b). In the latest housing boom, building focused on meeting the needs of those upgrading housing rather than low-cost starter homes for first-time buyers.

A decline in homeownership rates is now being observed in a number of homeowning countries, including Japan, Australia and New Zealand. The trend has not, however, been even across all age groups but is particularly pronounced in the rising cohort of younger people (Hirayama and Ronald, 2007; Burke, 2007; Morrison, 2008; Yates, 2007).

In New Zealand, rates have declined unevenly across the age groups, showing that the impact is being felt most by those between 25 and 29 and 30 and 34. Between 1986 and 2006 homeownership rates fell 17.9 per cent in the 25–29 age group and 17.7 per cent in the 30–34 age group (Government House Prices Unit, 2008). The next largest falls were in the 35–39 group at 15.5 per cent and the 40–44 group at 12.2 per cent. Homeownership for these younger age groups is thus lengthening, with consequences for when they are likely to be mortgage free. Such trends produce quite a different profile of wealth acquisition from that of those who entered homeownership in their early twenties. In the period between the census of 2001 and 2006, the only group to increase their rate of homeownership was those over 75 (MSD, 2008).

The structuring of tenure thus needs to be disaggregated so that cohort effects are clearer. One significant cohort effect that has been the subject of attention is the movement of the baby-boom generation, which has high homeownership rates into retirement. Important research questions here focus on accumulation through the life course of housing wealth and the impact of this on retirement years, wealth distributions, intergenerational equity and transfers and release through reverse-equity mortgages (Forrest and Murie, 1995; Hamnett et al., 1991; Thorns, 2008). The current projections suggest that the number of owner-occupier households in older age groups will increase and those under 40 are likely to decline by 17 per cent by 2016 (DTZ, 2005). Younger households have been particularly affected as the cost of entering the housing market has risen, with increases from 2000 to 2005 of 39–60 per cent (Grimes et al., 2007) and from 1996 to 2005 from 88 per cent to 131 per cent being sustained in the Auckland regional market. These changes may represent a lagged or permanent structural change. However, further research will be required to answers this question adequately (Morrison, 2008).

New Zealand has significant differences in homeownership rates by ethnicity. In 1986 the European rate was 76.4 per cent and by 2006 this had declined to 70.5 per cent. However, for the Maori population the rates were 49.2 per cent and 42.5 per cent in 2006 and for Pacific peoples the fall was from 44.4 per cent down to 34.1 per cent. So a similar trend has occurred across all major ethnic groups but starting from a different and lower base. A declining rate further opens up the gap between those owning across the major ethnic groups that comprise the New Zealand population. The cost of entering appears to be the most crucial factor across all groups, as these have been rising steeply during the latest boom period, up by 60 per cent from 2000 to 2005 and over the ten years from 1996–2005 up by 131 per cent.

In New Zealand research, one outcome of these changes identified is the emergence of an intermediate market defined as working households unable to purchase a dwelling at the lower-quartile house price under standard bank-lending criteria. The relative size of the intermediate housing market (IHM) is a measure of housing affordability for first-time buyers (DTZ, 2007, 2008). This group falls outside state assistance but has too low an income and accumulation potential to access the homeownership market as the cost of entering is prohibitive. The size of the intermediate market provides an indicative measure of the number of households being left behind by the housing market as they can no longer afford to buy a dwelling. The data show that the size of this market fell from 1996 to 2001, largely due to a 3.3 per cent fall in interest rates. However, between 2001 and 2006, due to a combination of higher house prices, up by 72 per cent, and a steady increase in interest rates, this segment of the market grew by 239 per cent (DTZ, 2007, 2008). The IHM numbers, therefore, more than doubled, from 72 300 to 187 000 between 2001 and 2006. Of this total 36 per cent were in Auckland. The IHM is concentrated in single- and two-parent households where there are two or fewer income sources, the reference person is under 40 and in a lower-income occupation. The size of this sector of the market is predicted to grow considerably over the next decade to 2016 as the recent boom and emerging downturn in the economy and housing market take effect. The total estimated numbers by 2016 could be between 165 100 and 282 332, depending on whether an assumption of low or high nominal house-price growth is made (DTZ, 2008).

ISSUES OF TRUST AND RISK

The financial meltdown and global economic crisis can be seen as yet another example of a systemic failure that appears to be increasingly a feature of late modernity. These failures show how greater risks are now surfacing and how these have contributed to the erosion of trust in the key institutions that provide social stability and cohesion. They encourage us to seek individual solutions to mitigate our risks and increase our sense of security; thus the increase in popularity of electronic alarms to guard against 'home invasion' and gated communities to ensure that there are 'people like us' in our neighbourhood (Dupuis and Thorns, 2008, 2009).

One of the most influential theorists in the sociological literature on risk has been Ulrich Beck, whose body of work has set the parameters of the debate around the nature of risk in contemporary Western societies (Beck, 1992a, 1992b, 1996a, 1996b). Beck's general thesis is that risk is the key feature that sets apart the current period of 'reflexive modernity' from earlier 'simple modernity' (or industrial society) and has been the basis of the fundamental changes that have occurred since the 1970s. Beck is not arguing that risk is new. There have always been risks. What is new is that the risks that characterized modernity have given way to the 'manufactured uncertainties' of late modernity (Beck, 1999). Beck notes the difference between modernity, when wealth and 'goods' were produced, and later modernity, when the production of 'goods' is accompanied simultaneously with the production of 'bads', or risks. In this literature the risks emanate largely from two sources: high-tech risks and ecologically based risks. What the current economic and financial crisis indicates is that we also need to extend this understanding to embrace these new risks. The character and complexity of these systemic risks have led Beck to describe the risk society as 'a catastrophic society' where catastrophes are brought about by the repeated crises of science and technology in which no one seems to be 'in control' any longer. The recent financial crisis and subsequent global recession is yet another example of the systemic risk of late modernity that undermines trust in our key institutions and the assumed knowledge of the experts that 'guide' our systems. Up until a few weeks before the meltdown in 2007 experts and central bankers were still indicating that the boom would continue and predictions of continuing growth were guiding policy-making. This certainty evaporated quickly, to be replaced by increasing levels of uncertainty.

In the latest crisis, failed experts were the financial experts and bankers (in the public and private sector) – the 'masters of the universe on Wall Street and in the city of London – who have been shown to have had a limited capacity to understand and correct the financial system thus dispelling their aura of "expertise" and thus leading to a significant decline in "investor confidence"' (Holland, 2008). What we see then is what Beck argues is a case of 'paradigm confusion', where the problems of late modernity are being confronted with the approaches of modernity. The financial meltdown is a systemic failure as the world has moved on and the instruments we are using are no longer appropriate or effective. This leads to a serious loss of trust in the experts and institutions that have shaped the present system and causes increased anxiety and desire to find security, both financial and personal, from tangible assets such as land and housing, and so further reinforces the drive for homeownership. An emerging and growing call to reassess the basis of our key economic models and measurements, many of which are still based on the manufacturing economies of the post-1945 world, to make them more fitting for the twenty-first century, can now be heard (see Stiglitz et al., 2009; Oxley et al., 2008).

THE MEANING OF HOME – THE SUBJECTIVE DIMENSION OF HOUSING

Home can be thought of as a centrally important site in which we interact and accommodate others, and from which we relate to the world around us. It is also a site that is affected by a host of externally generated influences. To appreciate the significance of home therefore requires an understanding of the subjective experiences of housing and neighbourhood and the social, economic and ecological forces that influence those experiences. Home is not just about the house but also about the land on which it is placed. For New Zealanders, the link with the land is important. For Maori (Tangata Whenua – people of the land) the land is where they find their roots and their sense of who they are as a people and their links with their past – their *whakapapa* (genealogy) – as well as with the present. It is a spiritual as well as an economic resource (Thorns et al., 2009).

Housing is thus connected to settlement and living. For European New Zealanders, as the majority live in single separate dwellings, their place is the house and the section (land). How they now relate to and use the outside space has changed over time and been subjected to global influences as many have increasingly turned this from an outside space to an extension of the rooms of the house and filled it with patios, barbecue areas, raised planters and outside entertaining and dining areas. A further aspect has been the tradition of the summer bach or second home, where vacations are spent close to the coast, lakes, rivers and bush, traditionally in simple do-it-yourself constructions, but increasingly now in more sophisticated and elaborate houses (Perkins and Thorns, 2006).

The meaning of home can be understood as a 'negotiated' reality: it is not something that is made and never changed, but is about process and how meaning evolved through the complex interactions of those present and those who are part of the household, often including the wider family/ *whanau*. The making of home for people is probably best described as 'work in progress', something that is never finished (Gorman-Murray and Dowling, 2007). Negotiation implies the sharing of power. However, this is not always the case in practice, and how the spaces within the houses were determined and used varies from cases where there is genuine negotiation to those where there is clearly dominance by one partner and forms of resistance by others, to those that could be characterized as resignation. Homes thus have to be seen as places where security, trust and shared meanings and understandings can be present, but they can also be places where conflict and the exercise of forms of domination and control can exist. Attention has been drawn in recent analysis to how dominant narratives of home have been very exclusive and emphasized the home as haven for heterosexual, white male humans rather than appreciating the range of household and family forms and increasingly diverse cultural practices and varying living arrangements that are present in our cities and neighbourhoods (Crabtree, 2009; Hayden, 1984; Friedman, 1998; Winstanley, 2001).

The home is the place of memories, a place where the objects that are displayed in the rooms and on the walls are part of the story of the individual and family journeys that have taken place. Possessions are linked to events; they are part of the family's history and persons who have been part of the family in previous generations (Marcoux, 2001). This is an ongoing process in which items for display are selected and discarded. In creating their sense of place, people use a number of important sources of information to gather their ideas about design, materials and available products, including lifestyle magazines, trade journals, professional designers, open days, show houses, television programmes and the Internet. This opens out the possibility that our conception of home and the design of our living arrangements are increasingly been influenced by global trends as much as local ones (Leonard et al., 2004). The emphasis on style over building appropriateness seems to have been encouraged here by the emphasis in the media upon lifestyle advertising that has celebrated the outdoor–indoor living and flow concepts and encouraged us to see the outside space as not just a 'garden' but as a living space to be enjoyed as part of a relaxed and contemporary lifestyle. Life-course change is an important aspect of home-making, and as people get older the importance of security and their health becomes more significant. People talk about how managing the household chores and maintenance of the property get harder as they get older. This factor becomes much more severe with the death of one partner.

Home as a special and significant space links us to thinking about how this relates to the wider set of spaces that people move through and engage with as they pursue their lives. Thus the neighbourhood and neighbours present a range of conceptual and methodological challenges and require some assessment of the continuing importance of place for the generation of meaning and identity for individuals and households. What is the range of activities that are still engaged in at the local level, and how are they maintained and organized? What is the relationship between the boundaries as seen by external institutions and agencies and those acknowledged by the locals living in a particular area?

The house–home is a central place where everyday life is constructed and lived out, where individuals and households search for and try to obtain their sense of security and craft their identity in a world that is increasingly shaped by growing uncertainty and risk. From this place they move out and engage with the neighbourhood and the wider city and region in which they are set. Global influences affect all these levels in varying ways: from reshaping our everyday lived experience and practices in our homes to reshaping the design of our neighbourhoods to revisioning and remaking the images of our cities and connections to the wider national and global worlds. People are increasingly aware now of the ecological environment and more knowledgeable about its value and fragilities as we move to create more sustainable living spaces. People live their lives within this set of contradictory pressures and demands. To meet the needs for shelter and to protect their assets in a world that appears to be increasingly unstable and subject to shocks and disruptions that are not predictable with any accuracy, people place emphasis on material success and individual responsibility. However, their capacity to do this is shaped by global financial institutions that are remote from individuals, their communities and local concerns.

CONCLUSION

The current financial and housing-market crises have disturbed many people's sense of security and trust in institutions, financial and political, to provide solutions for them. Understanding the strength and persistence of homeownership requires us to understand both its material and non-material dimension, and the function it provides for individuals and families and how these have been disrupted by the present crises. Recent events have shown the further erosion of trust in public institutions. The crisis places strains on these relationships and has increased the pressure to seek individual solutions. Crises cause both disruption and opportunities. They can be the circuit-breaker to open up new pathways for the future, or we can simply recover or retreat into our previous patterns of activity and behaviour once the initial crisis is over. In the analysis an attempt has been made to bring together a number of streams of the contemporary debate drawing on a wider spectrum of theory and analysis than the normally dominant economic discourses. Homeownership here provides a useful point for focus as it combines both material and non-material dimensions, and is central to our concerns for security and safety and the mitigation of risk through our own actions as we cease to have trust in many of the institutions of our society in late modernity.

The challenge for housing policy is to appreciate this larger joined-up canvas and create policies that seek to provide people with safe, secure, affordable places to live where they can craft their identities and feel empowered and enabled to become part of a wider neighbourhood and urban community, and rebuild the social capital that has been eroded. To achieve this we may need to rethink our preoccupation with homeownership and individual property rights as the solution and create a more varied set of arrangements and supports to meet the increasingly diverse needs of today's populations.

REFERENCES

Ansley, B. (2001), 'Home truths', *New Zealand Listener*, 20 January, pp. 18–23.
Arcus, Mathew and Ganesh Nana (2005), *Intergenerational and Interfamilial Transfers of Wealth*, Wellington: Centre for Housing Research, Aotearoa, New Zealand.

Beck, Ulrich (1992a), *Risk Society: Towards a New Modernity*, London: Sage.

Beck, Ulrich (1992b), 'From industrial society to the risk society: questions of survival, social structure and ecological environment', *Theory, Culture and Society*, **9** (February), 97–123.

Beck, Ulrich (1996a), 'World risk society as cosmopolitan society? Ecological questions in a framework of manufactured uncertainties', *Theory, Culture and Society*, **13** (4), 1–32.

Beck, Ulrich (1996b), 'Risk society and the provident state', in Scott Lash, B. Szerszinski and Brian Wynne (eds), *Risk, Environment and Modernity: Towards a New Ecology*, London: Sage, pp. 27–43.

Beck, Ulrich (1999), *World Risk Society*, Cambridge: Polity Press.

Burke, Terry (2007), 'Experiencing the housing affordability problem: blocked aspirations, trade-offs and financial hardships', Research Paper no. 9, Melbourne Australian Housing and Urban Research Institute.

Case, K.E. (2009), 'What are house prices telling us?', paper presented at the Housing Mortgages and Financial Turmoil Seminar, RMIT, February.

Crabtree, L. (2009), 'Housing as a social–ecological system: resilience, adaptive capacity and governance considerations', paper presented at the Australasian Housing Research Conference, Sydney, August.

Davidson, Alexander (1994), *A Home of One's Own; Housing Policy in Sweden and New Zealand, From the 1840s to the 1990s*, Stockholm: Almqvist and Wiksell.

DTZ New Zealand (2005), *Housing Tenure Aspirations and Attainment*, Centre for Housing Research, Aotearoa, New Zealand Wellington.

DTZ New Zealand (2007), *The Future of Home Ownership and the Role of the Private Rental Market in the Auckland Region*, Centre for Housing Research, Wellington.

DTZ New Zealand (2008), *The Intermediate Housing Market in New Zealand*, Centre for Housing Research, Wellington.

Dupuis, A. and D. Thorns (1998), 'Home ownership and the search for ontological security', *Sociological Review*, **46** (1), 24–47.

Dupuis, A. and D. Thorns (2008), 'Gating practices in a risk society', *Urban Policy and Research*, **26** (2), 145–57.

Dupuis, A. and D. Thorns (2009), 'Living with risk, living in risk: an analysis of the leaky building syndrome in New Zealand', paper presented at the Australasian Housing Research Conference, Sydney, August.

Ferguson, Gael (1994), *Building the New Zealand Dream*, Palmerston North: Dunmore Press.

Forrest, Ray and Alan Murie (eds) (1995), *Housing and Family Wealth in Comparative Perspective*, London: Routledge.

Friedman, Alice (1998), *Women and the Making of the Modern House: A Social and Architectural History*, New York: Harry N. Abrams.

Giddens, Anthony (1990), *The Consequences of Modernity*, Stanford, CA: Stanford University Press.

Gorman-Murray, A. and R. Dowling (eds) (2007), 'Home', *M/C Journal*, **10** (4), available at http://journal.media-culture.org.au/0708/01-editorial.php, accessed 23 April 2008.

Government House Prices Unit (2008), *Final Report of House Price Unit: House Price Increases and Housing in New Zealand*, Department of Prime Minister and Cabinet, Wellington.

Grimes, Arthur, Andrew Aitken, Ian Mitchell and Vicky Smith (2007), *Housing Supply in the Auckland Region*, Centre for Housing Research, Wellington.

Hamnett, C., M. Harmer and Peter Williams (1991), *Safe as Houses: Housing Inheritance in Britain*, London: Paul Chapman.

Hayden, Dolores (1984), *Redesigning the American Dream: The Future of Housing, Work and Family Life*, New York: W.W. Norton & Company.

Henderson, K. and G. Scobie (2009), 'Household debt in New Zealand', New Zealand Treasury Working Paper 09/03 Wellington, December.

Hirayama, Yosuko and Richard Ronald (2007), 'Baby boomers and baby busters and the lost generation: generational fracture in Japan's home owner society', paper presented at the APHRN Conference, Seoul, August.

Holland, K. (2008), 'America in turmoil as credit crisis firms its grip', *The Christchurch Press*, 22 September, p. A7.

Laing, R.D. (1969), *The Divided Self: An Extended Study of Sanity and Madness*, London: Tavistock.

Leonard, L., H.C. Perkins and D.C. Thorns (2004), 'Presenting and creating home: the influence of popular and building trade print media in the construction of home', *Housing Theory and Society*, **21** (3), 97–110.

Macfie, R. (2009), 'House of Pain', *New Zealand Listener*, 18–23 October, p. 10.

Mangin, Paul, Susan Thompson and Matthew Tonts (2008), *Qualitative Housing Analysis: An International Perspective*, Bingley: Emerald Publishing Group.

Marcoux, J.-S. (2001), 'The refurbishment of memory', in D. Miller (ed.), *Home Possessions*, Oxford: Berg, pp. 69–84.

Ministry of Social Development (2008), *The Social Report*, Wellington.

Morrison, Philip (2008), *On the Falling Rate of Home Ownership*, Wellington: Centre for Housing Research, Aotearoa, New Zealand.

New Zealand Labour Government (2005), *Building the Future: The New Zealand Housing Strategy*, HNZC, Wellington.

Olsson, P., C. Folke and F. Berkes (2004), 'Adaptive comanagement for building resilience in social–ecological systems', *Environmental Management*, **34** (1), 75–90.

Oxley, L., P. Walker, D. Thorns and H. Wang (2008), 'The knowledge economy/ society: the latest example of measurement without theory', *Journal of Philosophical Economics*, November, **20** (1), available at: http://www.jpe.ro/?id=revista&p=3.

Perkins, H. and D.C. Thorns (2003), 'The making of home in a global world', in Ray Forrest and James Lee (eds), *Housing and Social Change: East–West Perspectives*, London: Routledge, pp. 120–39.

Perkins, H. and D.C. Thorns (2006), 'Home away from home: the primary/ secondary home relationship', in Norman McIntyre, Daniel Williams and Kevin McHugh (eds), *Multiple Dwelling and Tourism*, Wallingford, UK: CABI, pp. 67–81.

PricewaterhouseCoopers (2009), 'New Zealand monetary policy and the residential housing market: a scoping study', Working Paper, Centre for Housing Research, Aotearoa, New Zealand Wellington.

Statistics New Zealand (2007a), *QuickStats About Housing, 2006 census*, Wellington.

Statistics New Zealand (2007b), *QuickStats About Population and Dwellings*, Wellington.

Stiglitz, J., A. Sen and J.-P. Fitoussi (2009), *Report of the Commission on the*

Measurement of Economic Performance and Social Progress, available at http://www.stiglitz-sen-fitoussi.fr/en/index.htm.

Stone, M. (2009), 'Housing and the financial crisis', paper presented at the Australasian Housing Research Conference, Sydney, August.

Thorns, D.C. (2008), 'Home ownership: continuing dream or approaching nightmare', paper presented at European Network of Housing Researchers Conference, OTB Research Institute, Delft, November.

Thorns, D.C. (2009), 'Housing booms and changes to housing affordability: finding solutions from the policy mix', *Journal of Asian Public Policy*, **2** (2), 171–89.

Thorns, D., Peggy Fairbairn-Dunlop and R. DuPlessis (2009), 'Biculturalism, cultural identities and globalisation: issues for Aotearoa New Zealand', paper presented at the AASSREC Symposium on 'Multiculturalism in a Globalising World', Bangkok, August.

Winstanley, Ann (2001), *Housing Home and Women's Identities*, PhD thesis, University of Canterbury.

Yates, Judith (2007), 'Affordability and access to home ownership, past, present and future?', Research Report No. 10, Melbourne, Australian Housing and Urban Institute.

10. The global financial crisis and its impact on households: the case of urban Vietnam

Hoang Huu Phe

INTRODUCTION: A TRANSITIONAL ECONOMY AND AN EMERGING HOUSING MARKET

Vietnam is a country in South East Asia with a total area of 331 690 km^2 and a population of 86 million (Census April 2009), making it the thirteenth most populous nation in the world. The country began its existence as a kingdom thousands of years BC. It fell under Chinese rule in 111 BC and regained its independence from China in AD 939. It went through the First Indochina War against colonialist France in the period between 1946 and 1954, which ended with the Dien Bien Phu battle, and the Second Indochina War, 1955–75, against the USA, culminating in the unification of the divided country in 1976. As a result of postwar economic mismanagement and the economic embargo imposed by the USA, the economy came to a near-collapse in the early 1980s.

For over two decades since the major policy change, or reform, in 1986 under the name of *Doi moi* (renovation), a centrally planned economy has gradually been replaced by what is now officially termed 'a market economy with socialist orientation'. Vietnam has now emerged as one of the most dynamic economies in the Asia-Pacific region. It maintained an average growth rate of 7.9 per cent over the period 1990–2000, and by late 2009 it finally shed its long-held status as a low-income country (with GDP per capita at just US$375 in 2000) to take on the new status of a medium-income country with a GDP per capita at US$1042. GDP growth rates are shown in Figure 10.1.

The *Doi moi* economic reform process, in its own way, has created 'profound enough effects' to qualify Vietnam as a transitional economy (Arkadie and Mallon, 2003). The three most important features of the *Doi moi* process are: (i) a gradualist, rather than 'big bang', approach; (ii) a relatively high rate of growth (as mentioned above); and (iii) a substantial

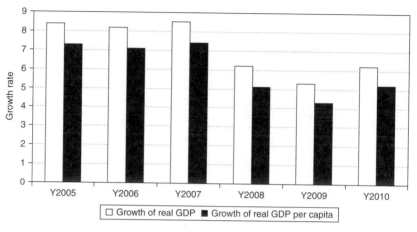

Source: Economist Intelligence Unit.

Figure 10.1 GDP growth rates, Vietnam, 2005–10

reduction of poverty. Between 1992/3 and 1997/8, the proportion of the poor in the population fell from 58 per cent to 37 per cent. By 2004, poverty was down to 20 per cent, and based on the poverty line of under one US dollar per day in PPP (purchasing power parity), the figure was less than 10 per cent.

As a mainly agrarian society of wet-rice growers, Vietnam has cultural traditions that place enormous importance on the links of the people to their land and therefore their homes, but during the turbulent historical times from the mid-1950s up to the beginning of *Doi moi* in 1986, housing was ranked third or fourth in priority, after industry and infrastructure (Hoang Huu Phe, 2002). The arrival of the market economy was to change all that.

In common with the situation in other transitional economies, the emerging housing market in Vietnam is characterized by the changes in two main aspects: (i) changes in the housing stock and (ii) changes in modes of housing production.

CHANGES IN THE HOUSING STOCK

The turbulent war years, with the tonnage of bombs dropped on the cities and the countryside in Vietnam exceeding that used during the Second World War in the whole of Europe, left severe scars both on the social consciousness as well as on the built environment. More than a decade after the war ended, the shortage of housing remained so serious in Vietnam that, in Central Hanoi districts, for example, the floor space per capita was under 4.2 m² (Hoang Huu Phe and Nishimura, 1990). After *Doi moi*, however, both the quantity and the quality of the housing stock underwent massive changes in line with the increase in economic output and efficiency.

Floor Space

In 1996, the average floor area per capita was 7.0 m² and the figure for 2000 was under 10 m² (Van, 2001). Between the two latest censuses, the housing space per capita in 2009 rose to 18.6 m² from 9.7 m² in 1999. It is worth noting that the Vietnam government's target for 2010 was specified at just 15 m². The big cities seem to be slightly ahead of the rest of the country, with Hanoi city reaching 20.8 m² and Ho Chi Minh 25.7 m² (Central Population and Housing Census Steering Committee, 2009).

Physical Quality

According to the 1999 census, the proportion of housing units with acceptable physical quality was 12.8 per cent, and the run-down units 22.64 per cent. In the 2009 census, the corresponding figures improved to 47 per cent for housing units with acceptable physical quality and only 7.4 per cent for run-down units.

Homeownership

Historically the homeownership rate in Vietnam has been very high due to the fact that around 85 per cent of the population lived in the countryside and the egalitarian, socialist policies before reform ensured that everyone had a minimal required shelter. Although the proportion of the urban population has increased to 29.6 per cent in 2009, the homeownership rate for the whole country remains at a very high level of 93 per cent (Census, 2009), a slight increase from 91.5 per cent in 2005 (HAIDEP, 2005). The proportion of owner-occupiers in big cities varies, from 82.6 per cent in Ho Chi Minh City, 86.3 per cent in DaNang, to 90.0 per cent in Hanoi and 92.6 per cent in Hai Phong. In the downtown areas of big cities, however, the proportion is thought to be much lower. A survey in 1989 conducted by the author in the Old City of Hanoi found that the proportion of private houses was only 37.6 per cent (Hoang Huu Phe and Nishimura, 1990).

CHANGES IN THE MODES OF HOUSING PRODUCTION

In the emerging economy of Vietnam, the ideological concept of housing as social service is gradually being replaced by market elements. Nevertheless, the process would seem to be one of 'trial-and-error' type responses rather than a well-designed course of development.

Housing as Social Service (Before 1989 and Until 1993)

The government's counter-inflation measures of 1989, including a reduction of state expenditure, a reduction of consumer subsidies and a relaxation of price controls, had succeeded in their purpose: to make prices matter for many goods in the market, including housing. Before that, housing was perceived and treated as a social service, to which everyone was theoretically entitled. In practice, housing in the form of basic accommodation, as provided to citizens, mostly state employees, is based on both needs and merits. The number of those who received government housing, however, never went above 30 per cent of the total number of state employees in any city.

Work-unit Housing (mid-1980s and 1990–96)

By the middle of the 1980s, partial solutions for the housing shortages were sought in the form of work-unit housing. It was not unusual for the ministries and large state-owned enterprises to set up their 'own funds' for the production of housing, which was distributed among the employees on the basis of needs and merits.

Joint Efforts by the State and the People (1989–93)

Another innovation in housing policy was tested, in the form of 'joint action by the government and the residents'. In this mode of housing provision, the state supported the residents by giving policy incentives and by investing in infrastructure for the existing residential areas, while the residents were largely responsible for building or improving their own homes.

Site-and-services Subdivision Schemes (1989–2000)

This mode of housing provision had some similarities with the 'site-and-services' approaches that were widely employed in other developing countries. Subdivided plots with basic infrastructure were sold to financially capable residents to build their own homes.

Project-oriented Housing Development (1996 Onwards)

This mode of housing provision is aimed at comprehensive development of the whole new urban residential blocks, including infrastructure. The task is given to powerful state-owned corporations with enough financial resources to ensure a smooth implementation of the projects. Except for housing development in the countryside and individual home construction and upgrading in big cities (one-third of the total), most of the new floor space in the country was added through the countless new urban areas projects invested and executed by these powerful state-owned corporations. The dynamics of this process is driven by the high rates of profit made possible by the huge advantages these corporations enjoy in obtaining land and capital from government sources.

As project-oriented housing development has become the dominant mode of housing supply, a few particular features of the housing market for new units in Vietnam can be identified:

- Large-scale housing projects require substantial finance resources, leading to a close relationship between the housing market and the financial market: a completely new feature in Vietnam's economic life (it was possible only after Vietnam joined the WTO (World Trade Organization), the move that has resulted in a real integration into the world's globalized economy).
- A large gap, or imbalance, exists between demand and supply, therefore the housing market is basically a 'seller' market rather than a 'buyer' market, and this is expected to last for at least a couple of decades into the future, judging from similar processes in higher-income economies, such as Malaysia and South Korea.
- This gap leads to a multiplicity of complaints about price-fixing by both private and government housing developers and about expensive housing beyond the reach of ordinary residents. A report of the Housing Expert Group under the government's Inter-Departmental Steering Committee for Housing and Real Estate stated that the real cost of producing 1 m² of floor space in a 20–25-storey residential tower block (VND16.5 to 17.5 million, or approximately US$970) is nearly a half of the selling price (VND28 to 32 million, or approximately US$1780) (Khanh Khoa, 2010).
- The profit rate is much higher for luxury housing projects, leading to a massive concentration of housing development for the high-income

submarkets, and the negligence of housing provision for low-income groups.

The changes in housing perception, housing stock and mode of housing production have shaped an emerging housing market that is vibrant and resourceful though still much less sophisticated compared with similar markets in a region known for very dynamic development of the real-estate markets. One of the most discernible weaknesses of Vietnam's housing market in the late 1980s–early 1990s was the lack of a functioning housing finance system, and that was to change radically later, as Vietnam entered the WTO in 2006. The changes described capture key features of the housing market in Vietnam when the global financial crisis struck.

THE GLOBAL FINANCIAL CRISIS AND VIETNAM

As Vietnam is a latecomer onto the development scene, the direct impact of the global financial crisis on the country is expected to be less severe compared with the more integrated economies in the region. This reasoning is based on three factors: (i) the Vietnam financial sector has little exposure to the kinds of assets in trouble; (ii) major international financial institutions have little investment in Vietnam; and (iii) Vietnam does not have much short-term overseas debt (Konishi, 2008).

The indirect impact of the global financial crisis on Vietnam, however, may be a very different story. Although it has a relatively small size and a low base, but a high level of integration into the regional and the world economy, Vietnam's economy has a very high measure of market openness, with the volume of import/export reaching 150 per cent of GDP. The FDI sector, while accounting for just 27 per cent of total investment volume, has contributed between 55 per cent and 77 per cent of total import/export volume (Rua, 2009). This interdependence makes the indirect impact of the global financial crisis on the Vietnam economy more severe than would otherwise be expected, due to the following factors (Konishi, 2008):

- the global economic slowdown reduces exports;
- the reduction in tourist arrivals;
- weaker FDI as companies have difficulties in organizing funds and see less urgency to expand production capacities; and
- declines in remittances and labour export.

What was anticipated has happened in the course of the spreading impact of the global financial crisis. Vietnam's nascent financial sector was not caught up with the contagion created by the sub-prime debacle in the USA. The global economic slowdown did reduce exports (14.2 per cent down from the 2008 figure) and tourist arrivals (down 11 per cent), reduced FDI flows (13 per cent lower than 2008), but perhaps due to the low-cost character of manufacturing and services, the impact of the global financial crisis was not enough to completely break the momentum of growth. Some scenarios of how Vietnam would get through the crisis were very pessimistic. It was feared, for example, that the GDP growth rate of around 8 per cent in recent years could turn into zero growth. In the end, with due discipline observed in fiscal and other macroeconomic policies and implementation, Vietnam finished 2009 with a growth rate of 5.2 per cent, higher than most predictions.

THE GLOBAL FINANCIAL CRISIS AND ITS IMPACT ON VIETNAM'S HOUSING MARKET

Except for self-help housing development, most of the registered housing developers in Vietnam lack financial resources, and are heavily dependent on outside funds such as bank loans and credit agencies, and this is probably the biggest risk in the market. After accession into the WTO in late 2006, between 2007 and 2009, the country attracted 4098 foreign investment projects with a total registered capital of US$114.15 billion, nearly 4.5 times higher than the target set for the entire period of 2006–10. A surge in both housing production and house prices was more or less in line with the international housing market movements. Before that, every year since the early 2000s, approximately 30 million m² of residential floor space was added to the housing stock, mostly in big cities.

The global financial crisis arrived in Vietnam in the early months of 2008. In that year alone, 50 million m² of residential space was added – the results of a bubble in 2007. The unusually high inflation rate, reaching 22 per cent, forced a reduction in household spending, leading to the freezing of the housing market. The high-end property sector suffered on average a price reduction of 40 per cent (see Figure 10.2). Some projects experienced price falls of as much as 60 per cent, such as in the Phu Xuan–Nha Be housing project in Ho Chi Minh city (Vietnam Real Estate Association, 2009), and many ongoing projects were forced to stop to wait for better times.

In 2009 the property market in Vietnam came closer to a semblance of what can be termed 'maturity'. A new phenomenon in 2009 was the consistently good performance of real-estate stocks – some of them had an increase of over 400 per cent. Property prices were quite stable. As

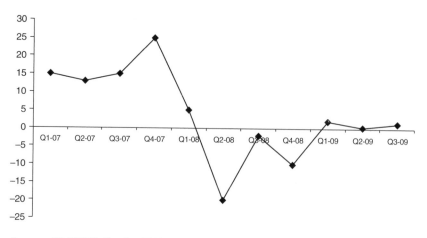

Source: VietREES, October 2009.

Figure 10.2   *Percentage changes in house prices in the high-end market segment*

Vietnam was one of the first countries in the world to come out of the crisis with very clear signs of recovery by the end of 2009, the real-estate and hospitality sector attracted a record amount of foreign registered investment, reaching US$7.6 billion in 2009 alone, next only to the most attractive sectors of food, beverages and residential services (US$8.8 billion) and putting manufacturing and processing into third place at US$2.97 billion (Nguyen Long Vân, 2010). The year 2010 brought, however, more uncertain prospects for the real-estate sector. While the high interest rates (up to 16–18 per cent) coupled with the high price for construction materials (steel, cement, etc.) left the higher ends of the residential market stagnant/ waiting, the medium and lower sectors seemed to be performing somewhat better (Ngoc Huân, 2010).

One of the unexpected impacts of the global financial crisis on the housing market in Vietnam is the role played by foreign direct investment (FDI) in channelling more financial resources into real-estate investment, which will certainly be concentrated only in housing projects at the high end of the market. This aggravates the imbalance between the demand and supply of affordable housing in the medium- and low-income categories, as mentioned earlier.

THE UNEVEN IMPACT ON HOUSEHOLDS IN VIETNAM'S HOUSING MARKET

In any urban region, the housing market is a complex system consisting of interconnected submarkets. Submarkets can be defined by different criteria; there are basically three types of submarkets: (i) geographically defined submarkets; (ii) structural submarkets; and (iii) demander groups' submarkets (Watkins, 2001). For the purpose of this chapter, it is most appropriate to refer to demander groups, that is, the income groups submarkets, which are roughly expressed in house-price parameters.

High-income Submarket

This submarket comprises the high-quality units produced, as a rule, by highly experienced foreign, domestic or joint-venture developers, in the new urban areas. In the domestic developer groups, the most important role is played by the SOEs (state-owned enterprises), or powerful state corporations, such as Song Da corp., HUD corp., Vinaconex JSC, UDIC. The private sector also contributes a substantial share (Bitexco, ACB, etc.). Customers for this submarket are well-to-do businesspeople, overseas Vietnamese and expats with the right to buy houses in Vietnam. House prices range from US$1500 per m^2 up to US$5000 per m^2 Many of the projects in this category are popularly known as the speculative sector.

Medium-income Submarket

Housing units of good quality are produced by institutional and private or joint-venture investors/developers as the groups mentioned above. Customers for this submarket are government officials with high salaries, people relocated from other urban areas to make room for new development, with substantial compensation money. House prices ranges from VND8 million (US$420) to under US$1500 per m^2.

Low-income Submarket

Housing in this group offers only basic amenities and usually low space standards (less than 50 m^2 per flat), with house prices on average less than VND8 million (US$420). This category of housing is made available for the low-income groups, a substantial part of which consists of government employees, the workers of FDI projects, university and vocational-school students.

THE UNEVEN IMPACTS ON HOUSEHOLDS

The first signs of the impact of the global financial crisis were registered in the high-income submarket of Ho Chi Minh City, which suffered on average a price reduction of 40 per cent (Vietnam Real Estate Association, 2009), and many ongoing projects were forced to halt. The speculative housing development in big cities before the crisis, in 2006–7, had pushed house prices to sky-high levels (up to US$5000 per m^2 for central city flats). They had been displacing lower-cost projects, but during the bursting of the market, these projects were forced to stay vacant because the finance flows suddenly stopped. Many of them had their licences revoked by the government. The demanders for this submarket, many of them buying for speculative purposes, have suffered heavily, especially in the midst of high interest rates. The households who are seeking housing units as owner-occupiers are faced with long delays and even cancellation of contracts to buy houses.

For the low-income submarket, the impact of the global financial crisis seems to be mixed. On the positive side, the stimulus package of the government, brought into play by the imperatives of the worldwide fight against a feared L-type recession, was explicitly addressed by the construction of low-cost housing for the urban areas (Ha, 2009). Measures to subsidize the interest rate for low-cost housing borrowings for state as well as private companies, and the introduction of building technologies to reduce the construction costs, were strongly encouraged. The transfer of urban land for the development of low-cost housing was also given priority. On the negative side, due to a lack of proper policies for low-cost housing, the government's stimulus schemes, introduced as a panacea for the improvement of housing conditions for poverty groups, never really got off the ground, for the following reasons. First, lending criteria meant that for low-income groups, loans were still beyond their means. Second, the low rate of profit discouraged developers, despite incentives such as exemption of payment for land use rights, four-year tax holiday for companies, and minimal VAT. Third, there was a shortage of land and a need for land pooling for development, despite government efforts.

Nevertheless, out of 64 provinces, 21 have sent proposals to register 198 projects for low-cost housing, an equivalent of 7.1 million m^2, or 166 390 flats, which could house 700 000 people. The year 2009, therefore, marks the beginning of a sustained drive for the production of low-income housing. Currently 24 low-cost housing projects for workers of the industrial zones are under construction.

The only bright spot during the 2008–09 financial crisis was that the submarket of the medium–low-cost owner-occupied housing (between US$300 and US$600 per m²) has flourished, due to the impact of the stimulus package from the government (Vietnam Real Estate Association, 2009).

CONCLUDING REMARKS

The global financial crisis caused massive disruption in the economic life of many countries, but Vietnam was affected more indirectly than directly, unlike other more financially sophisticated economies. Compared with other countries in the region, Vietnam escaped from the global financial crisis in late 2009 relatively early and less painfully, due to the lower level of exposure to financial excesses. Nevertheless the relative openness of the Vietnamese economy and, combined with it, an excessive dependence on FDI funding for high-income housing projects in the time of the global crisis and recession, could distort the balance between demand and supply and wreak havoc on the whole domestic housing market by the force of the impact transmitted through the interdependencies between submarkets.

The global financial crisis has therefore had an uneven impact on households in different submarkets/income groups. While the high-income submarket households were much less affected in terms of basic living conditions, they suffered greatly in terms of using their residential properties as a depository of value. Although the financial crisis unexpectedly opened a new, promising avenue for addressing the problem of housing for low-income groups through the use of the government stimulus anti-crisis package, the implementation of this drive was severely impeded by red tape and lack of consistent policies, as well as by a shortage of land for development.

The relative benefits gained by the medium-income submarket during the time of crisis are significant in the sense that this submarket covers a substantial range of effective demand for housing. The redirection of the flows of funds towards this market is supposed to neutralize the imbalance in the housing market.

Vietnam needs a functioning housing market as a prerequisite for a socially sustainable, equitable development process for the country, and the lessons learnt from the recent global financial crisis could be instrumental in building up material, technical and institutional capacities to cope with the excesses of the housing market, which are not always of Vietnam's own making.

REFERENCES

Arkadie, Brian Van and Raymond Mallon (2003), *Vietnam: A Transition Tiger?* The National Australian University, Canberra, Australia: ANE U Press.

Central Population and Housing Census Steering Committee (2009), *The 1/4/2009 Central Population and Housing Census: The Sample Results*, Hanoi, Vietnam.

Ha, N.M. (2009), 'An introduction to housing policy in Vietnam', paper presented at the Symposium for Housing, organized by Konrad Adenauer Stiftung and UN Habitat Vietnam.

HAIDEP (2005), 'Hanoi integrated development and environment program', research report funded by JICA.

Hoang Huu Phe (2002), 'Investment in residential property: a taxonomy of home improvers in central Hanoi', *Habitat International*, **26** (4), 471–86.

Hoang Huu Phe and Yukio Nishimura (1990), 'The historical environment and housing conditions in the "36 Old Streets" quarter of Hanoi', Research Paper No. 23, Human Settlements Development Division, Asian Institute of Technology, Bangkok, Thailand.

Khanh Khoa (2010), 'Real estate prices are always higher than real values', *Ha Noi Moi Newspaper* (The New Hanoi), Hanoi, 21 May.

Konishi Ayumi (2008), 'The global financial crisis: Vietnam prospects in 2009 and beyond', presentation and discussion at the AmCham Briefing Luncheon, Hanoi, 24 November.

Ngoc Huân (2010), 'The property sector in difficulties due to high interest rate', *Lao Dong Newspaper*, Hanoi, 4 May.

Nguyễn Long Vân (2010), 'Vietnam's real estate sector: the discernible upward moves', *Journal of Construction (Xay Dung)*, Hanoi, 10 February.

Rua, T.H. (2009), 'The theoretical and practical issues of responding to the global financial crisis: the Chinese and Vietnamese experiences', *Nhan Dan Newspaper*, Hanoi, 14 December.

Van, N.T. (2001), 'Vietnam Human Settlements Report', presented at UN Special Session on Human Settlements (Habitat II), New York, 7 June.

Vietnam Real Estate Association (2009), *Proceedings of Symposium on Housing Development Programs and Implementable Measures*, Ho Chi Minh City, August.

Watkins, C.A. (2001), 'The definition and identification of housing submarkets', *Environment and Planning A*, **33** (12), 2235–53.

11. Housing policy issues in South Korea since the global economic crisis: aspects of a construction-industry-dependent society

Soo-hyun Kim

INTRODUCTION

The majority of Korean people believe that the Korean housing problem is the worst in the world. Almost daily, the press reports problems of high house prices *vis-à-vis* income, the potential rise or fall of house prices, and the unstable lease market. According to one survey, 58 per cent of Korean households (65 per cent in Seoul) have felt and still feel stress or anxiety due to a sharp rise in house prices (KBS, 17 January 2007). The previous government administration (2003–07), headed by President Roh Moo-hyun, was subject to harsh public criticism for its inability to control house prices (*Hankyeoreh Newspaper*, 10 January 2008), despite domestic increases being lower than those of most other advanced nations in the world.

There are several reasons why Koreans are so sensitive about housing issues. First, real estate takes up 80 per cent of the total household assets; therefore one's entire fortune depends on the fluctuations of house prices. Also, Korea has experienced periodic sudden rises in house prices during the rapid economic development and metropolitan concentration process since the 1960s, adding to the sensitivity. Moreover, the high dependence of the Korean economy on the construction and housing industry magnifies the influence of change in the housing market from the perspective of economic management.

In such a situation, the Lehman Brothers collapse in 2008 also dealt a direct blow to the Korean housing market. As house prices had risen quickly in the 2000s, mainly for the preferred metropolitan regions, the economic shock was almost regarded as signalling the bursting of the bubble. In some local cities unsold houses accumulated, reaching 3 per cent of the total local housing stock. Responding to this, the Korean government introduced an aggressive pump-priming policy for housing industry with big tax reductions. This included direct purchase of unsold houses by the government, support for construction businesses, boosting housing supply through lifting limited development areas, and the revitalization of redevelopment projects through high-rise, high-density constructions. Past policies had focused on regulating the ownership of multiple homes to prevent rises in house prices but the current government, which came to power in 2008, encouraged this so as to increase house sales. Also, the government began to engage in large-scale public works and urban development projects to support the construction industry; the maintenance project for major rivers across the country and the plan for the new construction of five super-high-rise buildings over 100 storeys in Seoul are part of this.

As the result of such active policies, prices in the Korean housing market did not drop as much as expected. The period of house-price falls did not exceed 6 months, and for some regions it even surpassed the peak of 2006. Furthermore, the lease deposit for *Jeonse*, a unique housing lease system of Korea (further explained below), kept rising and now almost matches the level before the Lehman Brothers collapse. In terms of the supply of new housing or trade volume, the market is still not at its full capacity, but at least the prices in the Korean housing market do not appear to reflect the influence of the economic crisis.

Several issues arise in this process – first, concerns about a new bubble. That is, the housing-market bubble of the 2000s was supposed to subside naturally after the US sub-prime mortgage crisis, but due to governmental artificial pump-priming policy for the housing market, the bubble grew even more, rather than subsiding. Moreover, while critics argue that the construction/civil engineering industry already takes up too much of the Korean economy, the government relies on this sector to promote economic recovery.

The second issue is the criticism that the redevelopment project revitalization scheme has caused housing costs for the low-income bracket to increase as they are driven out of their homes. As a consequence of hastening the redevelopment projects for economic recovery, conflicts between tenants and redevelopment businesses have been frequently observed, and in January 2009, a fire occurred in Yongsan-gu, near downtown Seoul, during the repression of an anti-eviction conflict, killing six people.

Lastly, there is the issue of those with multiple homes, which is unique to Korea. Many Koreans regard those who own multiple homes as speculators and are antagonistic towards them, especially during periods when prices are rising. The government enacted policies to suppress multiple-home owners. Therefore some NGOs and the opposition party have claimed that since the economic crisis, if the government encourages the ownership of multiple homes, the unequal distribution of wealth will be deepened and the housing situation will deteriorate. On the other hand, the government and the ruling party have claimed that it is inevitable to permit multiple home ownerships in such a depression in the housing industry.

The purpose of this chapter is to examine such issues, which have been magnified since the economic crisis, and to suggest the tasks that Korean housing policy should aim for at this juncture. To achieve this, the chapter first outlines the general situation of the Korean housing market and the development of housing policy. Following that, the subsequent section explores the situation of the Korean housing market since the Lehman Brothers collapse and the corresponding government policies. Finally, the chapter summarizes the tasks ahead for Korean housing policy.

THE STATE OF KOREAN HOUSING AND HOUSING POLICIES

The State of Korean Housing

South Korea's rapid economic growth is well known. Its per capita GNI, which was only $278 in 1970, first exceeded $10000 in 1996 and reached $20000 in 2007. This rapid growth was often described as being miraculous, and Korea was referred to as one of the economic 'Tigers'. The Korean population grew in line with the economy, and metropolitan centralization intensified faster than in any other nation in the world.

This development was accompanied by a sudden increase in housing demand; however, housing supply could not keep pace with increasing demand. House prices in Korea (especially in Seoul) continued to rise and were at times referred to as an expression of 'The Real Estate Invincibility Theory'. A 'Ten-Year Cycle' theory also emerged, with the observation that house prices in Korea generally rose every ten years. When house prices rose faster than average income, housing PIR (price-to-income ratio) and RIR (rent-to-income ratio) also continuously rose. The relative proportion of income devoted to housing in the lower classes still continues to increase and this pressure is worsening (Kim, S.-H., 2008, p. 159).

High house prices and cyclical price increases have produced an obsession with real-estate property among Koreans. Real estate came to make up 77 per cent of total private assets and the ratio reaches 81 per cent if rent deposit (*Jeonse*) is included. This is an extremely high ratio relative

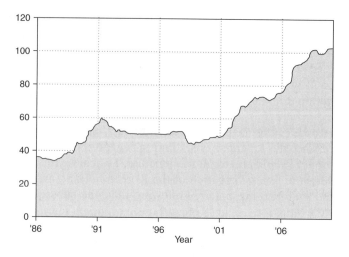

Source: Statistics of Kookmin Bank (http://land.kbstar.com/).

Figure 11.1   Changes in housing price (unit: index Dec. 2008 = 100)

to that of the USA (33 per cent), Japan (60 per cent), and the UK (54 per cent) (Park, D.-B., 2009). Real estate is, in effect, the sole form of private property. This means in turn that the public is inevitably sensitive to changes in house prices and that any change, whether increasing or decreasing, will become a top political issue.

In contrast to the high level of attention given to housing, the proportion of Korean people owning a private home has remained relatively constant; around 57 per cent for the last 20 years. This is due to increases in house prices, which has meant that families cannot afford to purchase a home. This ratio is about 10 per cent lower in Seoul compared to the rest of the nation. Although past government administrations have campaigned to increase homeownership, about 40 per cent of the nation (50 per cent in Seoul) are living in a home owned by someone else. Approximately 50–60 per cent of these people sign private leases through the unique Korean leasing system, which is called *Jeonse* (Table 11.1; see also Box 11.1).

The quality of Korean housing has improved significantly since the 1990s because of the increase in housing supply and a decrease in the average household size. The proportion of families living in housing that does not meet minimal government housing standards has decreased by 20 per cent in ten years – from 34 per cent in 1995 to 13 per cent in 2005. However, housing quality still lags behind that of other advanced nations. The pressure for reform is high, especially in older parts of the cities. For this reason many areas of Seoul are currently undergoing redevelopment.

Table 11.1 Changes in Korean housing tenure (national–Seoul) (unit: percentage of households)

Year	1985		1990		1995		2000		2005	
Region	National	Seoul	National	Seoul	National	Seoul	National	Seoul	National	Seoul
Owner-occupied (Homeownership)*	53.6	40.8	49.9	38.0	53.3	39.7	54.2	40.9	55.6 **(60.3)**	44.6
Private rented Jeonse	23.0	36.8	27.8	40.3	29.7	43.8	28.2	41.2	22.4	33.2
Monthly rent with deposit	10.1	17.5	8.2	10.6	10.3	13.5	10.7	14.4	15.1	18.5
Monthly rent	9.7	2.2	11.0	9.0	4.2	1.4	4.1	1.9	3.9	2.0
Public rented**					(1.6)	(2.0)	(1.7)	(2.5)	(2.1)	(2.9)
Free and others	3.7	2.7	3.1	2.0	2.5	1.4	2.8	1.6	3.1	1.6

Notes:
* As there are many owners living in others' homes as tenants, the homeownership rate is around 5% above owner-occupation rate. First calculated by KSO in 2005.
** Included in private rented sector. The figures in parentheses are the author's estimates.

Source: Korean Statistical Office (www.kostat.go.kr).

BOX 11.1   THE KOREAN LEASING SYSTEM

The Korean leasing system is the only one of its kind worldwide and is crucial in understanding the Korean housing market.

Leasing is conducted by paying the homeowner a deposit (*Jeonse*) of 30–70 per cent of the cost of the home in return for rights of use of the home. When the contract expires, the entire amount of the deposit is returned to the tenant. Therefore the homeowner in effect collects rent in the form of bank interest on the deposit paid and often uses this income as principal capital for business and so on. For homeowners seeking to purchase additional homes, they are able to match their costs to the price of the home minus the deposit they would receive when they lease the home; the leasing system is often used as a way to purchase more homes with small amounts of cash. This method has a significant leverage effect when house prices experience a sharp rise. In addition, some people who wish to purchase a home that is more expensive than the capital they currently hold often purchase an expensive home, remain living in a cheaper leased home. This is one of the reasons for the disparity between the proportion of Koreans who own a home and the proportion of Koreans who live in their own home.

The tenant in a leased home benefits in that he is able to live in an expensive home at relatively low cost. In addition, although tenants tie up a large amount of cash in deposit, the leasing system can be interpreted as a type of savings system in that the deposit can easily be converted to capital for purchasing a new home. In Korea's familial culture, many parents help their married children pay for their future homes by giving them a deposit to lease a home for newlyweds. Since the deposits are always large, lease tenants can quickly become home purchasers when housing costs rise. This is the most important reason why the housing market quickly heats up in Korea, where a mortgage system is not yet developed. The leasing problem generally becomes a social issue when deposit costs rise at the time of contract renewal, because the marginal cost is large and causes financial strain on tenants.

What is the future of the leasing system? The problem of the underdevelopment of a mortgage finance system is now being addressed. The future must therefore be seen from a different perspective. First, it is unlikely that the tendency to purchase homes that cost as much as cash-in-hand plus the lease deposit, which will be returned in the future, will disappear. This tendency gives weight to the belief that house prices will rise again in the future. The practice of helping children pay for a future home by paying for a deposit on an earlier leased home is also unlikely to disappear. The Korean practice of not levying gift tax in most of these situations must also be taken into consideration.

Another important trait of Korea is that long-term loans with real-estate collateral (a mortgage) do not play a significant role in the process of home purchasing. Of all capital used for purchasing homes, long-term mortgages make up only about 5 per cent, and, even including short-term loans, the proportion of bank loans in home-purchase capital remains at around 34 per cent on average. The largest sources of such capital are lease deposits (*Jeonse*), savings and familial support.[1] This means that the housing problems of the poor are inevitably serious, where house prices are excessive with respect to income and the financial system is underdeveloped. Moreover, governmental public housing policies are still in the early stages of development. The proportion of families living in public rental housing remains at around 3 per cent, and even with more homes supplied by the government beginning with the Roh administration, only about 6 per cent of families are projected to live in such homes by 2012.

Korea's Housing Policies

Korea's housing policies have the tendency to change rapidly according to changes in house prices. When prices increase, policies then increase supply while reducing demand – this is accomplished by raising taxes or tightening finance. When prices decrease, policies then lower taxes and actually encourage multiple-home ownership. This is, in large part, how the construction industry operates in the Korean economy, as well as the vital nature of real estate as private property. For the government, the housing market could neither be overheated nor depressed.

Particularly after the Asian foreign currency crisis that hit Korea at the end of 1997, the Kim administration (which gained power in 1998) reduced real-estate taxes and in effect encouraged multiple-home ownership.[2] The Kim administration also sought to nurture the construction industry and use it as a driver for economic recovery.

Korean house prices saw another sharp rise in the early 2000s because of the expansion of global liquidity and the Kim administration's economic stimulus package based on the construction industry. Beginning in 2003, the Roh administration strengthened government intervention in the housing market, increased property taxes and transference taxes for two or more houses. In addition, government policies also made it more difficult for multiple-home owners to receive bank loans when seeking to purchase another home.

In contrast, the Lee administration (beginning in 2008) came into power already dissatisfied with the high taxes in the real-estate sector. This administration used the global financial crisis and the subsequent stagnation of the Korean construction industry to make big cuts in housing taxes. The high taxes that were previously levied on multiple-home owners were eliminated, and policies encouraging multiple-home ownership (reminiscent of the Kim administration) again flourished.

As described, Korean housing policies (especially taxation policies) alternated between strengthening and amelioration, depending on the state of the economy. It is of course logical for the government to alternate between supporting and repressing policies according to economic fluctuations. However, the difference between the two types of policies in Korea is so marked that the policies 'jump' back and forth. Even institutions that must necessarily be fixed as a social norm, such as property tax, have changed rapidly according to changes in the economy. Many Korean people are distrustful and dissatisfied with the 'jumping' policies, but have shown an ambivalent attitude when the housing industry directly affects the economy. For example, there are protests against multiple-home owners when house prices rise, but these protests are silent when house prices either fall or are stabilized.

While Korean housing policies change in accordance with price trends, the issues of different forms of home possession have not garnered much interest in Korean policy-making or research. The issue of stabilizing homeownership or the issue of balance between the different forms of housing tenure, and the appropriate amount of public-housing supply, are not discussed at length. In this context, the role of the private rented sector in particular must be discussed first. Korea does not have a clear policy regarding private rental housing. Koreans regard private rental housing as a temporary housing tenure and policies have developed mainly in accordance with that perception.

HOUSING POLICIES AND ISSUES OF KOREA SINCE THE ECONOMIC CRISIS

Policy Changes and Market Situation since the Economic Crisis

In the previous section, the Korean housing market situation and the flow of housing policy changes were examined. The characteristic of Korean housing policy is that it has been very sensitive to business fluctuations. This is somewhat inevitable for government of any inclination due to the importance of the housing market and its political significance. The Lee administration that came to power in February 2008, however, appeared to have a different basis for its housing policy, as it tried to actively promote economic recovery.

At first, the Lee government in its 2007 election campaign criticized the tax system and loan regulation reinforcement policies during periods of house price rises, and claimed that it could lower prices only by increasing the housing supply and easing the tax system. Accordingly, since its introduction in early 2008, it began to discard the high property tax and transfer tax for those with multiple-home ownership, which were the core policies of the previous government. For this, the trial to reinforce the property tax on high-cost real estate was practically incapacitated,[3] and in the meantime, the heavy transfer income tax for multiple-home owners was greatly lowered in its amount and scope.

Along with this, regulations were eased in order to revitalize the project of redeveloping apartments over 20 years old into high-rise, high-density structures. The need to build public rental housing in the redevelopment process was regarded as unnecessary and discarded, and regulations were altered so that the sizes of newly built houses were now allowed to increase. Also, in old, low-rise residential areas, redevelopment projects were actively promoted as 'new town'[4] projects; in early 2008, moves to revitalize became widespread. All politicians were promising to quickly carry out 'new town' projects in their districts. Moreover, as the Lee government promised high economic growth, it suggested relying on the civil engineering/construction business as a means to achieve this. The construction of a grand canal (later reduced to the four major rivers maintenance project) and the expansion of construction such as roads and bridges in local areas increased substantially. Also, a construction plan for five high-rise buildings over 100 storeys high in Seoul's major areas was mooted.

Such policy trends were further strengthened after the Lehman Brothers collapse in 2008. At this time, direct support for unsold houses or weak construction businesses was added. As the number of unsold houses

Table 11.2   House-price changes over the previous month (%)

	Jan	Feb	Mar	Apr	May	Jun	Jul	Aug	Sep	Oct	Nov	Dec
2008	0.3	0.3	0.8	0.9	0.6	0.6	0.4	0.2	0.2	*−0.1*	*−0.4*	*−0.7*
2009	*−0.6*	*−0.3*	*−0.2*	0.1	0.1	0.2	0.3	0.3	0.7	0.4	0.3	0.1
2010	0.1	0.3	0.2									

Source: Statistics of Kookmin Bank (http://land.kbstar.com/).

under construction grew to 120 000, the government provided a 3 trillion KRW relief fund, and some houses were also directly purchased for public rental housing. Limits on development areas around Seoul were also lifted to strengthen the policy of supplying new apartments in the metropolitan area. Along with this, in contrast to the previous administration, which had built nearly 100 000 public rental units every year, the Lee administration reduced this by almost half and increased the number of houses for sale. The focus was on purchase rather than rental, mid–large size rather than small size, and the redevelopment of urban Seoul or nearby areas.

As the result of such an aggressive pump-priming policy for the construction sector and the housing market, the Korean housing market experienced only about six months of price falls after the Lehman Brothers collapse, and prices are rising or stabilizing again (see *italic* figures in Table 11.2). This is particularly surprising considering the concerns of late 2008. There was much concern that the American sub-prime mortgage situation and the international economic crisis would burst the housing-market bubble in Korea. Such a strong market recovery, however, is now criticized for posing even more difficulties, and various controversies have arisen in Korea.

Issues of Korean Housing Policy since the Economic Crisis

Concerns about a new housing bubble

Since 2008, several issues have arisen related to the economic crisis and the subsequent change in housing policies. The first is concern about a new bubble. The excessive housing bubble in the 2000s, which was supposed to subside naturally after the collapse of Lehman Brothers has grown larger due to the artificial housing-market recovery policies of the government. Moreover, the government has been criticized for its economic recovery package because the civil engineering/construction sectors are already too prominent in the Korean economy (Kim, S.-H., 2009b; Byun, C.-H., 2009).

Some scholars argue that the accumulated oversupply and decreased demand due to low fertility and ageing will lead to a prolonged depression and dramatic fall in the Korean housing market, and therefore the housing market recovery policy and supply expansion strategy are vulnerable to ultimately greater market downturn (Seon, D.-I., 2008, 2009; KKS Economic Research Institute, 2009). There is the possibility, some argue, of a bust similar to that of Japan in 1990. On the other hand, Kim, G.-W. (2009), Kim, J.-S. (2009) and others claim that the demographic structure of Korea has not yet reached the stage for a decrease in housing demand, and due to the accumulated undersupply since the economic crisis, in three to four years house prices may rise again, so that a dramatic drop will not occur. The government, while it also acknowledges 'the overly expensive housing cost' (President Lee, remarks in September 2008), is continuing the housing market recovery policy, arguing that it is necessary given the serious economic situation.

The bubble debate in Korea is ongoing. While it is very difficult to determine or predict a bubble, due to the high house prices relative to incomes and the experience of the sudden price rise in the 2000s, the bubble theory remains a sensitive issue. In early 2010, the question of whether Korea is experiencing a bubble or a bust is still the subject of major TV debates (MBC, 4 February 2010). What will happen in the short term is difficult to predict. What is clear is that, in the long run, the Korean housing market will enter a period of stability or decline. In the 2020s, low fertility and ageing will have a major influence on the house market, and it is expected to enter a long-term stable period. Therefore, how to manage the excessive bubble and at the same time reduce it gradually before that point is very important in housing policy; from such perspectives, the housing-market recovery policy of the Lee government is of some concern. That is, it is necessary to predict changes in the housing market over the next ten years and prepare the appropriate measures to accommodate such developments, but the government is pursuing policies based on the rapid growth period of the past.

Expansion of urban redevelopment projects and deterioration of the low-income class residence issue
The second issue is the criticism that the expansion of urban redevelopment projects permits excessive profits for the landowners and development businesses, thus creating wealth gaps, while the low-income class suffers from increased housing costs and will be driven out of their original communities (Kim, S.-H., 2009a). Especially in the case of Seoul, in 2003, when the current president Lee was serving as its mayor, 2406 hectares were designated to redevelopment as 'new towns',

Table 11.3   Comparison of the housing situation before and after 'new town' redevelopment projects

Classification	Before project	After project
Ratio of housing under 60 m² (exclusive area)	63%	30%
Ratio of housing under 500 million KRW of sale price	86%	30%
Ratio of housing under 40 million KRW of rental deposit	83%	0%
Average housing size (exclusive area)	80 m²	107 m²
Average housing price	390 million KRW	540 million KRW

Source: Advisory Committee for Housing Improvement of Seoul (2009).

representing 2.4 times the sum of all the redeveloped areas of Seoul so far (SDI, 2008).

Through such large-scale redevelopment projects, the housing stock could be improved, but most of the original residents had to leave the area due to construction of housing that they could not afford. In reality, when the cases of completed 'new town' redevelopment areas are examined, small/cheap housing disappears and large houses for sale are in the majority (see Table 11.3). The result is that 90 per cent of the original residents move out of the area. Moreover, as a number of redevelopment projects are in progress at the same time in the whole of Seoul, the lease prices for the low-income population are rapidly rising even for the areas not targeted for redevelopment (Seoul Metropolitan Government, 2007a, 2007b). In Seodaemun-gu, near downtown Seoul, the lease prices for cheap housing in the area were found to be increasing much faster than average in 2008 (Advisory Committee for Housing Improvement of Seoul, 2009).

As the circumstances for the poor deteriorate, protests against development are increasing. Not only tenants, but also poor homeowners are conducting meetings, demonstrations and lawsuits against the increasing economic burden and compulsory evictions (Kim, N.-G., 2009). Policy-makers and some academic scholars acknowledge that the current redevelopment involves deterioration in the housing situation of certain classes and increases housing costs. Thus it is required to resolve the lease-rise issue according to the progress of simultaneous redevelopment projects, especially after the Yongsan protests (referred to earlier). The Lee administration, however, remains unchanged in its belief that the expansion of housing supply is the only way to resolve the housing problem in Korea (i.e. high prices) and continues to promote the expansion of Seoul's redevelopment projects. Therefore there are no fundamental changes other than adjusting the promotion timeline for project districts and controlling corruption.

Multiple-home owners and policy for private rented housing

While it may be difficult for foreign scholars to understand, the issue of those owning multiple homes is very important for Korean housing policy, and moreover, for public opinion. Especially when house prices are increasing, these homeowners are seen as the major culprits of price hikes and social pressure increases to suppress the phenomenon. The government actually created measures to increase taxation for people who owned multiple homes in the early 1990s and also during the Roh administration, when house prices saw a sharp increase.

Property taxes are normally managed as local taxes by regional administrators. However, during the aforementioned periods, these taxes were raised and some parts of them were incorporated into national taxes. In addition, the Roh administration raised the transfer income tax for second homes to 50 per cent, and required 60 per cent for third homes and beyond, which normally exempted those who have only one home. Progressive scholars and political parties often see 'single-home ownership as a value to be pursued, and multiple-home ownership as something to be overcome' (Sohn, N.-G., 2008, 2009; Byun, C.-H., 2008). The Democratic Labour Party in particular has proposed a policy restricting multiple-home ownership itself. There is also the expectation that if multiple-home ownership is repressed, the extra homes will stabilize the housing market by increasing supply.

On the other hand, scholars who emphasize market economics point to the various penalties imposed on multiple-home owners (e.g. in taxation) as an 'obsession with the policy of one family–one home', and claim that this must be eliminated (Kim, G.-H., 2008; Lee, C.-M., 2008). They claim that housing supply could actually be repressed by the stigma attached to multiple-home ownership. When the housing industry is weak or the economy is suffering, the upper classes must purchase extra homes in order to continuously fuel housing supply. These extra homes end up back on the market as private rental housing.

These two positions were clearly and politically articulated after the 2008 economic crisis when the Lee administration eliminated the taxes levied on multiple-home owners and promoted economic recovery centred on the construction industry. The majority party, the Grand National Party, claimed that the tax burden on multiple-home owners had become overly penalizing and that real-estate speculation would not occur even if taxes were eliminated. In contrast, minority parties such as the Democratic Party and the Democratic Labour Party attacked the tax decreases and labelled them as 'tax cuts for the rich', and warned that the 'house-rich' would gain extreme benefits with house-price rises. However, under severe economic circumstances, taxes and financial repression of multiple-home owners were mostly eradicated.

While the discussion of whether to suppress or pragmatically accept the ownership of multiple homes continues, surprisingly, there is no discussion about the income that multiple-home owners make when they lease their extra homes. The ownership itself of multiple homes is criticized, but no one raised the issue of the management of those extra homes. About 40 per cent of all families in Korea live in privately leased homes, but only about 3 per cent of all the private rental housing is registered.

Furthermore, lease taxes are virtually nonexistent, and the restriction on raising lease prices by more than 5 per cent is ineffective because the home-owner can simply find a new tenant after the first contract is over (typically two years). Rent regulation systems that can be seen in other advanced nations, including registration of leased homes, taxation on lease income and fair rent according to region, are absent or unenforced in Korea.

Financial regulations and taxation on multiple-home owners have lost public trust because of the instability in the housing sector. It is thus necessary to approach the problem from the perspective of the social role of the private rental housing resulting from multiple-home ownership. That is, the income earned by multiple-home owners from leasing their extra homes should be taxed instead of increasing transfer taxes.

CONCLUSION: TASKS OF KOREAN HOUSING POLICY

Koreans tend to believe that they are experiencing the worst housing situation in the world. As house prices have risen dramatically, and 80 per cent of household assets are locked in real estate, the fluctuations of house prices has become a key political issue. Therefore the concern about housing prices falls since the economic crisis forced the Korean government to rely on traditional pump-priming policies. That is, it cut taxes for housing and tried to lower the burden of bank loans. In addition, the relief loan support for the construction sector and the active housing supply policies for government were introduced.

As a result, the Korean housing market, against expectations, recovered quickly. Price recovery alone, however, cannot address the underlying problems of the Korean housing market. Rather, price recovery signals even greater danger of a subsequent bursting of a larger bubble. Also, expansion of redevelopment projects raises the issues of the deteriorating housing circumstances of the low-income class. These issues were politically magnified, especially by encouraging the ownership of multiple houses as a way of pump-priming the housing industry. In this context, it is broadly accepted by progressive scholars that Korean housing policy has the following four core tasks (Kim, S.-H., 2009b).

First, housing policy must not be used as a main tool for economic recovery. The development and utilization of real estate are closely related to the entire economic structure so that the policy cannot be enacted without such considerations. If, however, housing policy is used excessively as a means for economic recovery, the economy becomes distorted, and unnecessary resources flow towards the housing area. It may seem to be immediately effective, but in the end house-price fluctuation returns and the living standards of the general population deteriorate even further.

Second, a structure must be established where unearned income does not occur through real estate. The best method is to construct a tax system where excessive profit cannot be generated from ownership and trading of real estate. It is particularly urgent to actualize property tax, which is still low compared to advanced nations.

Third, the low-income population needs to be supported so that appropriate housing can be secured. As economic polarization is deepening, those who cannot acquire housing via the market is increasing. Due to the demolition of existing cheap housing through redevelopment or 'new town' projects, the housing-cost burden is further increasing for this class. Accordingly, the livelihood of this class must be protected through public rental housing, rent-support systems and resettlement support for existing tenants in the case of redevelopment projects.

Fourth, housing policy should attempt to achieve a balance of ownership/private rented/public rented. Policy focusing only on ownership has proven to be very vulnerable in this economic crisis. Ownership, private rented and public rented respectively all have roles to play. Public rental housing is the most costly and hard to manage, but is the most effective way to provide housing for the most economically vulnerable households. Private rented housing is helpful in relation to recent trends where single-person households and housing mobility are increasing. However, private renting has received almost no political attention because it is locked behind the ideological screen of houses owned by multiple-home owners. Because of this, the private rented sector is the least developed area in Korean housing policy.

In this context, the issue of multiple-home ownership must be examined practically rather than ideologically. The task of actualizing lease income tax and maintaining the lease regulation system to the level of advanced nations is just as urgent. This perspective differs from that of those scholars who emphasize the role of the market because this is not to simply acknowledge multiple-home ownership, but to stress the need to modernize the private rented sector.

NOTES

1. That is why Korean banking system is safe even if house prices drop. This was the case in the Asian financial crisis and in the current crisis as well.
2. At that time, Korea experienced an astonishing house-price crash, the first in its history. It collapsed about 14 per cent in 1998.
3. Compared to 2007, when part of the property tax was made national, the collected amount of integral real-estate tax dropped to less than half that for 2009.
4. 'New town' here does not mean constructing a new city on the outskirts of a large city, but developing an old section into a new residential area.

REFERENCES

In Korean

Advisory Committee for Housing Improvement of Seoul (2009), 'Document for public hearing held by Seoul Metropolitan Government', 15 January.
Byun, Chang-Heum (2008), 'Politics of desire and Lee, Myung-Bak administration's real estate policy', *Memories and Prospect*, **19**, 63–94.
Byun, Chang-Heum (2009), 'Housing market expansionism and housing policy of the Lee administration', in Lee, Jeong-Jeon et al. (eds), *Real Estate Crisis*, Seoul: Humanitas, pp. 152–80.
KBS (Korean Broadcasting Corporation) (2007), 'Hope to be homeowners?', *In-depth 60 Minutes*, 17 January.
Kim, Gyung-Hwan (2008), 'Revision of real estate tax: the half success', *Maeil Business Newspaper*, 9 January.
Kim, Gyung-Woo (2009), *Catch the New Housing Boom*, Seoul: Hans Media.
Kim, Jong-Seon (2009), *New Housing Boom will Turn Up in 2011*, Seoul: Vision Korea.
Kim, Nam-Geun (2009), 'Development for profit and human rights violation, people's solidarity for democracy', *Citizens and the World*, **15**, 227–39.
Kim, Soo-Hyun (2008), *Principles and Issues of Housing Policy*, Seoul: Hanul Academy.
Kim, Soo-Hyun (2009a), 'Understanding of new town and its alternative, people's solidarity for democracy', *Citizens and the World*, **15**, 208–26.
Kim, Soo-Hyun (2009b), 'Housing policy for coexistence', in Lee, Jeong-Jeon et al. (eds), *Real Estate Crisis*, Seoul: Humanitas, pp. 263–84.

KKS Economic Research Institute (2009), *Burst of Economic Bubble and Long-term Recession*, Seoul: Human & Books.

Lee, Chang-Moo (2008), 'A way to normalize housing market', paper for National Assembly Conference.

Munhwa Broadcasting Corporation (MBC) (2010), 'Where to? Housing market in 2010', *100 Minutes' Debate*, 4 February.

Park, Deok-Bae (2009), 'Household asset is in danger', Hyun-Dai Economic Research Institute Report, 2 August.

Seon, Dae-In (2008), *Housing Bubble Bust is Impending*, Seoul: Hankook Business Newspaper Press.

Seon, Dae-In (2009), *Dangerous Economics*, Seoul: Deonan.

Seoul Development Institute (SDI) (2008), *Strategies for Implementation of New Town Projects in Seoul*.

Seoul Metropolitan Government (City of Seoul) (2007a), *Studies on Demolition of Low Price and Small Housing*.

Seoul Metropolitan Government (City of Seoul) (2007b), *A Method of Improving Resettlement Rate of Original Resident in New Town Project*.

Sohn, Nak-Gu (2008), *Society of Real Estate Class*, Seoul: Humanitas.

Sohn, Nak-Gu (2009), 'Real estate class and Korean society', in Lee, Jeong-Jeon et al. (eds), *Real Estate Crisis*, Seoul: Humanitas, pp. 210–37.

12. Towards a post-homeowner society? Homeownership and economic insecurity in Japan

Yosuke Hirayama

INTRODUCTION

With the outbreak of the global financial crisis triggered by the US sub-prime mortgage meltdown, people's fortunes relating to homeownership are now being affected by an increasingly insecure economy (Schwartz and Seabrooke, 2009). Over the past two decades, many societies have undergone the sustained expansion of property ownership under volatile economic conditions. This has drawn increasing attention to the significance of the role played by housing economies in shaping social processes (Doling and Ford, 2003; Forrest, 2008; Ronald, 2008). However, wider economic changes do not necessarily produce the same outcome, but are mediated by the indigenous social, economic, political, institutional and policy contexts of particular countries and, thus, create diverging effects on housing and social transformations. The impact of the current financial crisis on property ownership has also differed between different countries.

Japan provides an acute case in relation to how economic instability affects homeownership. The housing system in postwar Japan has consistently driven the growth of the owner-occupied housing sector and nurtured the creation of a 'homeowner society', where many households have successively ascended the housing ladder towards achieving property ownership (Hirayama, 2007). Immediately after the 'bubble economy' collapsed at the beginning of the 1990s, however, Japan entered a noticeably prolonged period of enduring recession with minimal or negative real growth in GDP, rising unemployment rates and reduced real incomes. Although the Japanese economy eventually began to recover in 2002, the economic upturn was not particularly strong and did not serve to improve the household economy. Moreover, Japan again began entering a severe recession in 2008, having become involved in the global financial crisis. There has consequently been an obvious decline in the cycle in which the large majority of households have ceaselessly followed a conventional housing path into homeownership (Hirayama, 2010a). Japan's contemporary housing situation is now raising questions as to the extent to which 'homeowner societies' can be maintained and whether a 'post-homeowner society' will emerge or not.

This chapter explores the sustainability of Japan's homeowning society with particular reference to the prolonged economic turbulence. The focus is on the structural decline in the cycle of successive moves by people who have followed the conventional housing path to the homeownership sector. The stagnated economy has progressively prevented many households from climbing the property ladder. Increasing numbers of individuals and households have thus begun to follow non-conventional housing paths in response to changes in the housing economy. However, various responses to economic fluctuations have not necessarily been effective in improving housing conditions. The chapter begins by looking at the changing economic context of the Japanese housing system. It then moves on to analyse the ways in which more turbulent economic conditions have affected the attainment of homeownership and the accumulation of housing assets, demonstrating a decline in the cycle of moves up the property ladder. The chapter finally highlights individual and household strategies responding to economic changes in terms of securing housing and accessing homeownership.

JAPAN'S HOMEOWNERSHIP AND THE ECONOMIC CONTEXT

The Japanese government has been explicitly inclined towards facilitating middle-class homeownership since the immediate postwar period (Hirayama, 2007). Of the various housing policy measures, the provision of the Government Housing Loan Corporation's (GHLC) low-interest loans was particularly aimed at expanding the owner-occupied housing sector. Since the 1960s the level of owner-occupied housing has been maintained at around 60 per cent, representing its position as the dominant housing tenure. After the bubble burst, however, the deep recession began to erode the economic pillar of homeownership. Subsequently, the global financial turmoil has further undermined the system of expanding property ownership. This section explores the economic context of transformations in Japan's homeowning society.

Since the early 1990s, the post-bubble recession has played a key role in disintegrating the homeownership-oriented housing system. The overall economy became deflationary and a decrease in income has made it more difficult for many renters to enter the homeownership market. The real prices of land and housing dropped sharply, leading to a notable increase in the number of homeowners trapped in negative equity (Forrest et al., 2003; Hirayama, 2003, 2007). Some developed countries had experienced house-price deflation before the onset of the sub-prime crisis. Decreases in house prices during the pre-sub-prime crisis period were usually observed for relatively short periods. In the UK, house prices began to drop in 1989 but started to rise again in 1994. The prices of new housing in the USA, which began decreasing in the late 1980s, started to increase again in the early 1990s. In Japan, however, the fall in residential land prices, which began in 1991, was extraordinarily prolonged. When Japan's post-bubble recession came to an end in 2001, the subsequent economic recovery was expected to stimulate an upturn in the housing market. However, rises in the price of residential land were only seen in Tokyo and a few other large cities during the short period from 2006 to mid-2008. Residential land prices continued to drop throughout the rest of the country even after the post-bubble recession ended. Consequently, the Japanese homeownership economy has been substantially reorganized.

Post-bubble stagnation has also encouraged the government to re-orientate housing policy towards a more neoliberal model. Compared to Western countries, particularly those that are Anglo-Saxon, the introduction of neoliberal policies was remarkably slow in Japan (Forrest and Hirayama, 2009). While the liberalization of policy started in the early 1980s in the UK and the USA, the Japanese version of neoliberal policy began to emerge only in the mid-1990s. Unlike Western countries, which had experienced a prolonged recession since the oil crisis in the early 1970s, Japan's economy had maintained a relatively strong performance until the bubble burst. This accounted for the delay in reorganizing policy. However, the post-bubble economic downturn fuelled the reorientation of housing policy. The interest rates on residential mortgages set by the private banking sector, which had been regulated by the government, were liberalized in 1994. The government subsequently began to form a mortgage-backed security market. The GHLC, which had been the core of traditional housing measures, was abolished in 2007. This signified an especially important shift in the postwar history of Japanese housing policy. While the Japan Housing Finance Agency was established as the successor to the GHLC, it withdrew from the primary mortgage market and thereafter only dealt with the secondary market of mortgage securities.

The global financial crisis provoked housing deflation in many countries. However, the way in which the crisis has affected housing and mortgage markets has differed according to the economic and policy contexts of particular countries. Until the sub-prime crisis, many Western countries had undergone long periods of unprecedented housing inflation since the mid-1990s (Kim and Renaud, 2009). The global economic crisis has thus brought about acute downward shifts in house prices in these countries. Of the advanced economies, Japan, along with Germany and Switzerland, have been an exception to the trends in house prices that many other countries have experienced, where housing prices have been almost continually decreasing since the 1990s. While the turmoil in the global economy has translated into downturns in dwelling prices in large cities in Japan (where house prices had risen since 2006), it has dealt an additional blow to the prolonged stagnation in the housing economy in smaller cities where house prices had continued to drop since the early 1990s.

Japan's homeowner society, which has long been in the grip of stagnation, is now being challenged by the new economic crisis. In many advanced countries, particularly Anglo-Saxon countries, where neoliberal policies on deregulating capital markets have been in place for some time, financial institutions have been greatly affected by the sub-prime crisis. By contrast, the direct impact of the sub-prime meltdown on the Japanese banking sector has been relatively limited, implying that Japan has delayed forming a mortgage-backed security market (Forrest and Hirayama, 2009). However, Japan's export-based macroeconomy has been seriously damaged by economic downturns in overseas countries, particularly the USA, and by the rapid appreciation of the Japanese yen. The bankruptcy of Lehman Brothers Holdings Inc. in September 2008 provided a trigger for throwing the Japanese economy as well as many other economies into a crisis-level recession. Annualized GDP growth rates in Japan were recorded at minus 12.3 per cent from October to December in 2008 and minus 11.4 per cent from January to March in 2009. The worsening macroeconomic situation has led to unprecedented drops in housing new starts, property transactions and house prices, further undermining the foundation of the homeowner society.

The new economic crisis has prompted the Japanese government to intervene in the housing market. Housing policy in postwar Japan has explicitly been implemented as an economic policy measure (Oizumi, 2007). Greater numbers of GHLC loans were granted when the economy became stagnant – after the first oil crisis in the early 1970s, after the second oil crisis in the late 1970s, after the beginning of the recession related to the Plaza Accord in 1985, and after the bubble collapsed in the early 1990s. This had created stimulating effects on economic recovery through accelerating construction of owner-occupied dwellings. Neoliberal housing policy, which involved the dissolution of the GHLC, meant less government intervention in the housing market. With the extraordinary downswing in the macroeconomy caused by the global financial crisis, however, since 2009 the government has begun to implement a series of housing measures to encourage the economy to recover. This is best represented by the policy on reducing mortgage-liability-related tax for home purchasers to an unprecedented extent. Nevertheless, the deflationary economy, with a decrease in incomes, has waylaid the government's emergency plan that was aimed at increasing the number of housing purchases and thus no recovery in the housing market has yet been seen.

It is also noticeable that demographic changes peculiar to Japan have linked with unstable economic conditions to accelerate fluctuations in the homeownership market. It was not only the economic bubble but also the moves of the baby-boomer-generation households up the housing ladder that encouraged the volatility in housing prices (Hirayama, 2007). Many baby-boomers, who were born in the last half of the 1940s, entered the homeownership market by the early 1980s and produced a large-scale demand for dwellings, which triggered the subsequent rise in house prices. By the early 1990s many baby-boomers had become homeowners, which encouraged the drop in house prices during the post-bubble period. The end of the post-bubble recession brought the upward shift in house prices in Tokyo and some other large cities in the mid-2000s. This was again implicated in demographic changes. The second baby-boomer generation, who were born in the first half of the 1970s and included the offspring of the baby-boomer generation, began to enter the homeownership market in the early 2000s, supporting the upturn in house prices in large cities. The direct factor that caused the subsequent downturn in the property market was the occurrence of the global financial crisis. However, an increase in second baby-boomer households who had achieved property ownership accelerated the downturn in housing prices. Housing-market movements have thus characteristically been implicated in not only economic but also demographic processes.

Moreover, the total population of Japan began to decrease in 2006. This is because Japan has one of the lowest fertility rates in the world. According to the 2006 estimate by the National Institute of Population and Social Security Research, the population, which was 128 million in 2005, will decrease to 90 million by 2055. This will be accompanied by an accelerated increase in the proportion of older people. The percentage of those aged 65 or more, which was 20.2 per cent in 2005, is forecast to increase to as much as 40.5 per cent by 2055. The number of households is also predicted to begin decreasing in 2015. The second baby-boomer generation was the last large cohort of first-time homebuyers. Since the global financial crisis, the Japanese housing economy has become more stagnant. This is now being combined with demographic changes to encourage a further decline in investment in housing.

DECLINE IN THE SOCIAL CYCLE

Since the early 1990s, continued stagnation has led to an apparent decline in the social cycle in which many people have successively moved towards accessing homeownership and accumulating housing assets (Hirayama, 2010a). In terms of entering the homeownership market, economic transformations have particularly affected younger groups (Forrest and Hirayama, 2009; Hirayama and Ronald, 2008). Older generations climbed the property ladder relatively nimbly before the bubble. Since the rise and fall of the bubble restructured the housing economy, however, younger generations have increasingly been confronted with more disadvantageous conditions in purchasing housing. Between 1983 and 2008, the level of homeownership decreased significantly, from 24.9 per cent to 11.8 per cent for households with a head aged 25–29, and from 60.1 per cent to 47.0 per cent for those aged 35–39. Despite the drop in the level of homeownership for younger households, the average level of homeownership for all households has hovered at around 60 per cent. This is due to an increase in the proportion of the older population having higher homeownership levels. Although owner-occupation has continued to be the dominant housing tenure, routes onto the property ladder have become increasingly constricted for younger generations.

The tendency for younger cohorts to delay accessing the homeownership market can be attributed largely to the 'casualization' of the labour force, with a substantial decline in wages. In response to the post-bubble recession, and within the context of a more competitive business environment, increasing numbers of corporations, struggling for survival, have carried out large-scale restructuring and downsizing of personnel. Moreover, neoliberal policy has involved the deregulation of employment practices. The labour market has thus been reoriented around declining stability in employment with associated rapid increases in the number of short-term contracts, part-time workers and temporary employees. The impact of labour-market reorganization has not been equally spread across generations, but has concentrated on younger cohorts (Genda, 2001). According to the Employment Status Survey, of all employees, the average percentage of non-regular employees (part-time, temporary and dispatched employees) rose from 15.8 per cent in 1982 to 33.0 per cent in 2007. During the same period, the percentage of non-regular employees aged 20–24 increased more sharply from 11.4 per cent to 43.1 per cent.

It is also necessary to look at a rapid increase in younger people who have delayed marriage and thus their establishment of independent families. Unlike some Western countries, where not only family households but also single people tend to aspire to homeownership, most people do not purchase a house until marriage in Japan, where acquiring an owner-occupied home is strongly linked to establishing a family. The increase in unmarried individuals has thus meant a decline in housing purchases. According to the Population Census, between 1980 and 2005, the percentage of unmarried people in the 30–34 age group rose from 21.5 per cent to 47.1 per cent for males, and from 9.1 per cent to 32.0 per cent for females. Furthermore, worsening economic conditions have deprived young individuals of opportunities to get married and establish their own families. There has been a clear correlation between the unmarried rate and economic status. The Employment Status Survey in 2002 revealed that the percentage of unmarried men aged 30–34 in regular employment was 41 per cent, while the figure for those in non-regular employment was notably high at 70 per cent (MHLW, 2006).

The economic conditions for purchasing a dwelling have become increasingly disadvantageous due to a combination of a decrease in incomes and an increase in mortgage-repayment costs (Hirayama, 2010a). The collapse of the bubble encouraged deflation in house prices. However, the decline in incomes has translated into smaller deposits and therefore larger mortgage liabilities. The supply of GHLC mortgages was expanded to a record high level in the first half of the 1990s, and interest rates since the 1990s have remained at extraordinarily low levels due to policies to stimulate the economy. This has effectively led housing purchasers to take out larger housing loans. Consequently, despite the drop in housing prices, the burdens of mortgage repayments have increased. Younger households with lower incomes have been plunged into particularly disadvantageous economic conditions in terms of purchasing a house. Of owner-occupier households with a head aged 34 or less, the percentage of those whose monthly housing costs to disposable income was 20 per cent or more increased from 18.7 per cent in 1989 to 36.6 per cent in 2004 (Hirayama, 2010a).

Before the bubble burst, the homeownership-oriented housing system was implicated in the capital-gain-based economy, where owning a house was a particularly efficient means of accumulating assets. Renters entering the homeownership market as first-time buyers were able to expect an appreciation in the real value of properties they were acquiring, while those possessing a house could have prospects of moving to a better house using the property as a stepping stone. Indeed, capital gains fuelled the system of propelling people towards the top of the property ladder. Since the bubble collapsed, however, most residential properties have continued to fall in value, with an increase in capital losses.

Almost all households that have purchased a dwelling within at least the past two decades have experienced devaluation of their property. The extent of housing depreciation has varied between different types of

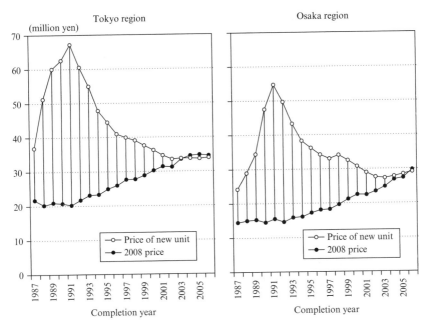

Note: Tokyo region includes prefectures of Saitama, Chiba, Tokyo and Kanagawa. Osaka region includes prefectures of Shiga, Kyoto, Osaka, Hyogo, Nara and Wakayama.

Source: Tokyo Kantei.

Figure 12.1 Capital losses on typical condominium units of 70 m²

dwelling, and the rate at which housing prices have fallen has been greater in second-hand housing than in newly built housing, and in condominiums rather than in single-family dwellings (Hirayama, 2005). The scale of capital losses generated on condominiums has thus been substantial. As shown in Figure 12.1, the average price of a newly built condominium with a floor area of 70 m² was 67.2 million yen (£448 000 [£1 = ¥150, November 2009]) in the Tokyo region in 1991. This fell to 20.3 million yen (£135 000) by 2008, generating a capital loss of 46.9 million yen (£313 000). In other words, the value of condominiums purchased during the peak of the bubble has fallen sharply by some 70 per cent. This also holds true for the Osaka region (see Figure 12.1).

The asset conditions of homeowners have been undermined with an increase in outstanding mortgage debts and a decrease in gross residential-property assets (Hirayama, 2010a). As seen in Figure 12.2, of owner-occupier households with a head aged 35–44, the percentage of those

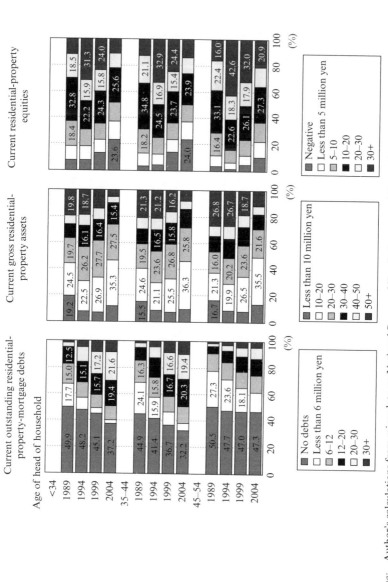

Source: Author's calculations from microdata on National Survey of Family Income and Expenditure

Figure 12.2 Changes in outstanding mortgage debt, gross assets and equities on residential properties of owner-occupier households

whose current outstanding mortgage debts were 12 million yen (£80 000) or more continued to increase from 14.6 per cent in 1989 to 49.0 per cent in 2004, while the percentage of those with a residential property whose current gross value was 30 million yen (£200 000) or more increased from 40.4 per cent in 1989 to 46.5 per cent in 1994 and then decreased, with the post-bubble economic downturn, to 28.0 per cent in 2004. There has been an increase in owner-occupiers with heavier mortgage liabilities who have retained properties whose values have dropped. Consequently, increasing numbers of homeowners have become trapped in negative equity. The maximum levels of loan-to-value ratios in Japan have been high as 80–100 per cent, which has encouraged the increase in negative housing equity. From 1989 to 2004, the percentage of owner-occupier households with negative housing equity rose from 8.0 per cent to 23.6 per cent for the 34-or-less age group, and from 3.6 per cent to 24.0 per cent for the 35–44 age group (see Figure 12.2).

There is no doubt that the new global financial crisis is further worsening economic circumstances pertaining to property ownership. A decline in the stability of employment and income is beginning to discourage an increasing number of renters from entering the owner-occupied housing market while a sharp drop in house prices is leading to a further increase in homeowners with negative equity. This implies a decrease in the extent to which homeownership status is pervasive and normative in Japanese society. There has also been an increase in mortgage defaults, signifying the beginning of a new era characterized by higher risks with regard to the maintenance of homeownership. As mortgage defaults increased, the GHLC was pressed to launch a series of new schemes to assist borrowers with difficulties in repaying their housing loans. As a result, increasing numbers of borrowers have been permitted to extend mortgage-repayment periods. Mortgage defaults are expected to further increase due to the current economic crisis.

The neoliberal housing policy involving the abolition of the GHLC has imposed more risks relating to mortgages on individual housing purchasers, particularly those on lower incomes. This has been responsible, at least partly, for the increase in mortgage defaults. Unlike the GHLC, which provided all borrowers with mortgages under homogeneous conditions in terms of interest rates, loan limits and guarantee fees, private banks have supplied more diverse mortgage commodities under varied lending conditions. This has encouraged lower-income housing purchasers to take out riskier housing loans. According to a survey of those who procured a mortgage in 2006, which was carried out by the Japan Housing Finance Agency, the percentage of those who borrowed all the necessary principal without making a deposit in purchasing a house was 21 per cent among higher-income people who earned 8 million–20 million yen annually, and 39 per cent for lower-income people who earned 4 million yen or less. The initial interest on a variable-rate mortgage is lower than that on a fixed-rate mortgage. However, variable-rate mortgages are riskier due to uncertain interest levels in the future. The survey revealed that the percentage of borrowers without deposits was 20 per cent for those who chose a fixed-rate housing loan but higher at 32 per cent for those who took out a variable-rate loan.

INDIVIDUAL AND HOUSEHOLD RESPONSES

Remaining in Parental Housing

How then are individuals and households coping with the prolonged economic stagnation in securing housing? A decline in the use of the traditional housing ladder has discouraged increasing numbers of individuals and households from following a conventional housing path and instead encouraged them to devise non-conventional ways of accessing housing (Hirayama, 2010a). Various responses to the less stable housing economy have involved: remaining in parental housing; continuing to live in rented housing; forming dual-earner households in purchasing a house; and waiting to inherit parents' houses. However, it is also important to look at a wide range of limits imposed on these responses in terms of accessing adequate, affordable housing. This section examines a variety of individual and household strategies relating to securing housing.

A new phenomenon for younger generations has been a notable increase in parental-home dwellers or 'parasite singles' – young unmarried adults who continue to live in parents' houses (Yamada, 1999). Younger groups have been particularly affected by the longstanding economic stagnation in terms of ascending the housing ladder. This has led many unmarried individuals to remain in parental homes. According to a combination of various data obtained from the Population Census, between 1980 and 2005, the percentages of parental-home dwellers rose from 24.0 per cent to 41.3 per cent for the 25–29 age group, and from 8.2 per cent to 24.8 per cent for the 30–34 age group (Hirayama, 2010a). Until the mid-1990s, the aftermath of the bubble economy generated an image that young adults living in parental homes indulged themselves by consuming luxury goods without having to incur housing costs or food expenses (Yamada, 1999). Since the late 1990s, however, with the prolonged post-bubble recession, the economic instability of parental-home dwellers has attracted increasing attention (Shirahase, 2005). A survey of young adults living in their parents' homes, conducted by the National Institute of Population and Social Security Research (2001), found that many parental-home dwellers were non-regular employees who did not have sufficient income to leave home to establish an independent household. It is thus reasonable to regard the increase in parental-home dwellers not as a phenomenon reflecting young people's dependent attitudes but as a consequence of their economically rational strategies for securing places in which to live.

The increase in parental-home dwellers has been made possible by a particular form of intergenerational relationship. The sustained promotion of homeownership has encouraged the current generation of parents to acquire their own spacious home, which has enabled the younger generation to live with them. The housing conditions of young adults living in their parents' homes are thus likely to be relatively stable and a large majority of them are assumed to occupy their own private rooms in the house. However, the economic circumstances surrounding 'parasite singles' are not necessarily stable (Hirayama, 2010a). The incomes of households involving unmarried young adults tend to decrease with advancing age due to their parents' retirements. Regardless of whether or not parental-home dwellers are 'parasitic', their parents' incomes, which they may have relied on, unavoidably decline. If parental-home dwellers are in secure employment, an increase in their own incomes with advancing age is likely to compensate for the decrease in their parents' incomes. However, many parental-home dwellers are casual workers on low wages.

Living in a Rented Dwelling

In response to economic changes in housing circumstances, there has been an increase in households that have continued to live in rented dwellings. In Japan, the provision of public rental housing has traditionally been residual (Hirayama, 2003). Private rented housing has thus occupied the main position in the rental market. As has been discussed, the economic burdens imposed by purchasing a house have become heavier while the value of most property assets has continued to decline. Therefore increasing numbers of households have relied on the private rented sector. Between 1983 and 2008, the percentage of private rented housing increased from 33.5 per cent to 57.0 per cent for households with a head aged 30–34, and from 18.4 per cent to 31.1 per cent for those aged 40–44. However, many renters have experienced disadvantages in terms of physical conditions and housing costs. As argued earlier, the government has traditionally operated a tenure-discriminatory housing system, concentrating on expanding middle-class homeownership. There has almost been no government support for improving private rented housing. This has been based on the assumption that private rented housing provides a temporary foothold on the lower rungs of the housing ladder and that many households move out of private rented dwellings after a short period and acquire their own homes. With transformations in the housing economy, however, an increasing number of households have begun to live in private rented housing for longer periods, meaning an increase of those in disadvantageous housing conditions.

Within the context of the prolonged stagnation, the deflationary economy with a decrease in real incomes is likely to promote a drop in market rents. Nevertheless, real rent levels have risen. The main factor behind this is the reduced availability of low-rent housing (Hirayama, 2010a). In Japan, many 'non-professional' property owners have managed rented dwellings. Although providing private rental housing has not been particularly profitable, many individuals or families who hold land have constructed rented housing as a sideline without having to invest in site acquisition (Morimoto, 1994). This has made the supply of low-rent housing possible. The rents of multi-family housing in wooden structures have been set at particularly low levels. While dwellings of this type have mostly been substandard in terms of floor area and amenities, they have functioned as low-cost shelters for low-income renters to live in. However, the number of existing low-rent private rental dwellings has substantially decreased due to structural ageing or dilapidation.

Moreover, in the late 1990s the government began to restructure the private rented housing market in alignment with neoliberal policy. The intention was to 'modernize' the system of providing and financing rental housing while establishing a more 'professional' and profitable market for investments in private rented housing. This led to major amendments to the Housing Lease Act in 1999. Before this amendment, tenants' security of tenure was protected and thus landlords could not easily evict them. However, with this amendment, it is now possible for owners to rent their houses for more limited periods and thus more accurately calculate their prospects of making profits. The government has also sought to establish a rental-property-security market. This requires yields from security investments to be more predictable. As a consequence of the new policy to 'modernize' the private rented housing sector, low-rent dwellings provided by non-professional landlords are declining while higher-rent dwellings financed by more professional investors are on the increase.

Forming a Dual-earner Household

There has been an increase in married couples who form dual-earner households in purchasing a house (Hirayama and Izuhara, 2008). Wives' participation in the workforce is a pervasive household strategy responding to changes in the economic circumstances of those entering the homeownership market. The establishment of families in Japan has traditionally been based on the 'male breadwinner family' model (Yokoyama, 2002). Nevertheless, continued economic stagnation has weakened the stability of male employment and incomes, and has consequently encouraged a decrease in household incomes. This has resulted in increasing numbers of married women entering the paid workforce (Iwama, 2008). Changes in the housing market have also made it more rational for married couples to form dual-earner households in accessing homeownership. As the economic burdens imposed by purchasing a house have become heavier, many women have increasingly been expected to earn substantial incomes. In addition, a rise in the age for first-time marriages has meant shorter periods in which mortgages can be repaid. This has further pressed married couples to earn dual incomes to finish repaying their mortgages earlier.

According to the National Survey of Family Income and Expenditure, the percentage of dual-earner households against all households including married couples, from 1989 through 2004, rose from 28.7 per cent to 41.3 per cent for the 25–29 age group, and from 38.0 per cent to 41.4 per cent for the 35–39 age group. Dual-earner households are more likely to live in owner-occupied housing compared to single-earner households. For example, in the 35–39 age group, the level of homeownership in 2004 was 69.1 per cent for dual-earner households and 58.1 per cent for single-earner households. The implication is that the entry of women into the workforce has become more decisive in enabling homeownership to be accessed.

It is, however, worth emphasizing that women are still disadvantaged in the labour market. With the increased significance of gender equality as a policy issue, the Equal Opportunity Act enacted in 1985 and the major amendments to this in 1997 and 2006 provided an institutional framework for enhancing women's status in the labour market. The enactment of the Basic Law for a Gender-Equal Society in 1999 also meant that gender equality became a public policy priority. These legislative institutions forced corporations to abandon gender discrimination in employment practices. However, they developed new employment categories in which employees, who accepted company orders such as work-related moves and longer working hours with higher salaries and greater employment stability, were considered *de facto* men. This system has effectively maintained *de facto* gender discrimination in employment practices. Moreover, neoliberal labour policy, which has encouraged the 'casualization' of the workforce, has affected women rather than men, resulting in the 'feminization' of casual employment. The 2007 Employment Status Survey indicated that the level of non-regular employees aged 25–29 was 39.9 per cent for women and 18.3 per cent for men. Therefore incomes earned by women have remained at low levels. While increasing numbers of dual-earner households have succeeded in entering the homeownership sector, to what extent women's economic status will be improved remains unseen.

Waiting to Inherit Houses

In mature homeowner societies like Japan, which have accumulated a huge amount of family-housing wealth, the role played by intergenerational relations has become increasingly significant in housing and social processes (Hirayama, 2010b; Izuhara, 2010). While, on the one hand, younger generations have experienced a more sluggish economy and faced difficulties in ascending the property ladder, on the other, an increasing number of young people are expected to inherit the housing assets of their parent's generation. A high level of homeownership among older generations combined with decreasing fertility has meant increasing possibilities for the next generation to inherit residential properties. Older households also maintain homeownership partly to bequeath property assets to their children. According to the Survey on People's Consciousness about Land Issues in 2008, approximately half the respondents who wished to own land and housing expressed the intention to bequeath assets to their offspring as the main reason they wanted to own real-estate properties.

Younger households are thus likely to have the option of waiting to inherit their parents' housing instead of purchasing a home with the burden of loan repayment. Nevertheless, there are limits to this 'waiting for inheritance' strategy in terms of improving the housing situations for younger people (Hirayama, 2010b). The offspring generation is unlikely to inherit housing property until they become considerably older due to increasing longevity that delays property succession. Younger households therefore tend to acquire their own housing rather than waiting to inherit their parents' properties. In addition, inherited housing does not necessarily effectively improve the housing circumstances of the younger generation. There are many households who do not live in a parental house they inherited because its location and physical condition are not necessarily attractive.

Furthermore, inequalities relating to housing properties within the older generation are increasingly being passed down to the next generation (Hirayama, 2010b). The housing and asset conditions of young households in the future will partly be determined by whether their parents own a house and whether they can inherit it. According to research on the possibility for urban renters to inherit housing, renters with relatively high incomes tended to have good prospects of inheriting housing while most low-income renters did not have any possibility of inheriting residential properties (Sonoda, 2000). There will thus be an increasing number of families accumulating property assets over generations while low-income families will own only limited housing assets.

Within the framework of intergenerational relations, *inter vivo* asset transfer, in addition to inheritance, plays a role in encouraging the younger generation to access homeownership. In response to the new economic crisis caused by the global turmoil in financial markets, in 2009 the government, with the intention of stimulating economic recovery, substantially reduced taxes on gifts in cases where parents financially support their children in purchasing housing. However, this tax policy to promote *inter vivo* asset transfer has further exacerbated inequalities with regard to homeownership opportunities for younger generations. Wealthy parents are more likely to support their children in entering the homeownership market while parents with limited assets cannot help their offspring to purchase a house.

CONCLUSION

There has been a social cycle of successive moves up the property ladder in postwar Japan that has played a central role in maintaining the homeowner society. This chapter, however, has demonstrated that the post-bubble recession and the subsequent occurrence of the global financial crisis has exacerbated the conditions for acquiring owner-occupied housing and accumulating property assets. Increasing numbers of individuals and households have begun to follow non-conventional housing paths, responding to the decline in the traditional housing ladder. However, the chapter has pointed out various limits imposed on people's diverse responses to worsened economic conditions in terms of securing housing.

These findings prompt us to revisit the question of whether a new era of a 'post-homeowner society' will appear or not. Private ownership in Japan continues to occupy the main position as the dominant housing tenure. In this sense, Japan's homeowning society will probably be maintained in the foreseeable future. However, homeownership in present-day Japan is completely different from before. For the past two decades, most owner-occupied houses have consistently generated capital losses and an increasing number of homeowners have been trapped in negative equity. An owner-occupied home in today's Japan holds no promise of capital gain.

Moreover, younger generations are now increasingly being excluded from routes that could take them into the homeownership sector. The effectiveness of the homeownership-oriented housing system has undoubtedly been undermined. This suggests that Japan is arguably entering a period of 'post-homeownership'. With the decline in the cycle that has underpinned the maintenance of the homeowner society, the government is now pressed to reconsider the organization of housing policy and improve the conditions of not only the owner-occupied housing sector but also the rented housing sector. Many developed countries, which experienced prolonged periods of unprecedented housing inflation, have now begun to enter a new period with a more precarious economy. It is not certain at present how the current global financial crisis will affect homeownership systems. However, an examination of Japan's experience implies the importance of questioning to what extent homeowning societies are sustainable.

REFERENCES

Doling, John and Janet Ford (eds) (2003), *Globalization and Home Ownership: Experiences in Eight Member States of the European Union*, Delft: Delft University Press.

Forrest, R. (2008), 'Globalisation and the housing asset rich: geographies, demographies and policy convoys', *Global Social Policy*, **8** (2), 167–87.

Forrest, R. and Y. Hirayama (2009), 'The uneven impact of neo-liberalism on housing opportunities', *International Journal of Urban and Regional Research*, **33** (4), 998–1013.

Forrest, R., P. Kennett and M. Izuhara (2003), 'Home ownership and economic change in Japan', *Housing Studies*, **18** (3), 277–93.

Genda, Yuji (2001), *Shigoto no Naka no Aimai na Fuan [The Vague Uneasiness of Work]*, Tokyo: Chuo Korou Shinsha.

Hirayama, Y. (2003), 'Housing and social inequality in Japan', in M. Izuhara (ed.), *Comparing Social Policies: Exploring New Perspectives in Britain and Japan*, Bristol: Polity Press, pp. 151–71.

Hirayama, Y. (2005), 'Running hot and cold in the urban home ownership market: the experience of Japan's major cities', *Journal of Housing and the Built Environment*, **20** (1), 1–20.

Hirayama, Y. (2007), 'Reshaping the housing system: home ownership as a catalyst for social transformation', in Yosuke Hirayama and Richard Ronald (eds), *Housing and Social Transition in Japan*, London: Routledge, pp. 15–46.

Hirayama, Y. (2010a), 'Housing pathway divergence in Japan's insecure economy', *Housing Studies*, **25** (6), 777–97.

Hirayama, Y. (2010b), 'The role of home ownership in Japan's aged society', *Journal of Housing and the Built Environment*, **25** (2), 175–91.

Hirayama, Y. and M. Izuhara (2008), 'Women and housing assets in the context of Japan's home-owning democracy', *Journal of Social Policy*, **37** (4), 641–60.

Hirayama, Y. and R. Ronald (2008), 'Baby-boomers, baby-busters and the lost generation: generational fractures in Japan's homeowner society', *Urban Policy and Research*, **26** (3), 325–42.

Iwama, Akiko (2008), *Josei Shugyo to Kazoku no Yukue [Working Women and Family]*, Tokyo: Tokyo University Press.

Izuhara, Misa (ed.) (2010), *Aging and Intergenerational Relations: Family Reciprocity from a Global Perspective*, Portland, OR: Policy Press.

Kim, K. and B. Renaud (2009), 'The global house price boom and its unwinding: an analysis and a commentary', *Housing Studies*, **24** (1), 7–24.

Ministry of Health, Labour and Welfare (2006), *Rodo Keizai Hakusho [Government White Paper on the Labour Economy]*, Tokyo: National Printing Bureau.

Morimoto, Nobuaki (1994), *Toshi Kyoju to Chintai Jutaku [Urban Rental Housing]*, Kyoto: Gakugei Shuppan Sha.

National Institute of Population and Social Security Research (2001), *Setai nai Tanshinsha ni kansuru Jittai Chosa [Survey on Parental Home Dwellers]*, Tokyo: National Institute of Population and Social Security Research.

Oizumi, E. (2007), 'Transformations in housing construction and finance', in Yosuke Hirayama and Richard Ronald (eds), *Housing and Social Transition in Japan*, London: Routledge, pp. 47–72.

Ronald, Richard (2008), *The Ideology of Home Ownership: Homeowner Societies and the Role of Housing*, Basingstoke: Palgrave Macmillan.

Schwartz, M. Herman and Leonard Seabrooke (eds) (2009), *The Politics of Housing Booms and Busts*, Basingstoke: Palgrave Macmillan.

Shirahase, Sawako (2005), *Shoshi Korei Syakai no Mienai Kakusa [Invisible Inequalities in Low Fertility, Aged Society]*, Tokyo: Tokyo University Press.

Sonoda, M. (2000), 'Shutoken ni okeru kosodate setai no jutaku sozoku no kanosei to soreni kanrensuru jutaku juyo no tokusei [The effect of the intergenerational transfer of the house on the housing need for young family household], *Meiji Daigaku Riko Gakubu Kenkyu Hokoku [Research Report, School of Science and Technology, Meiji University]*', **23**, 23–30.

Yamada, Masahiro (1999), *Parasaito Shinguru no Jidai [The Time of Parasite Singles]*, Tokyo: Chikuma Shobo.

Yokoyama, Fumino (2002), *Sengo Nihon no Josei Seisaku [Public Policy for Women in Postwar Japan]*, Tokyo: Keiso Shobo.

13. Business nearly as usual: the global financial crisis and its impacts on households in Hong Kong

Ngai-Ming Yip

INTRODUCTION

The most recent economic crisis is perhaps the deepest recession since the 1929 world depression. The stock market reacted even more bleakly than the 1929 depression with a 50 per cent fall from April 2008 to early 2009 compared with only a 10 per cent fall 80 years ago. Although rescue packages of various countries have prevented panic and the market has recovered sharply in early 2009, the stock market in mid-2009 had still fallen 30 per cent below its peak in April 2008. At the same time the collapse in demand had reduced the volume of world trade by 20 per cent in June 2009, 15 months after its peak in April 2008. In the 1929 depression, it only fell by 10 per cent over the same time span (Eichengreen and O'Rourke, 2009).

With an open and globalized economy, Hong Kong has inevitably been hit severely by the recent crisis. From mid-2008, all economic indicators reacted negatively – GDP plummeted, trade nosedived, house prices dropped and the stock market collapsed. Yet from early 2009, the shoots of recovery began to emerge, first in the property market then in consumer confidence, the stock market and the economy, although there is little evidence of a quick recovery in imports and exports. It also seems that Hong Kong has not suffered much in the global credit crunch and its resulting devastating economic chaos or the collapse of housing markets found in some Western countries.

Of course, Hong Kong is not alone in this region, in which impacts of the current financial crisis appears to have been much milder. It seems that lessons may have been learned from the Asian financial crisis, which triggered a more profound transformation in the region's financial institutions and heightened people's awareness of risk. In addition, the continual growth of the Chinese economy has created a stabilizing force in the region and Hong Kong has benefited from the spillover effects. This chapter attempts to summarize the changes in the economy and the housing market since mid-2008 and tries to make sense of such changes in the light of the lessons learnt from the Asian financial crisis in 1997, as well as the influence of the China factor in mitigating the impacts of the recent financial crisis.

IMPACTS OF THE 2008 GLOBAL FINANCIAL CRISIS ON THE ECONOMY OF HONG KONG

With a high degree of embeddedness in the global economy, Hong Kong unsurprisingly felt the immediate effects as the global financial crisis exploded in the autumn of 2008 following the downfall of several big financial institutions in the USA. Hong Kong, one of the biggest trading ports in the world, responded almost instantaneously regarding imports and exports. The downturn started in the autumn of 2008, when demand in the biggest markets began to shrink, a month-by-month reduction of 16.5 per cent in total exports. A corresponding year-by-year drop of 5.3 per cent was recorded in November 2008 when a modest growth in imports and exports was then expected. The worst scenario came in the first quarter of 2009, during which the year-by-year reduction in export was over 20 per cent. Imports were hit even harder. January 2009 saw a year-on-year contraction of 27.1 per cent. Such a huge contraction was caused by the sharp decline of demand in Hong Kong's major trade partners, which were deeply affected by the economic crisis. For instance, exports to the USA, the UK and Germany, three of the top four trade partners (the other is Mainland China) all experienced a much higher reduction than the average.

The depressing performance in trade, one of the most important economic activities of Hong Kong, inevitably translated into a plunge in GDP. The economy began to turn downwards in the last quarter of 2008 with a year-on-year contraction of GDP of 2.6 per cent in real terms. In the first quarter of 2009, GDP dropped by 7.8 per cent. Although it was considered to be much less adversely affected than most of its neighbours (e.g. the Singapore economy plummeted by 12.5 per cent in the last quarter of 2008), it was still the second-largest contraction since the third quarter of 1998, when the Asian financial crisis began to bite. Although the economy has recovered slightly since then, with a year-on-year contraction of 2.4 per cent in the third quarter of 2009, the chance of a positive overall economic growth in 2009 was expected to be extremely dim (APEC Study Centre, 2009).

With the economic slump taking hold, it is not surprising to find that the rate of unemployment began to soar in the last quarter of 2008 and peaked in the second quarter of 2009 with a seasonally adjusted figure of 5.4 per cent. Although this is a very modest level of unemployment compared to the historically worst period at the peak of SARS in 2003, it nevertheless indicates a rather rapid jump from the 3.3 per cent level in mid-2008. As would be expected, deterioration in the labour market affected wage levels in real terms: they experienced a slight drop of around 1 per cent from the last quarter of 2008 until the second quarter of 2009, the most recent statistics that are available (Census and Statistics Department, 2009).

The Hang Seng Index began to fall from the second quarter of 2008 and accelerated downwards in the fourth quarter of the year (Hang Seng Index, 2009). Yet notwithstanding the gloomy outlook for the economy, the stock market began to rebound, with rescue plans in major markets being introduced and market confidence being restored. A U-turn was observed from the middle of the first quarter of 2009 and since then it has recovered more than it lost.

House prices also began to level off in mid-2008 when the sub-prime crisis in the USA worsened, after a steady rise for five years from the ebb of the bust cycle in mid-2003. Prices plummeted 20 per cent in the last quarter of 2008 when the crisis exploded. However, this pattern had been reversed by the end of 2008 and momentum gathered pace towards the third quarter of 2009. It slowed down a bit when the Hong Kong government began to intervene in October 2009.

LESSONS FROM THE 1997 ASIAN FINANCIAL CRISIS

The Asian financial crisis was a traumatic experience for Hong Kong. Not only was the economic blow devastating, it also changed the way the people of Hong Kong looked at economic growth and investment risk. In 1997, the economy suffered the biggest decline since the Second World War. GDP shrank by 6 per cent in real terms in 1998 and the unemployment rate in 1999 jumped to 6.2 per cent, nearly three times its average level of 2–2.5 per cent during the earlier years of the 1990s. In fact, the biggest impact was on house prices, which dropped by one-third in 1998 alone. In addition, Hong Kong also suffered price deflation until 2004. The worst year was 1999, when consumer prices deflated by 6 per cent. The outbreak of SARS added another blow to the delicate recovering economy and pushed house prices further downwards. Yet it also marked the beginning of housing-market recovery; this market had then fallen by nearly two-thirds from its historical peak in mid-1997.

The collapse of the housing market in 1997 also pushed many home-owners into negative equity, particularly those who had bought in the housing boom. Negative equity was a new phenomenon in Hong Kong. Even the media at first could not find a corresponding term in Chinese. It was also a completely new experience for homeowners, as Hong Kong had never encountered any serious setback in the housing market since the 1970s, when homeownership began to proliferate among the middle class. The degree of negative equity was also alarming. When the Hong Kong Monetary Authority first did a survey on the extent of negative equity, it discovered that 65 000 mortgage borrowers with around HK$127 billion (US$16.3billion) were in negative equity, which constituted respectively 14 per cent of all mortgage borrowers or nearly one quarter (23 per cent) of total outstanding mortgage loans (HKMA, 2001). With the outbreak of SARS in 2003, house prices slid even further, and this pushed 105 697 mortgage borrowers with outstanding loans of HK$165 billion (US$21.2billion) into negative equity in mid-2003 (HKMA, 2003), a two-thirds increase over the level of 2001.

House prices began to pick up after the ebb of the price boom in 2003 and eased the problem of negative equity. In early 2008, just before out-break of the recent financial crisis, negative equity was about to disappear, with only 953 cases. But this deteriorated quickly in the second half of 2008, with a tenfold increase of negative-equity loans (15 times in terms of loan value) to 10 944 borrowers and HK$24.8billion (US$3.2billion) outstanding loans by the end of 2008.

At the peak, nearly one-third of mortgage borrowers were in negative equity and unable to pay off their debts even after selling their assets. It is surprising, therefore, that mortgage default was still under control. Mortgage default was a non-issue in the banking industry before the Asian financial crisis; the banking regulator did not even bother to collect the statistics regularly. When such figures were first reported in 1998, the mortgage delinquency ratio (loans in arrears in the previous 90 days) was only at 0.3 per cent. Although the level of negative equity and unemployment had both soared since then, the ratio increased to 1.33 per cent by 2001 and fell thereafter to a negligible 0.04 per cent in October 2009. Even among mortgage loans in negative equity, the delinquency rates were not particularly alarming – reaching 2.62 per cent in the fourth quarter of 2002 (HKHA, various years).

Conservative lending policy is perhaps one important factor accounting for the low delinquency rate (and consequentially low repossession rate). In fact, the banking regulator (Hong Kong Monetary Authority) had already instructed commercial banks to tighten mortgage lending as early as 1992 as a proactive measure to contain the risk of a property bubble. A ceiling loan-to-value ratio was set at 70 per cent and, in practice, the banks were even more conservative in their mortgage lending policy. For instance, in mid-2007 at the height of the house boom, the loan-to-value ratio of outstanding loans was only 52 per cent (HKMA, 2008) and was 61.8 per cent in mid-2001 when the housing market hit rock bottom. It then stabilized at around the 60 per cent level and, most recently, was 63.4 per cent in October 2009 (HKMA, 2009). At the same time, the banks were also being instructed to adopt a prudent policy in assessing the repayment ability of borrowers and a ceiling repayment-to-income ratio of 50 per cent was often adopted. In practice, the ratio was believed to be far lower than the permitted ceiling level.

Low loan-to-value and income to repayment ratios offer a comfortable cushion and help stabilize the market in times of price fluctuations. This helps to contain default risk even during an extreme market environment (e.g. the worst market bust in 2003). For instance, even for the most vulnerable loans (properties in negative equity), the loan-to-value ratio of such loans could still be contained at a modest level – at an average of 128 per cent (HKMA, 2003). This would not create urgency for the banks to rush for repossession. Instead, rescheduling of repayments was often the common practice for default loans.

The conservative attitude of the banks is also reflected in their receptiveness towards mortgage-related financial products. Securitization of mortgage loans is very limited in Hong Kong and nearly all mortgage loans are in the form of variable-rate mortgages (which offer the least risk for the banks). With the intention of developing a market for securities, the Hong Kong government set up the Mortgage Corporation (HKMC), which mirrors the state-guaranteed mortgage-loan securitization model of the USA. However, the banks were not enthusiastic since they did not have any urgent need for funds. Hence, by the end of 2008, the HKMC possessed only 67 322 mortgages worth HK$29.9billion (US$3.8billion), just 5 per cent of the outstanding mortgage loans held by commercial banks in Hong Kong. There has been no progress in motgage-backed securities since then.

Coincidentally, the unenthusiastic attitude of the banks towards security-related mortgage products and the timing of the Asian financial crisis may have helped Hong Kong to avoid the devastating sub-prime crisis that hit most economically advanced countries. Many countries have benefited from the expansion of cheap credit, particularly in the property market, and Hong Kong would have been expected to follow suit. On the one hand, it is tempting for a financialized economy to employ innovative financial instruments to boost mortgage borrowing (Montgomerie, 2008), and on the other hand, the high property prices of Hong Kong and the escalating financialization of the economy (Smart and Lee, 2008) should also have pushed Hong Kong in such a direction. Yet the conservative banking sector was slow to react to new financial instruments and at the same time a depressed property market after the Asian financial crisis also generated no space for additional credit. Hence these circumstances meant that Hong Kong missed out on the era of thriving sub-prime expansion and avoided the devastating consequences.

SUPPORT FOR THE HOUSING MARKET AND THE CHINA FACTOR

In the latter half of 2008, house prices began to rebound, just in time to give a supportive boost to the recovering economy amidst unclear external economic prospects. Although such a rebound was regarded by many commentators as merely sandcastles created by speculation, the mild recovery may indeed have solid underpinnings. In fact house prices had emerged out from the bust cycle in mid-2003 and had doubled by mid-2008 (Figure 13.1), just before the outbreak of the financial crisis. This was partly fuelled by the improving economy, which experienced a V-shape recovery after 2004 but was largely pushed by the successful

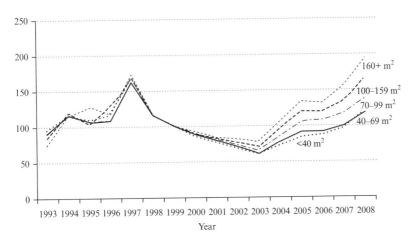

Source: Department of Rating & Valuation (various years).

Figure 13.1   House price index by flat size, 1993–2008 (index 1998 = 100)

control in supply and the improvement of the vacancy rate. Completion of new flat units was at a historic low level in both 2007 and 2008, at 10470 and 8780 flats respectively. It is expected that production will bounce back to 14470 and 12600 units in 2009 and 2010. Yet, even so, the levels are less than half of the peak of housing production at 35322 in 1999 (Department of Rating & Valuation, 2009, 2000). Whilst the unsold new dwellings accumulated from the Asian financial crisis a decade ago have begun to be absorbed by the market (only around 5000–6000 units left in the market (Centaline, 2009a)), the expectation of gradually rising demand has fuelled the anticipation of a supply shortage and further pushed up house prices.

In fact, the expectation of increased demand is well founded. An improving economy has helped to build the confidence of homebuyers and release the potential purchase capacity that had been deterred by the severe market conditions in the property market bust in 2003. The BRE (Building and Real Estate) confidence index in the property market produced by the Hong Kong Polytechnic University shows a marked improvement in homebuyer confidence from 564 in late 2003 to 703 in early 2007 (the earliest and the latest figures that have been produced) (RCCREE, 2007). The market for small flats, which have the lowest financial risk, was the earliest to rebound, later followed by the high-end market. Yet it is the latter market segment, whose participants are often investors and speculators, that created the momentum for a rapid market recovery.

Swift economic recovery after 2003 has also brought a substantial improvement in the affordability for homebuyers. In mid-2008, when house prices of small and medium-sized houses had recovered much of their value after the Asian financial crisis and reached three-quarters of their historical peak price of 1997, affordability for homebuyers had improved substantially compared to its worst level at 1997. Measured by the crude aggregate indicator of median income to median house price, notional affordability has improved by more than double in 2008 compared with 1997 (Figure 13.2). The burden of actual mortgage repayments has also improved marginally. The median mortgage repayment-to-income ratio fell from 30.7 per cent in 2001 to 28.6 per cent in 2006 (Census and Statistics Department, 2007a). A low-interest-rate environment, which was created by the economy-stimulating packages and relaxed monetary policy, was also one strong underpinning for the improvement of affordability. The low mortgage rate, in fact one of the lowest in Hong Kong's banking history, has substantially reduced the burden of homebuying. In addition, households in Hong Kong also have the capacity to borrow more. Household debts as a proportion of GDP (in which mortgages constitute a large proportion) has fallen from 61.5 per

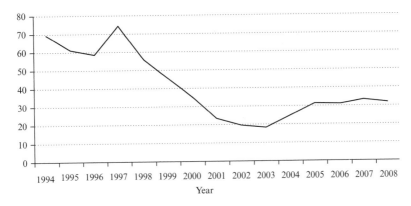

Note: The index is the proportion of monthly mortgage repayment to household's income, assuming the household earns the average household income of the relevant year and bought a flat at the median price with a 20-year mortgage at the prevailing interest rate.

Source: Centaline (2009b).

Figure 13.2   Affordability of first-time buyers (1994–2008)

cent in 2001 to only 52.7 per cent in 2006, a level comparable to that of the mid-1990s (Mastercard, 2008).

The China factor is perhaps another forceful underpinning for the housing market. With a tough environment in international trade, China was still determined, and was able, to sustain a high rate of growth in both 2008 and 2009. With Hong Kong increasingly embedded in the thriving Chinese economy, optimism about economic recovery has run high. Yet the most direct impact of such optimism is the inflow of hot money into Hong Kong seeking opportunities for investment when conventional investment markets have been depressed. It was estimated by the Hong Kong government that HK$500billion (US$64billion) of hot money has been transferred to the local economy since the recent economic crisis, which has pushed up both the stock and the housing market. The Heng Sang Index has doubled from its lowest (at 10 676) in 2008 to nearly 23 000 in mid-November 2009 and has then fluctuated between 20 000 and 22 000 from November 2009 to March 2010.

Although much of the hot money may be short term and concentrated mainly in the stock market, some of it has stayed in property as long-term investment or is targeted at immigrating to Hong Kong via the capital investment route (which requires over HK6.5million (US$0.83million) for at least two years). Most of these investors demand housing at the high end of the market. In fact, prices of luxurious apartments in mid-2009 have already exceeded their historic peak of mid-1997 (Department of Rating & Valuation, 2009; Centaline, 2009a).

HOUSING 'SAFETY NET'

Hong Kong has not then entered into the kind of predatory mortgage business found in the sub-prime market of the USA for low- to middle-income homebuyers as public housing has offered a housing safety net for these households and greatly reduced the attractiveness of sub-prime mortgages. Public rental housing has been acting as housing of last resort for the low-income groups since its inception in the mid-1950s and publicly assisted homeownership has offered middle-income households cheap owner-occupied flats for the last 40 years.

In 2009, nearly one-third (29 per cent) of households lived in public rental housing (HKHA, 2009), with rents at only at half to one-third of the market level. Enjoyment of the public rental housing sector is means tested and it is successful in targeting the poorest one-third of households. With a big boost in production in the late 1990s, the waiting time for public rental housing has been shortened to less than three years, although there is still a long waiting list of over 100 000 households.

At the same time, public housing for sale has been constructed since the late 1970s for middle-class households. As house prices in Hong Kong are very high, homeownership has been a burden even for middle-income households. For instance, a requirement for 30 per cent of downpayment for a mortgage has already created a constraint for first-time buyers, and the burden of regular repayment also appears to be equally taxing. For instance, in the boom years in the first half of the 1990s, a first-time buyer whose income was at the median of the income spectrum had to spend around two-thirds to three-quarters of their income in repaying the mortgage for a flat in the median price range (Centaline, 2009b). Yet the stringent income limits for public rental housing have also stripped the opportunities for middle-income households to access public rental housing. This has trapped many middle-income households between the market and state sectors.

The Home Ownership Scheme (HOS), a publicly assisted homeownership scheme, was set up to fill such a gap. From 1976 until 2003, when the scheme was under pressure from big developers to be halved, a total of over 345 000 flats (or around 14 per cent of the housing stock) were constructed (HKHA, various years). Designed as shared-equity homeownership for households who earned around the median income, HOS helped to reduce both the income and wealth constraints in home buying as the selling prices of HOS flats were often at 40–60 per cent of the market level. With a guarantee of buy-back in the first five or ten years, HOS buyers could enjoy a preferential mortgage interest rate as well as a longer repayment period and effectively reduce the burden of repayment.

Shared equity is perhaps the most important assistance for low-income homebuyers, as it also helps to share the risk of homeownership investment, particularly in times of economic uncertainty. At same time, it also secures a future dividend for the government when the assets appreciate (Lee and Yip, 2001). However, buyers of HOS flats appear to enjoy the certainty and stability brought by the shared-equity homeownership rather than perceive it as a step on the housing ladder. Only a few of them sold their flats on the open market after the sale embargo. In fact, only around 65 000 or 14 per cent (Hong Kong government, 2008) have been sold on the open market.

The selling of public housing (Tenant Purchase Scheme, TPS) can also help to realize the dream of homeownership for middle- to low-income households. Launched in 1998 to allow sitting tenants to buy their flat at a discount of up to 78 per cent of market value, around one in six rental flats or 113 000 units had been sold by 2003 when the scheme was stopped together with the moratorium of the HOS. TPS operates in the same way as HOS, with the shared-equity ratio of around 50 per cent to 60 per cent (with an additional discount as a gift for early take-up). The shared-equity arrangements for HOS and TPS have eased both the income and wealth constraints for homebuyers as well as offering a housing safety net for the lower and middle-income renters and owner-occupiers who are the major target of sub-prime mortgages in other countries. Hence this partly explains the limited development of the sub-prime mortgage market in Hong Kong and the avoidance of one of the important triggers for the crisis in the banking sector.

UNEVEN IMPACTS ON DIFFERENT SOCIAL GROUPS

Despite the intensity of the current global financial crisis, job losses were much less drastic than during the Asian financial crisis a decade ago. This may be a combined result of the employment-boosting programmes of the government, the rebound of the asset markets as well as the high level of confidence of employers towards the prospect of economy recovery (Government Economist, 2009). The financial service sector, which was heavily hit in the current crisis, has only suffered a very short-term blow. Despite a sharp reduction in business receipts in the second half of 2008,

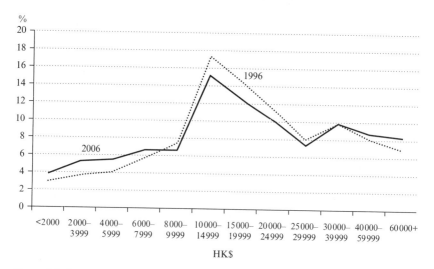

Note: Median household income in 2006 and price index were respectively 1.5 per cent and 4 per cent lower than in 1996.

Source: Census and Statistics Department (2007c).

Figure 13.3   Household income distribution (1996, 2006)

the sector achieved a modest recovery in 2009. The shedding of jobs at the beginning of the crisis in 2008 had been reversed by 2009 and, in fact, there was a growth in jobs in late 2009 compared with the pre-crisis level (Government Economist, 2009). In the current crisis, the sector quickly reacted by a sharp salary cut for their employees in order to contain staff costs. This was a much bolder response than it made in the Asian financial crisis. With confidence picking up, there was also an apparent rebound in salary levels in the sector towards mid-2009.

The sudden but short-lived impact on the financial sector reflects the relatively limited effect of the recent financial crisis on Hong Kong's high-income employees. Similarly, other high income workers such as managers, professional and semi-professionals were also the least affected in terms of unemployment and wages. On the contrary, job losses for the semi-skilled workers whose work depends more on the export market, were hit the hardest by the financial crisis, although this sector is now relatively small. Service and sales workers were also hit by the contraction in tourism and retailing when the crisis reached its peak in early 2009, but the recovery in the asset markets contributed to a limited recovery.

The rapid recovery for high-income workers *vis-à-vis* their poorer counterparts in such a serious crisis reflects a longer-term trend of a widening income gap between the rich and the poor in Hong Kong. Whilst average incomes hardly changed between 1996 and 2006, more households have moved to each end of the income spectrum. The income distribution has become flatter, which indicates a greater diversity between the rich and the poor (Figure 13.3). The Gini coefficient of income distribution, which stood at 0.518 in 1996, had further worsened to 0.533 by 2006 (Census and Statistics Department, 2007a). This has put Hong Kong on a par with the USA (Gini coefficient at 0.45 in 2007) (CIA, 2010), as one of the most unequal places in the developed world.

With the moratorium of the assisted homeownership scheme (the HOS) and the retrenchment of public rental housing, the housing safety net for poor and lower-middle-income households has been seriously weakened. Poorer households are now more exposed to the vulnerability of the housing market in the context of widening inequalities. With no assisted homeownership flats and fewer public rented flats as a buffer, the more volatile private housing market becomes the only choice for middle-class homebuyers or poorer renters.

CONCLUDING REMARKS

Given its open economy and dependence on international trade and investment, Hong Kong is extremely vulnerable to changes in the world economy. Increasing financialization of the world economy and the aspiration of Hong Kong to become a world-class financial centre have deepened such risk. Hence, with the most important pillars of the economy of Hong Kong – the financial industry, the property market as well as international trade – being hit severely at the beginning of the current financial crisis, there was the potential for the crisis to deal a heavy blow to the local economy. Hence the relatively mild and (still at the time of writing) short-lived negative impacts of the current financial crisis on the local economy may come as a surprise.

It has been argued that the current financial crisis in fact has structural roots. The regulation school has predicted that a finance-led growth regime's success will inevitably unfold into a major structural crisis (Boyer, 2000). Yet increasing financialization has also created a more socially embedded global finance system (Montgomerie, 2008) in which local factors are important mediating forces. Hence the current financial crisis, despite its apparent 'global' outlook, should also be understood in the context of the local 'urban problematic' (Dymski, 2009). Thus, the recent social and economic circumstances of Hong Kong as well as the recent trajectories are keys to an understanding of the impacts of the recent financial crisis.

Against such a context, the Asian financial crisis in 1997 as well as its aftermath are significant, *inter alia*, in shaping a very different social and economic landscape. The Crisis in 1997 triggered the longest recession in Hong Kong since the Second World War. The burst of the property bubble shed 70 per cent of the asset value of properties (at the lowest point of the slump), cut the production of new housing by over 80 per cent and pushed over one-third of homeowners into negative equity. A lesson about the risk of a speculative property market was learnt. Not only is the society now more sensitive to the risk of asset bubbles; commercial banks are also more prudent about expanding into risky business, particularly the mortgage for low-market properties, even if this constrains their profits.

Perhaps more by luck than by design, a sluggish economy after the Asian financial crisis also created a relative surplus of funds, which made mortgage-backed securities unattractive to local investors despite the enthusiasm of the government in employing such instruments to boost the local securities market. With such extremely cautious practices, Hong Kong has not been as deeply involved as other countries in risky mortgage-backed financial instruments or sub-prime mortgages, although this may have meant that Hong Kong missed out from benefiting from the expansion of the financial sector, where cheap credit was available. The (still) thin engagement of Hong Kong with the recent credit expansion may have indeed saved Hong Kong.

Despite the sudden price drops in the second half of 2008, the property market had soon recovered in early 2009. This offers one vital sustaining factor for the recent recovery. In fact, such a rebound matched the long-term upward trajectories of the housing market from its rock bottom in 2003. The recent financial crisis produced an unexpected blow to confidence and led to a short-term adjustment, while more sustainable factors, underpinned by the orchestrated effort of the government and major developers to curb both land supply and the production of new flats in order to generate the expectation of a future shortage, soon helped to restore confidence in the market. The China factor was and is also a strong maintenance force for recovery. With a rapid growth amidst worsening world economic prospects, China has become a strong magnet for both foreign investment and short-term hot money. With the local economy increasingly embedded in the development of China, Hong Kong gained both the market confidence as well as the hard investment necessary for economic recovery.

The absence of any extensive impact of the recent financial crisis on poor and middle-class households can also be attributed to the existence of a large public-housing sector. With high housing costs and skewed income distribution, the housing problems of the low-income households have always been a sensitive social issue. The public-housing programme, which supplies rental flats for those on low incomes and assisted homeowner-ship for the lower-middle-income group, has acted as a social stabilizing force. Although such policies also suppress the growth of homeownership in Hong Kong compared with its neighbours (Hong Kong has a 'low' homeownership rate of only 53 per cent), it also prevents the expansion of a predatory mortgage market for the low-income and socially vulner-able to satisfy their desire for homeownership. This also partly explains the low rate of mortgage defaults and repossessions during economic recession as middle-income households are less vulnerable to economic hardship given the high saving rates and low debt levels among such households.

But, although the current financial crisis has not had a deep impact on the general economy of Hong Kong, nor generated a particularly harsh effect for particular groups, it has widened further the income gap that has been deteriorating over the last two decades. The high-income groups appear to be unaffected by the crisis, with even the hardest-hit financial sector showing a very robust recovery. However, the service industry and the trade business sectors, which accommodate much of the low-paid workforce, have had a longer road to recovery. This acts to further intensify the division between the rich and poor. With an increasingly neoliberal approach to housing policy, with the moratorium of assisted homeownership and the reduction in public rental housing production, the housing safety-net has been greatly weakened. Newly formed house-holds, the young and the singles are finding themselves facing a growing affordability gap. In the near future, it will be difficult to further expand homeownership, particularly among lower income groups, without expos-ing them unnecessarily to more risky financial markets.

REFERENCES

APEC Study Center (2009), 'HKU announced 2009 Q4 HK macroeconomic forecast', available at http://www.hku.hk/press/news_detail_6030.html, APEC Study Center, University of Hong Kong, accessed 25 November 2009.

Boyer, R. (2000), 'Is a financial-led growth regime a viable alternative to Fordism? A preliminary analysis', *Economy and Society*, **29** (1), 111–45.

Census and Statistics Department (2007a), 'Median monthly domestic house-hold mortgage payment and loan repayment, median mortgage payment and loan repayment to income ratio and median outstanding period of mortgage payment or loan repayment by type of housing, 2001 and 2006, population by-census 2006 table E108', available at http://www.bycensus2006.gov.hk/en/data/data3/ statistical_tables/index.htm#E1, accessed 23 November 2009.

Census and Statistics Department (2007b), 'Population by type of housing, 1996, 2001 and 2006, population by-census 2006 table E101', available at http://www.bycensus2006.gov.hk/en/ data/data3/statistical_tables/index.htm#E1, accessed 23 November 2009.

Census and Statistics Department (2007c), 'Household income distribution in Hong Kong', available at http://www.bycensus2006.gov.hk/FileManager/EN/Content_941/06bc_hhinc_slides.pdf, accessed 25 November 2009.

Census and Statistics Department (2009), 'Unemployment rate by industry and occupation', available at http://www.censtatd.gov.hk/hong_kong_statistics/statistical_tables/index.jsp?charsetID=1&subjectID=2&tableID=012, accessed 27 November 2009.

Centaline (2009a), 'Centaline city leading index', available at http://hk.centanet.com/icms/ template.aspx?series=174, accessed 1 December 2009.

Centaline (2009b), 'Affordability ratio', available at http://hk.centanet.com/icms/ICMServlet? attachImage=true&contentType=application/vnd.ms-excel&attachment=18528, accessed 22 November 2009.

CIA (2010), 'CIA: the World Factbook', available at https://www.cia.gov/library/publications/the-world-factbook/, accessed 14 April 2010.

Department of Rating & Valuation (2000), 'Hong Kong property review'.

Department of Rating & Valuation (2009), 'Hong Kong property review 2009', available at http://www.rvd.gov.hk/en/publications/hkpr09.htm, accessed 22 November 2009.

Department of Rating & Valuation (various years), 'Private domestic price indices by class (territory-wide)', available at http://www.rvd.gov.hk/en/doc/statistics/his_data_4.pdf, accessed 17 November 2009.

Dymski, Gary A. (2009), 'Afterword: mortgage markets and the urban problematic in the global transition', *International Journal of Urban and Regional Research*, **33** (2), 427–42.

Eichengreen, Barry and Kevin H. O'Rourke (2009), 'A tale of two depressions, 1 September 2009', available at http://www.voxeu.org/index.php?q=node/342, accessed 30 November 2009.

Government Economist (2009), 'A comparison on economic performance between the current crisis and the 1997–98 Asian financial crisis', available at www.hkeconomy.gov.hk/en/pdf/box-09q2-1-1.pdf, accessed 23 November 2009.

Hang Seng Index (2009), available at http://hk.finance.yahoo.com/q/bc?s=^HSI&t =2y, accessed 6 December 2009.

HKHA (2009), 'Hong Kong Housing Authority (HKHA) housing in figures 2009', available at http://www.housingauthority.gov.hk/hdw/content/document/en/aboutus/resources/statistics/HIF2009.pdf, accessed 10 November 2009.

HKHA (various years), 'Hong Kong Housing Authority (HKHA) annual report', Hong Kong: Hong Kong Housing Authority.

HKMA (2001), 'Survey on residential mortgage loans in negative equity, 16-Oct-2001, Hong Kong Monetary Authority (HKMA)', available at http://www.info.gov.hk/hkma/eng/press/category /resident_index.htm, accessed 25 November 2009.

HKMA (2003), 'Survey on residential mortgages in Hong Kong, 11 Nov 2003,

Hong Kong Monetary Authority', available at http://www.info.gov.hk/hkma/eng/press/category/ resident_index.htm, accessed 16 November 2009.

HKMA (2008), 'Survey on residential mortgages in Hong Kong, 29 Dec 2008', Hong Kong Monetary Authority, available at http://www.info.gov.hk/hkma/eng/press/category/ resident_index.htm, accessed 16 November 2009.

HKMA (2009), 'Survey on residential mortgages in Hong Kong, 25 Nov 2009', Hong Kong Monetary Authority, available at http://www.info.gov.hk/hkma/eng/press/category/ resident_index.htm, accessed 16 November 2009.

HKMA (various years), 'Residential mortgage loans in negative equity (quarterly reports)', Hong Kong Monetary Authority, available at http://hk.centanet.com/icms/attachmentDownload.aspx?download/174-1451-16646/affordability.xls, accessed 15 November 2009.

HKMA (various years), 'Survey on residential mortgages in Hong Kong', Hong Kong Monetary Authority, available at http://www.info.gov.hk/hkma/eng/press/category/ resident_index.htm, accessed 16 November 2009.

HKMC (2008), *Hong Kong Mortgage Corporation 2008 Year Book*, available at http://www.hkmc. com.hk/, accessed 18 November 2008.

Hong Kong Government (2008), *Hong Kong Year Book 2008*, available at http://www.yearbook. gov.hk/2008/en/pdf/E11.pdf, accessed 18 November 2009.

Lee, J. and Ngai-Ming Yip (2001), 'Home ownership under economic uncertainty – the role of subsidized sale flats in Hong Kong', *Third World Planning Review*, **23** (1), 61–78.

Mastercard (2008), Shocks and Resilience – Hong Kong's Dynamic Household Credit Market, Mastercard World Wide Insight, 2008 Q2, available at http://www.insightbureau.com/insight_reports/mc_insights/2008_Q2_Hong_Kong_Household_Credit_Market.pdf, accessed 20 November 2009.

Montgomerie, Johanna (2008), 'Bridging the critical divide: global finance', *Finalisation, and Contemporary Capitalism, Contemporary Politics*, **14** (3), 233–52.

RCCREE (2007), 'BRE confidence index for residential property', Research Centre for Construction and Real Estate Economics (RCCREE) Hong Kong Polytechnic University, available at http://www.bre.polyu.edu.hk/research/bre_index/ intro/Intro.htm, accessed 2 February 2010.

Smart, A. and J. Lee (2008), 'Financialisation and the role of real estate in Hong Kong's regime of accumulation', *Economic Geography*, **79** (2), 153–71.

14. The impact of the financial crisis on China's housing market

Jianping Ye and Chao Sun

INTRODUCTION

Unlike that in most Western countries, China's real estate market has a relatively short history. It was established in 1994 when the process of housing reform got under way and has gradually developed since then. Although the second-hand housing market in China has now attained a considerable scale, it is newly constructed housing that constitutes the greatest portion of the market. In parallel, although China's finance and real-estate sectors are increasingly interdependent, this is still in its initial state of development. On the one hand, the housing market is supported mainly from bank credit than from other sources. On the other hand, bank credit is too concentrated in real estate. For instance, in 2008 more than one-third of the total credit of the bank of China was in real estate.

The sub-prime mortgage crisis that originated in the USA after August 2007 evolved into a global financial tsunami, and inflicted enormous damage upon the world economy. With global economic integration, China's economy could not be totally immune from these developments. From the macroeconomic data of the second half of 2008, it is evident that the financial crisis had some impact upon China's economy, with a slow-down of China's economic growth and a sharp decrease of import–export volume. As regards the real-estate industry, meanwhile, China's housing prices declined, real-estate investment decreased, newly constructed housing (calculated by floor area) shrank and housing trading volumes dropped. However, after February 2009, China's real-estate market revived rapidly, with a dramatic rise in both housing trading volume and housing prices. For instance, in September 2009, the average transaction price of newly constructed housing in Shenzhen was 20940 yuan per m², the highest in Shenzhen's history. This compared with 10770 yuan per m² in February 2009, a rise of 94 per cent over that period.

Thus, after the outbreak of the financial crisis in the second half of

2008, China's real-estate market underwent a rapid fall followed by an equally rapid recovery. The extent to which these abnormal phenomena originated from the financial crisis is worth further scrutiny since during this process a range of policies was implemented at various government levels. These included, at the central level, a 4 trillion yuan stimulus scheme and a plan to strengthen the support for ten industries, and, in big cities like Shanghai, Nanjing and, Beijing, local governments targeted the rescue programme at the real-estate sector. For instance, there were more favourable policies on tax and fees for the second-hand housing market, subsidies for house purchase, more relaxed lending for second homes and developers were allowed to defer payment on various land-related charges. This chapter will explore whether these policies, intended to counteract the anticipated recession, were able to reverse the downward movement of the housing market.

THE IMPACT OF THE FINANCIAL CRISIS

Nationwide

Given the changes in GDP growth in China, it is clear that the financial crisis is indeed negatively affecting China's macroeconomy. The previous high-speed growth rate maintained over several years has fallen by around 3 per cent, from 11 per cent to 8 per cent. These worsened economic conditions are mainly due to the shrinkage of import and export trade, with a consequent impact on other economic sectors. However, the real-estate economy has not been so obviously affected. The enterprises most severely hit by the financial crisis have little direct connection with supply and demand in the housing market. Thus the decrease of the economic aggregate has not seriously affected the housing market.

The other profound influence of the financial crisis lies in its acceleration in the transformation of the Chinese economic structure. China should have experienced a much more severe depression. However, the implementation of the '4 trillion' programme by the Chinese government has increased investment in fixed assets substantially, which compensated for the loss from the shrinkage of import and export trade. The dominant policy aim has been to increase the level of domestic demand and investment in the national economy. Moreover, for a newly developed housing market such as in China, the consumption and investment of real estate plays an important role.

Fixed-asset investment played a significant role in the economic recovery in the second and third quarter, 2009. From 2004 to the third quarter of 2009, fixed-asset investment showed a continuous growth rate above 20 per cent. The fixed-assets investment – GDP ratio rose above 50 per cent in the last two quarters. Moreover, real-estate investment has represented a relatively high proportion of this fixed-asset investment. Indeed, against the background of the financial crisis, the real-estate industry has served as a major driving force for national economic growth and thus received more policy support than before the financial crisis. Therefore the effect of the financial crisis did not occasion a major recession. On the contrary, on the supply side, market upward momentum was maintained.

It should also be noted, however, that the investment-led recovery derived mostly from the government's direct or indirect investment, that is, in essence, in the form of government purchases. There was relatively limited investment from the enterprise sector. The Chinese government depended mainly on an expansionary fiscal policy and loose monetary policy to revitalize the economy. Nevertheless, regardless of the route taken to deal with the crisis, it would appear that the potential impacts were dealt with effectively. First, during this period the unemployment rate has remained at below 4.3 per cent, indicating a very limited impact on company and job losses. Second, the consumer price index has fluctuated within a narrow range, suggesting little effect on the overall cost of living. Third, the per capita disposable income of urban residents increased by 9 per cent – people earned more after than before the crisis. Generally, therefore, the principal economic fundamentals affecting housing demand were not negatively affected by the outbreak of the financial crisis. Disposable income of residents increased and the inflation rate remained at a relatively low level. Thus the consumption capacity among both renters and owners was not seriously affected.

Loose monetary policy did, however, increase the broad money supply. Before the first half of 2008, the growth rate of China's broad money supply was maintained at around 20 per cent. In 2008, with concerns growing about the problem of excess liquidity, rising inflation and soaring asset prices, notably house prices, the central bank adopted a tighter monetary policy. It raised the benchmark interest rate and statutory reserve requirement. This reduced the growth of the money supply to some degree (Han et al., 2007; He, 2007). However, with the financial crisis spreading, there was a significant change in the domestic economic situation, with imports and exports shrinking and GDP growth slowing down. In order to stimulate investment and consumption, and promote economic growth, the central bank in 2009 once again relaxed monetary policy and interest rates fell to their lowest level since the second quarter of 2004, Broad money supply's growth rate expanded above 25 per cent and came close to 30 per cent from the second quarter of 2009. Thus, although the surge of the money supply played a significant role in stimulating economic growth, it also raised the risk of excessive liquidity.

And in China there is a perennial bidirectional linear causality relationship between the development of China's real-estate market and its financial market (Pi and Wu, 2004: Xie and Zheng, 2006). The increase of financial assets can considerably promote the rise of aggregate investment of the realty market. Financial policies, such as the adjustment of market interest rates, the banks' policy of real-estate loans and the adjustment of mortgage loan interest rate can influence the investment and price of the real-estate industry, and can also enforce macroeconomic regulation and control by implementing monetary policies to affect the real-estate market (Cao, 2005; Wang and Guo, 2007; Zeng et al., 2008).

THE HOUSING MARKET

In the USA the financial crisis exploded in the real-estate market and then rippled through the financial market, spreading to the entire economy. But in China the pattern was rather different, with the impacts falling mainly in two areas. First, as a country highly dependent on foreign trade, the export-oriented economy contracted with the international economic situation. Second, and perhaps more importantly, the financial crisis affected investors and consumers' confidence and expectations of the future. Just as in Southeast Asia in 1998, despite a well-functioning economy, investors took fright and capital fled, resulting in a self-realized panic.

There was a clear reduction in the demand for housing in the second and third quarters of 2008, reflected in the decline of both residence sales by floor space, real-estate investment and new construction by floor space – only half the volume of 2007. But neither the purchasing power (per capita disposable income) nor housing prices showed any significant change at that point. That was the situation in both first- and second-tier cities' housing markets. However, the first-tier cities' housing markets were more affected by the international situation, and the second-tier cities' were affected by the first-tier cities. The panic was transmitted.

However, there is only limited evidence that these developments were wholly caused by the global crisis. Ever since 2007, China's real-estate market had appeared to be overheating, housing affordability problems were increasing and the national economy was faced with potential inflation risks. In order to cool the market, the Chinese government adopted a tight monetary policy and introduced a series of new regulations in relation to land policy, tax policy and real-estate credit policies. For instance, the initial instalment required for a mortgage as a percentage of

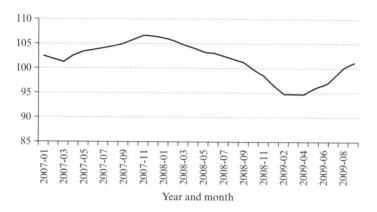

Figure 14.1   National real-estate indices, 2007–09

the purchase price was raised from 20 per cent to 30 per cent and capital ratio requirements for real-estate corporations were strictly controlled in order to control credit levels. Therefore in China the impact of measures to cool down an overheated housing market overlapped with the impact of the financial crisis. Prices were already falling, affecting investor confidence before the global crisis. Thus it is difficult to distinguish the impact of the credit crunch and the more generalized crisis from the impact of the specific, deflationary policies implemented by the Chinese government.

However, although there was a marked reduction in investment in the housing market, consumer demand was maintained to a significant degree by the momentum of China's urbanization process. This is a key factor in explaining why the housing sales area (floor space) and sales volume declined in 2008, while house prices maintained a rising trend until August compared with the same period the previous year. After September 2008, the trends in the real-estate market were reversed and house prices began to decline, reaching their lowest point in February 2009 (see Figure 14.1). As early as May, however, house prices had started to rise again, and increased by more than 10 per cent in July and August. Essentially, there was strong underlying consumer demand. After a short period of consumer caution, and fuelled by the stimulation package, prices rapidly revived. After the second quarter of 2009, the effects of the market-stimulation polices began to have very evident effects. Both the sales area and sales volume were not only higher than in the same period in 2008, but even higher than the period before the outbreak of the financial crisis (2007). Government intervention in the real-estate market gradually restored consumer confidence and released the strong house-purchase demand, which had been postponed in the wait-and-see period.

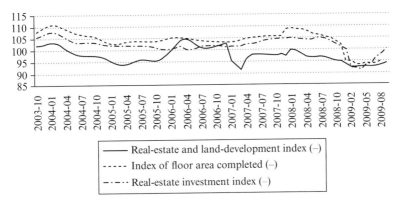

Figure 14.2 Supply in the housing market

The impact of the financial crisis on the residential property market's supply side is more substantial in real terms, but because of hysteretic adjustment of the supply side, the fluctuation in the supply side appears later than the demand side.

As mentioned above, consumers' expectations affected by the financial crisis also transferred to the supply side. The wait-and-see emotion formed in the residential market led to a huge drop in sales and a slowdown and even a decline in growth rate of the real-estate market prices. This slowed down the process of new construction and extended construction periods, with developers postponing deadlines for putting new housing on the market. Figure 14.2 shows that after the second quarter of 2008, the year on year growth rate of completed floor space of residential housing construction continued to decline significantly, becoming negative in the fourth quarter of 2008. But after the Chinese government announced the 4 trillion yuan investment scheme, a huge amount of capital began to flow back into real estate, an industry regarded as a pillar in the promotion of economic growth. Once the industry had the strong support from the state and the banking sector, the scope and scale of credit increased and demand was re-energized. Indeed, it was particularly real-estate investment that took the lead in generating a strong market recovery.

There is a further factor that must be noted in relation to the impact of the financial crisis. This relates to the reduced supply in the residential sector because of China's increasingly scarce land resources and the corresponding tight regulation of urban land use. After a period of extensive and rapid urbanization, for both environmental reasons and because of more limited land supply, urbanization cannot continue to accelerate in the same way. The demand for land for new residential construction faces a bottleneck and has entered a period of relative scarcity, with a continuous shortage of sites to cope with the growing cities. This is evident above from the decline in the real-estate land development area since 2007. Land-supply constraints have therefore also aggravated the supply problems of the housing market.

Particularly in China's large, first-tier cities such as Beijing and Shanghai, a period of extensive urban development has already exhausted most of the land resources surrounding the cities. There is very limited potential for further urban expansion on this model. The only way for these first-tier cities to continue to develop is through renewing the old urban zones. But for developers, this path involves much higher costs and other difficulties. The financial crisis accelerated the migration of real-estate developers from first-tier cities to second-tier cities in search of higher profit margins and a more abundant supply of land.

DIFFERENCES BETWEEN THE FIRST- AND SECOND-TIER CITIES

In the first tier cities such as Beijing and Shanghai, their physical scale and population size generate substantial internal demand for housing. Also, as global cities, their real-estate sectors attract international as well as domestic investment. For these reasons, the housing markets of the first-tier cities were overheating in terms of real-estate investment for some time before the global financial crisis.

With the onset of the financial crisis, the impact in the first- and second-tier cities was somewhat different. As international cities, the first-tier cities were greatly influenced by the global situation. With the double impact of the macroeconomic controls to cool the markets and the financial crisis, after the second half of 2008, housing prices in the first-tier cities fell significantly and both the sales area (floor space) and sales volume began to decrease dramatically. However, as can be seen, this decline was relatively short-lived as the government stimulation policies began to take effect. Moreover, as is evident from Figure 14.3, the nominal decline in house prices was negligible, less than 1 per cent. By the third quarter of 2009, prices in the first-tier cities were again on an upward trend.

The pattern in the second-tier cities in China was considerably less volatile, with a relatively stable pattern throughout 2007 and well into 2008. Thereafter, there was a more modest and shorter period of house-price falls, with prices recovering in parallel with the upward trend in the lead cities. Development in the second-tier cities is more closely linked with the

Figure 14.3   *First- and second-tier cities' real-estate price indices,*
2004–09

regional markets and local investors, so the overall impact of the financial crisis was significantly smaller than in the first-tier cities. In those secondary cities, development trajectories are primarily affected by the local economic situation rather than by global circumstances, and the housing markets rarely attract consumers and investors from other regions. Thus both before and after the crisis these markets remained relatively stable. From the first quarter of 2007 to the third quarter of 2008, the sale prices in the real-estate market showed a steady growth of around 6–7 per cent. Even after the financial crisis, although the growth rate of real-estate sales price went down, the overall trend was still upward.

Although housing markets in second-tier cities are mainly sustained by local demand, local buyers seem to have overreacted when the economic crisis affected the first-tier cities. Panic about an expected crisis overshadowed the actual impacts of the crisis itself. Yet it was soon clear that rescue measures by both the central and local governments were having an immediate effect in stabilizing house prices in the first-tier cities. Not only was confidence in the housing markets of the second-tier cities quickly restored, but effective demand from consumers, previously suppressed by the high house prices, was subsequently released to fuel a further round of price increases.

Hence the impacts of the recent financial crisis on China's housing market were not as big as expected. The apparent downturn of both the economy and the housing markets was short-lived, and a quick recovery was evident. Indeed, it was the housing market that acted as the driving force and locomotive of economic recovery.

CHINESE CHARACTERISTICS

China was able to control the downturn generated by the crisis through its major interventions in the macroeconomy. The main effect of the crisis was on investor confidence. Although there was capital flight from the country, this did not produce any significant economic impacts because of the country's huge foreign exchange reserves. And when the Chinese government's macro regulation policies began to take effect, investor optimism soon returned.

From a macroeconomic perspective, China's characteristics contrast strongly with those of the USA and other developed countries. The share of total consumption in GDP is relatively small with the major portion derived from net exports, investment and government procurement. Therefore, in an economic downturn, the government was able to stimulate economic growth through increased investment, especially government investment. Even if people are not willing or able to spend money, the government can spend for them. The latter strategy is distinctly easier for a government than encouraging consumers to expand their personal consumption. And the funds for investment and government procurement came from either the bonds issued by the government, or from the enormous savings in China. According to official statistics,[1] the level of China's household savings has remained high for the past ten years, rising from 5 trillion yuan in 2001 to the current 25 trillion yuan. The scale of these savings provided a major funding source for the investments that contributed to rapid economic recovery.

China's housing market also has a number of distinct features driving it forward and generating continuing and growing demand. First, rural–urban migration is on a massive scale and each year a substantial additional urban population is created. Bearing in mind that China has a population of 1.3 billion, a 1 per cent per year urbanization rate means that, annually, 1300 million people will enter cities and their housing demand cannot be met from the existing stock of dwellings. This requires new building at unprecedented levels. Second, the mismatch between supply and demand is further exacerbated because of urban redevelopment and urban expansion. In both the first- and second-tier cities, the redevelopment of older inner areas and the urbanization of the rural peripheries involve the displacement of a large number of existing residents. Moreover, this process of redevelopment, rebuilding and the expropriation of land can only be achieved through the provision of reasonable compensation and arrangements for the displaced residents by the government. The provision of newly built houses is often an important part of the compensation. Third, although, in recent years, the average per capita living space has been increased to 26 m² per capita, inadequate distribution means that a large section of urban populations is still living in accommodation below those space standards. These people want to improve their space standards. These three elements of housing demand differentiate the housing market in China from that in the developed countries. Moreover, ever since it was announced that China would hold the Olympic Games in 2008 and EXPO in 2010, the housing markets in first-tier cities such as Beijing and Shanghai have maintained an upward trajectory (Shih and Ye, 2008). China's housing market is therefore still very immature in relation to supply and demand, with an enormous numerical disparity between dwellings and households in the expanding cities.

As stressed earlier, the development of the housing market is highly dependent on bank credit. In response to the financial crisis, the banks relaxed their credit limits, which, given the substantial underlying demand, quickly helped the housing market out of its depressed state. In addition, the rapid recovery was achieved through the two key elements of the government's policies. There was substantial new investment in the construction of infrastructure, affordable housing and so on, thereby stimulating economic growth. And a series of preferential policies to stimulate the market generated more effective demand. In 2008, the downward trends in the housing market were partly the product of tighter monetary and credit policy. When the policy shifted direction, the market recovery occurred naturally. Moreover, and crucially, because of China's political and economical system, both central and local governments have substantial control over the banking system and the Chinese government has a much greater desire and ability to regulate the market economy than those of Western countries.

EXPECTATIONS FOR THE FUTURE

In general, the financial crisis did not seriously China's affect housing market. Any downward trend was short-lived. The reasons for that are mainly the Chinese government's timely response and the firm and favourable macroeconomic adjustments. But the government's response also involves some potential future difficulties.

First, in order to promote economic recovery, the government has again adopted a loose monetary policy to increase the money supply. Although China has survived the financial crisis through new investment, in the long run there are the dangers of rising inflation and excess liquidity that existed before the crisis. Also, the loosening of credit restrictions may have boosted economic growth but has created more long-run risks for the banking sector. Moreover, the stimulation of economic growth is still primarily derived from direct government investment, with a large amount of enterprise and private capital still lying idle. For China, the next stage of economic development must involve a greater deployment of non-government investment.

Second, the government's regulatory policy in the real-estate market has helped the demand side to readjust after the financial crisis. However, as a direct consequence of these policies, prices have returned to an upward trend rather than experienced a steady decline. The current prospect is therefore one of increasing rather than decreasing affordability difficulties for many urban households.

Third, real-estate regulations and controls are mainly aimed at the demand side of the market, while there is little regulation and control on the supply side. Given the ever-burgeoning demand side pressures, it is likely that the gap between supply and demand will continue and possibly become increasingly serious. Thus the next set of regulatory policies needs to give greater attention to the promotion of supply-side development in the housing market. Again, this will require the guiding of more enterprise and private capital into the real-estate sector rather than overly relying on direct government investment.

NOTE

1. Intranet Business Express: http://202.112.118.59/index/index/index.asp.

REFERENCES

Bai, J. and P. Perron (1998), 'Estimating and testing linear models with multiple structural changes', *Econometrica*, **66** (1), 47–78.
Cao, F.M. (2005), 'Finance policy on real estate market from twice mortgage adjustment', *Zhejiang Economy*, **15**, 52–3.
Han, D.M., M.Z. Tu and K. Cao (2007), 'Real estate bubble and monetary policy', *China Soft Science*, **6**, 9–16.
He, C. (2007), 'Relationship between real estate price and monetary policy', *Finance Theory and Practice*, **3**, 22–5.
Pi, S. and K.P. Wu (2004), 'The causality between real estate market development and economic growth: an empirical analysis to China', *Management Review*, **3**, 8–12.
Shih, Y.N. and J.P. Ye (2008), 'Housing price volatility demand and supply in an

emerging market: evidence from Beijing holding Olympic Games 2008', proceedings of CRIOCM 2008 International Research Symposium on Advancement of Construction Management and Real Estate, pp. 431–6.

Wang, L.F. and F. Guo (2007), 'Research on dynamic impact of macro economy on real estate price – on the basis of VAR', *Research on Financial and Economic Issues*, **11**, 15–19.

Xie, H. and L. Zheng (2006), 'Effect of monetary policy on real estate market: theory and policy', *Finance Theory and Practice*, **1**, 24–8.

Zeng, H.L., Z. Zeng and J. Wu (2008), 'Impact on asset price from monetary policy: an empirical analysis to China', *Finance Development Research*, **10**, 22–6.

15. Concluding discussion – where to now?

Ray Forrest

The dominant message flowing from the preceding chapters is that a so-called global financial crisis has had widely varying impacts across the world in relation to both institutions and households. There is not a simple continuum ranging from severe to minimal impact, but it is evident that the experiences of homeowners in Iceland or Hungary contrast strongly with their counterparts in, say, Australia and the Netherlands. At the same time, for the moment at least, it seems that predictions of a pervasive and structural crisis in the global economy were premature, as were concerns about large-scale hardship and property losses among homeowning households. However, taken collectively, the chapters suggest the need for considerable caution in judging the level of pain that may ultimately emerge. It remains too early to say, with the potential for further economic disruptions, and with the effects of the 2007 crisis continuing to ripple through economies, labour markets and housing systems.

The other general comment concerns the organization of the chapters in this book. We gave considerable thought as to how best to group the various country analyses, hoping that some clear thematic principles would emerge from the discussion and debate at the associated symposium. This proved elusive, or, more accurately, explanations and analyses are rooted in combinations of factors that encompass local institutional structures, policy histories and practices, demographics, tenurial structures and developmental paths. This latter aspect posed a problem for many of the authors in providing an explanation and exploration of the household impacts within the limited confines of a chapter. Whilst in some cases the key explanatory factors can be fairly easily exposed, in other cases the path-dependent nature of the impacts requires ideally a longer historical account in relation to policy and institutional development.

In the end, a quasi-geographical grouping proved as good as any other. It is 'quasi' in the sense that the UK and the USA seemed appropriate points of departure as representing the countries at the epicentre of the recent crisis. And at least in housing-market terms, it was European countries that were most directly affected by the immediate fallout from the sub-prime crisis and credit crunch. The impacts in Asia and Australasia were generally indirect and less severe. Even Japan fits this pattern, as the recent crisis merely exacerbated an already depressed and vulnerable housing market rather than provoking a new crisis. This geographical organization also captures to a considerable degree the global pattern of securitization and toxic loans, and the extent to which housing markets were vulnerable to the financial meltdown. Whilst it is not the case that all European housing systems were heavily immersed in securitization, it is certainly the case that Asian economies were not. We can now proceed to offer some general observations arising from the collection.

First, it is evident that housing systems that are more globally integrated, more extensively financialized and more dominated by homeownership are prone to a new set of risks and vulnerabilities. The consequences of these risks and vulnerabilities are not, however, shared equally by institutions and households. In the ensuing chaos of the global financial crisis, while some of the major institutional casualties were bailed out by their governments, providing solid empirical evidence for what had previously been mainly theoretical arguments for the 'too big to fail' thesis, others went to the wall. Similarly, among households there were winners and losers, both within and across societies. Within societies, where there were substantial direct impacts of the crisis in terms of housing, the main casualties were typically the younger, more recent and highly leveraged lower-income households. The winners were typically more mature mortgaged homeowners and more affluent recent buyers benefiting from falling interest rates or more preferential mortgage deals. However, unlike the case for the institutional casualties, assistance for homeowners in difficulties has often been very limited. Their collective plight did not threaten more endemic, structural failure of the financial system.

Second, there is not one simple pattern in relation to the severity of the impact of the crisis and the degree of exposure of households that corresponds neatly to any existing classificatory schema rooted in welfare-regime types or more simple measures of the degree of commodification such as the level of homeownership. For example, there has not been a common liberal, Anglo-Saxon experience–the Australian or New Zealand experience contrasts with that of the UK or the USA. Iceland could be regarded as one of the heavy casualties with high exposure to innovative financial products, securitization and toxic assets. Ireland would not, however, be far behind, but there the driving force for more lax lending behaviour was more intense competition among mainstream lenders rather than securitization. Similarly, Hong Kong, erroneously regarded as a bastion of free-market capitalism and a key player in global financial flows, escaped virtually unscathed. Indeed, most of its indicators remained stubbornly positive even at the height of the crisis. The explanation for this resides in a combination of regulatory measures, the experience of the previous Asian financial crisis, the power of its retail banking sector and the existence of a large public rental sector. And Japan, with a relatively low level of homeownership by international standards, a high degree of state support for homeownership (until recently), with little if any exposure of institutions or households to securitization and a very conservative attitude to housing equity and savings has experienced a housing-market crisis and numerous household casualties for 15 years. Basically, there are too many contingent factors in play. Policy histories, demographics, different institutional practices, underlying patterns of housing demand and tenure structures coalesce and collide with the global economic downturn to produce quite different outcomes.

Third, and linked to the previous point, one reading of the contributions to this book would suggest that the impact on households, at least in terms of explicit statistical evidence, has been relatively modest. Falls in house prices, housing transactions, GDP, incomes or even employment do not necessarily translate directly into household casualties in terms of repossessions or arrears or other measures of housing stress. They are often lower than might be expected given the general economic conditions. In some countries there have been significant levels of housing stress. Foreclosure rules and practices in the USA have seen high levels of bankruptcy and eviction. In Hungary, foreclosures in 2009 were double those of the previous year. Elsewhere, such as in the UK and Iceland, lenders and government have developed rescue schemes or restructured loan payments to try to limit the levels of repossessions and evictions. But the impact has also been affected by factors such as the relative cost of owning and private renting, the overall pattern of exposure of homeowners to falling house prices and unemployment and the role of social rental tenures. In Ireland, for example, job losses have so far been concentrated in sectors with below-average levels of homeownership and younger owners tend to be in the higher income bands and, so far, able to cope with large mortgages. There is also a large group of older outright owners who are a product of past sales of public housing that involved heavy discounts. As the chapter on Ireland shows, this process can create a tranche of low-debt/outright owners with a low level of vulnerability to economic downturns and financial blow-outs. In other cases, in the Netherlands and most notably Hong Kong, the survival of large social rental sectors has meant that lower-income households were not so heavily exposed to the economic downturn. And in the Netherlands, despite a substantial increase in the level of homeownership, extremely high levels of household debt and high loan-to-value ratios, lending criteria based on ability to pay and robust mortgage-guarantee schemes have limited the impact on households. However, as suggested earlier, many of the contributors think that the worst may yet be to come, with the effects on jobs still uncertain, with high levels of household debt and with inadequate welfare safety-nets in some countries. A further downturn in housing markets could push more home-owners into difficulties. Equally, market recovery could involve higher levels of forced sales and foreclosures.

Fourth, governments have mattered in a variety of ways in determining the outcomes. Most obviously, the bail-outs of the big financial institutions through massive use of tax revenues in countries such as the USA, the UK or the Netherlands were a key moment in shaping the overall trajectory of the crisis – and a moment in which the consequences of market failure became collective national responsibilities. This can be interpreted in different ways. References to nationalization in this context suggest a reassertion of state control and intervention in the financial sphere, and a significant riposte to neoliberal market ideology. Alternatively, and this has been a particularly prominent element of public debate in the USA, the scale of the bailout and the negotiations that brought it about can be seen as reflecting the hegemony of the finance sector and its colonization of key Treasury posts. Thus it can be argued that far from being weakened by the crisis, corporate finance interests have become more embedded in government – the marketization of government rather than the government of markets.

Also, while the dominant policy discourse in Europe is one of austerity and retrenchment, some other governments, notably in Asia, such as China, Korea and Vietnam, formulated and implemented substantial stimulation packages to counter the effects of the crisis on trade. Much of this investment was focused on the real-estate sector, with attendant risks of excess price inflation and future bubbles. The impacts of these injections of state funding have been varied in relation to the impact on households. In Vietnam, the financial crisis mainly affected the luxury end of the market, which had been the focus of domestic and overseas investment to the neglect of middle-, and particularly low-income housing. The stimulation package has, however, concentrated on more affordable housing and provided the opportunity, and necessity, to build cheaper housing and potentially widen access. It could be argued therefore that the financial crisis has had a progressive impact on housing opportunities as FDI deserted the more speculative luxury end. In China, where the effects of the crisis were more indirect, hitting trade rather than the property markets, the household impact had different dimensions. There were modest (by Western standards) price falls in the more internationally connected cities on the east coast. Again, it was the higher-end, commercial housing sector that experienced a short period of price falls, affecting more affluent households that can afford such properties. The huge injection of state funding soon reversed this decline. But given that much of the housing being constructed in the major cities is way beyond the reach of average Chinese households, the impact of the crisis could be seen as involving little distributional impact in terms of access to homeownership. Those hit hardest by the decline in overseas trade were, in the main, lower-income unskilled workers rather than homeowners. Throughout the crisis, the second-tier cities, more embedded in domestic labour and property markets, experienced little impact.

Fifth, many of the chapters refer to the prospect of falling homeownership rates among particular cohorts. In some situations the overall rate of homeownership will continue to grow as large cohorts of ageing, homeowing baby-boomer households flow across population structures. A rising overall level of homeownership may well conceal highly divergent intergenerational patterns. In countries such as Japan, Iceland, Ireland, the USA and the UK, a varied combination of less benign economic conditions, the fallout from the era of neoliberal financial innovation and changing housing policies indicates particular difficulties for younger generations, and particularly aspiring lower-income households. In some cases, such as in New Zealand, the UK and the USA, overall homeownership rates are already falling. Often, these trends preceded the 2007 crisis, although they are now likely to become more marked. Moreover, as some analyses indicate, the casualties from the recent crisis may find it difficult to re-enter homeownership because of their damaged financial circumstances and their credit record – particularly in a period when lenders are seeking other lower-risk opportunities, when risk has been 'repriced' and lenders seek prime rather than sub-prime borrowers, and when mortgage finance remains tight. Also, there may be attitudinal shifts among a younger generation and necessary changes in housing choices and strategies. Renting may become more attractive if rental markets expand, leases are more affordable and some of the favoured attributes of homeownership can be found in the rental sectors. As the US analysis shows, whilst the relative advantages of owning and renting are typically couched in monetary terms, it is non-monetary factors that may be more important in tenure decisions – at least among some households. Post-crisis, the housing debate is therefore as much about the future for renting, and particularly private renting, as it is about the future for homeownership. This issue is especially prominent in the discussion of the Korean housing situation.

This scenario raises a number of issues about future housing policy, and about more fundamental processes of social stratification and inequality.

The drive to extend the market for homeownership can be variously presented as a social objective to extend the benefits of homeownership to a wider cross-section of the population (the spread of middle-class opportunities and lifestyles, etc.) or as the relentless logic of commodification through financialization (the economic objective). This progressive shift in the framing and content of the homeownership 'project' was alluded to in Chapter 1. The development of sub-prime loans and more lax lending criteria at one time seemed to be a virtuous combination of the two – offering new profitable opportunities for corporate finance and extending homeownership to previously excluded households. Unfortunately, some recent recruits to homeownership have clearly made a quick exit and many others have only a precarious foothold. Moreover, although there are examples of prolonged and substantial falls in house prices, the underlying pattern is of continuing and severe affordability problems. This is particularly evident in China, Vietnam and Korea, but there are more pervasive upward pressures on house prices in relation to factors such as declining household size, the purchasing power of the baby-boomer generation and low levels of construction activity before the global downturn. The absence of financial innovation and sub-prime lending, and the impossibility of gaining access to homeownership for lower-income households, could be seen as a blessing – especially if there is an alternative of affordable and high quality public or private rental housing. However, unless Japan provides a glimpse of a more general future for homeownership in which asset values will remain depressed and the economic attractions of homeownership diminish, 'protection through exclusion' is a recipe for growing social divisions and inequality. In other words, if privatization policies have run their course (where they have been possible through the existence of large public rental sectors) and market-driven, high-risk, low-initial-cost borrowing is unsustainable, what is to be the new housing strategy to reduce the gap between older and younger generations and between high-income and low-income households? The transfer of swathes of state housing has produced very high levels of homeownership in the transitional economies of Eastern Europe and China. Financial innovation provided a further boost, most notably in the USA. But the pattern of change in terms of levels of homeownership suggests a real and sustainable level of satisfactory homeownership (satisfactory in terms of condition, cost, marketability, etc.) nearer 60 per cent. If declining levels of homeownership among younger generations is to be reversed and homeownership opportunities for lower-income groups are to be extended, government-backed homeownership schemes of some form would seem essential. Alternatively, a consequence of the recent crisis may require a rethink of the social objectives of housing policy – one that transcends the homeownership bias characterizing many national housing policies over recent decades.

A sixth observation linked to the above concerns the broader familial and intergenerational dimensions of the crisis. The recent dominance of neoliberal ideas has asserted the role of the market in housing opportunities – atomized households seeking the best mortgage deals in highly competitive finance sectors. However, rising barriers to entry in relation to price and deposit have put more pressure on parents to assist their offspring. The flight from higher-risk lending, higher loan-to-value ratios and soaring house prices in countries such as China will increase these pressures, requiring younger households to find higher deposits. The contrast between resource-rich and resource-poor families will increase in terms of housing trajectories. A further familiar dimension is the issue highlighted in the US chapter. Where do the casualties go? As the US chapter shows, family and friends represent the most common destination for those evicted from owned or rental homes. This is likely to be generally the case in countries without adequate social safety-nets to reduce eviction or without available social housing. If the number of refugees from homeownership increases, families will have to shoulder a greater burden. We have already observed the pattern of delayed family formation among young people. A less evident impact of the crisis on households, therefore, is likely to be a further accentuation of a process of familization in relation to housing opportunities that has been under way for some time – acknowledging, of course, existing cultural differences in housing practices and social norms particularly between Eastern and Western societies. The intergenerational aspects of the impact of the crisis also extend beyond the issue of vulnerable younger homeowners or aspiring young entrants but encompasses the reduced financial circumstances of some low-income seniors. This was a point raised in the introductory chapter and also alluded to by Berry in his discussion of the Australian situation.

There are two final observations to make. First, secondary economic shock waves promise further episodes of housing market and economic instability. These secondary waves include the rising interest rates in the pipeline (already emerging in some countries) and the fiscal austerity packages being introduced to reduce public-sector deficits. Rising mortgage interest rates and rising public-sector unemployment threaten a new and potentially larger wave of household casualties evidenced in repossessions and arrears. Second, there are the more subtle social and psychological impacts of the crisis on homeowners and prospective homeowners and the wider political ramifications. Previous crises, which have been more geographically contained, have typically provoked discussions of changing attitudes towards homeownership. In general, these discussions have been short-lived. Housing markets have recovered, prices have begun to rise again and the normal cycle of more generous lending and excessive borrowing has returned. These episodes have been more closely associated with Western, capitalist housing markets and, as the chapters in this book demonstrate, homeownership systems are highly varied in relation to their developmental histories and institutional foundations.

The 2007 crisis and its aftermath have, however, raised a broader set of questions concerning the relationship between corporate finance and homeownership. This concerns the supposedly more intimate and special nature of house as home – and the erosion of the belief and past experience among households that house purchase involved a different kind of relationship between borrower and lender compared to the purchase of other commodities. In the past this was reflected in the differentiation of lenders for house purchase from the mainstream institutions, in the various forms of special state support for homeownership and often in the lived experience of the treatment of homeowners who found themselves in difficulties. Reactions to the crisis in terms of government responses and the attempts by some corporate lenders to mitigate, or at least delay, the worst impacts on households capture a continuing tension between the social nature of home as a supposedly secure and intimate space and its increasingly financial anonymization. Put simply, losing your home is rather different from having your car repossessed, and the political and social impact of home repossessions or rising arrears on any significant scale is considerably more destabilizing. This relates to the observations by Thorns about the loss of trust in banks and other financial institutions and the social unrest reported in the Hungarian and Icelandic accounts. The impact on households goes further, then, than a simple count of the proportion of purchasers deemed to be in difficulty on various measures and beyond debates about the need for more or less financial regulation. It concerns the changed relationship between homeowners and the institutions that finance their purchase. The global financial crisis has highlighted the stark contrast between an ideology of homeownership that promulgates ideas of security, stability and belonging, and the more precarious realities of globalized financialization and more intense market competition.

Appendix: selected key indicators

Country	GDP growth rate (%)			Harmonized unemployment rate (%)			Central government debt of GDP (%)		
	2007	2008	2009	2007	2008	2009	2007	2008	2009
Australia	4.8	2.2	1.0	4.4	4.2	5.6	5.2	4.9	8.1
China	13.0	9.0	8.7	4.0	4.2	4.3	18.9	15.6	18.2
Hong Kong	6.4	2.4	−3.0	4.0	3.6	5.4	8.9	13.9	18.1
Hungary	1.2	0.6	−6.7	7.4	7.8	10.0	61.3	68.2	72.7
Iceland	5.6	1.3	−6.6	2.3	3.0	7.2	23.2	44.3	87.2
Ireland	6.0	−3.0	−7.5	4.6	6.4	11.9	19.8	27.7	46.0
Japan	2.3	−1.2	−5.3	3.9	4.0	5.1	164.2	178.0	192.1
Korea, South	5.1	2.2	0.2	3.2	3.2	3.6	29.7	29.0	32.6
Netherlands	3.6	2.0	−3.9	3.2	2.8	3.4	37.8	50.1	49.9
New Zealand	2.9	−0.1	−1.4	3.7	4.2	6.1	20.4	20.6	27.5
UK	2.6	0.5	−4.8	5.3	5.6	7.6	42.6	61.3	75.1
USA	2.1	0.4	−2.4	4.6	5.8	9.3	35.6	40.0	53.1
Vietnam	8.5	6.2	5.3	4.6	4.7	2.9	43.3	48.8	52.3

Notes and sources: GDP growth rate is from *The World Factbook*, available at https://www.cia.gov/library/publications/the-world-factbook/fields/2003.html?countryName=Australia&countryCode=as&regionCode=au&#as, accessed 5 July 2010.

Harmonized unemployment rate is from OECD Report, except the non-member countries, available at http://www.oecd.org/dataoecd/43/20/41261417.pdf.

Harmonized unemployment rate of Hong Kong is from Census and Statistics Department, the Government of HKSAR, available at http://www.censtatd.gov.hk/gb/?param=b5uniS&url=http://www.censtatd.gov.hk/hong_kong_statistics/statistical_tables/index_tc.jsp?tableID=006; harmonized unemployment rate of China is from National Bureau of Statistics of China, available at http://www.stats.gov.cn/tjsj/ndsj/2009/indexch.htm; harmonized unemployment rate of Vietnam is from General Statistics Office of Vietnam and *The World Factbook*; available at http://www.gso.gov.vn/default_en.aspx?tabid=467&idmid=3&ItemID=8639.

Central government debt of GDP is from OECD Report, but the data of non-member countries, including China, Hong Kong and Vietnam, is from *The World Factbook*, available at http://stats.oecd.org/Index.aspx?datasetcode=GOV_DEBT.

Index